The Reparable
and the Irreparable

The Reparable and the Irreparable

Being Human in the Age of Vulnerability

Johann Michel

Translated from the French by
Nicolas Carter

LEXINGTON BOOKS
Lanham • Boulder • New York • London

Published by Lexington Books
An imprint of The Rowman & Littlefield Publishing Group, Inc.
4501 Forbes Boulevard, Suite 200, Lanham, Maryland 20706
www.rowman.com

86-90 Paul Street, London EC2A 4NE

Originally published in French as *Le réparable et l'irréparable. L'humain au temps du vulnérable*.

Éditions © Hermann 2021.
English translation © 2023 by The Rowman & Littlefield Publishing Group, Inc.

All rights reserved. No part of this book may be reproduced in any form or by any electronic or mechanical means, including information storage and retrieval systems, without written permission from the publisher, except by a reviewer who may quote passages in a review.

British Library Cataloguing in Publication Information Available

Library of Congress Cataloging-in-Publication Data

Names: Michel, Johann, 1972- author.
Title: The reparable and the irreparable : being human in the age of vulnerability / Johann Michel.
Other titles: Réparable et l'irréparable. English
Description: Lanham : Lexington Books, [2022] | Includes bibliographical references and index. | Summary: "What do repair and reparation tell us about human beings? They speak to our (natural) vulnerability, our (moral) fallibility, and our (social) incompleteness, but also about the many capabilities we draw upon to mitigate these shortcomings. It is from the heart of human finitude that repair and reparation draw meaning"-- Provided by publisher.
Identifiers: LCCN 2022037100 (print) | LCCN 2022037101 (ebook) | ISBN 9781666906868 (cloth) | ISBN 9781666906875 (epub)
Subjects: LCSH: Reparations for historical injustices--Philosophy. | Compensation (Law)--Philosophy. | Healing--Philosophy. | Philosophical anthropology.
Classification: LCC KZ6785 .M5313 2022 (print) | LCC KZ6785 (ebook) | DDC 340/.115--dc23/eng/20221005
LC record available at https://lccn.loc.gov/2022037100
LC ebook record available at https://lccn.loc.gov/2022037101

For Emmanuelle Vassal

Contents

Acknowledgements		ix
Introduction		xi
1	This Vulnerable Flesh	1
2	The Fragmented Mind	47
3	Fault and Offense	93
4	The Measurement of Harm	131
5	History in Debt	179
Conclusion		217
Bibliography		221
Index		231
About the Author		235

Acknowledgements

I owe a debt of gratitude to Gwenael Gouerou, Bernadette Aubert, Jean-Claude Gens, Hélène L'Heuillet, Janine Barbot, Nicolas Dodier, Marie Delbard, Pascal Sommer and Louis Casteilla for their rereading, their comments and their support.

All translations are our own, unless otherwise indicated.

Introduction

Since the second half of the twentieth century, Western societies have seen an unprecedented increase in movements, demands, and policies in favor of reparations. The historical catastrophes that shook the last century are both the immediate origin of this groundswell and its founding paradigm. The prophetic age of bright new dawns collapsed, leaving in its wake an era of mourning. Then came the time for reparation. In one sense, the contemporary era invented the concept of reparation as a response to radical evil. But in one sense only. This book seeks to take the true measure of the contemporary historicity of reparation and, at the same time, to grasp it in its full anthropological depth.

Policies of reparation and processes of reparative justice are only one facet of how the concept of repair can be expressed and enacted. It is a global phenomenon but has no unified form. Indeed, there are so many ways in which ideas of repair and reparation are expressed, at different levels: one can mend a damaged object, heal a wound, redress an injury, make amends for an offence . . . The Latin root *reparare*—to prepare again, restore, refresh, recover—portends its semantic plurality. And in the plurality of its uses, the concept of repair points at the same time to something fundamental about what it means to be human. My aim here is to understand repair/reparation both in its specific registers of givenness and constitution (biological, social, legal, political, etc.) and as a universal of the human condition. In the footsteps of Marcel Mauss, the aim is to probe the idea of repair from the anthropological perspective of the "total man" (in all its biological, social, legal and political aspects).[1] Due to the multiplicity of uses of the cognate terms "reparation," "reparations," and "repair" in highly complex specialist fields, the "positive knowledges" (sociology, neuroscience, psychology, law) necessarily play a significant role in enabling us to grasp the language, concepts and implications. There is as yet no general philosophy of reparation and repair. My aim here is to bring it into existence, as part of a systematic dialogue with the natural and social sciences.

What does reparation tell us about human beings? It tells us about their (natural) vulnerability, their (moral) fallibility, their (social) incompleteness . . . but also about the many capabilities they draw upon to mitigate the effects of these shortcomings. It is from the heart of human finitude that reparation draws its meaning. Of course, people don't spend all their time making repairs. When do we repair? When does *homo* become *reparans*? The need, desire or duty to repair arises when a set of events or actions modifies the initial state of an organism, thing, person, or group in a harmful way. And what exactly is "repair"? It is a set of (biological) dispositions, (material) systems, ordinary (social) techniques, and specific (legal) procedures designed to recondition (a thing), treat and heal (an organism), or compensate (for an offence, an injury or a crime). And yet not every detrimental change of state necessarily entails a reparative process: we can pick at scabs, leave an object broken, refuse to apologize for an offense. On a more global scale, however, organic and social life would be impossible without reparative exchanges; free rein would be given to death (natural organisms) or to the permanent war of all against all (social organisms). Can we even conceive of a society in which all harm suffered (insults, material damage, crimes . . .) would remain without consequences and without effect? At the political scale, repair, in the form of reparations, is after all seen as one of the instruments of peace within societies. The refusal to make reparation—which may be justifiable when one is wrongly accused and the refusal is not down to stubbornness, denial or dishonesty— inevitably comes up against social mechanisms of reparation, from ordinary injunctions, such as apologizing, all the way up to the grand reparative institutions shaped by positive law.

More generally, repair can be thought of as one of the basic modalities of regulation of human life, as a set of responses and reactions following an injury, loss, offense, or crime. The reparative process is invoked, and sometimes imposed, because natural, social or individual organisms are faced with temporary or structural imbalances, dissymetries or amputations as the result of an accident, a catastrophe, or external aggression. Reparation, in other words, performs what Antonio Damasio calls a "homeostatic function" in specific fields of regulation (biological homeostasis, psychological homeostasis, social homeostasis, legal homeostasis, etc.):

> The elaboration of moral rules and laws and the development of justice systems responded to the detection of imbalances caused by social behaviors

that endangered individuals and the group. The cultural devices created in response to the imbalance aimed at restoring the equilibrium of individuals and of the group. The contribution of economic and political systems, as well as, for example, the development of medicine, responded to functional problems that occurred in the social space and that required correction within that space, lest they compromise the life regulation of the individuals that constituted the group.[2]

In its homeostatic function, the purpose of reparation is to mitigate, compensate for, or nullify an injury, an affront, or a privation. This gradation of the reparative process (mitigate, compensate, nullify) is essential to understanding the differential gap that separates the initial, damaged state from the post-repair state. Certain procedures, certain imaginaries, certain intentions seek quite simply to erase this gap, almost as if nothing had happened, as if reparation could take us back to the *status quo ante*. This book, however, sets out to systematically explore the place of the irreparable as an irreducible part of any process of repair, albeit to different degrees. The irreparable points to a state of affairs that we cannot remedy; it is frequently associated both with the irreversible and with the inexorable, that is, the impossibility of going backwards, of reversing the course of history, or of a process. The irreparable would lose its heuristic power, however, if it came to imply the intervention of a higher power or a historical necessity written in advance, as part of some great teleological, metaphysical or theological script. If counterfactual history tells us anything, it is that social and even biological processes could have taken very different directions. The irreparable means that mitigating and compensating for the loss of something can never erase the past, as though the harm had never happened: every repair, to some extent, leaves a residue, a vestige of the irreparable. There is never a pure and simple return to the initial state. A mark, however small, will always remain on the thing repaired; a trace on the body, even if healed, in the form of a scar; a feeling of some kind, even if there are "no hard feelings," after an offense, even if forgiven. The irreparable is the mark that time leaves on the affected being.

And yet the reparable and the irreparable, each in its own domain, are not givens, set in stone once and for all: what was once thought to be irreparable (certain disabilities, for example) may, thanks to scientific and technological advances, prove amenable to repair, at least in part. Yesterday's irreparable can become tomorrow's reparable and, of course, yesterday's reparable can, when circumstances change, become tomorrow's irreparable. The aim of this investigation is to comprehend the reparable and the irreparable as relative and correlative concepts.

Does the persistence of the irreparable, from a moral viewpoint, mean that the guilty must eternally strive to make reparation? Can we conceive simultaneously of the insistence of the irreparable and the possibility of redemption? How can we break the cycle of debt and unleash new initiatives without erasing the period of injury? How can the irreparable manifest itself other than through resentment and other dark passions? These are among the ethical questions that any anthropology of repair must grapple with.

Though all the manifestations of repair may share a common core, their implications, effects and modalities vary profoundly from one model to another, from organic (self)-repair, to reparative justice, to the many forms of reparation: religious, moral, legal and political. Already at the scale of living things, all organisms, human and non-human, repair themselves at least to some extent. Self-repair (along with self-conservation, self-regulation and self-construction), Canguilhem tells us, is one of the criteria that set living things apart from mere matter. What distinguishes organic self-repair is its spontaneous character. It owes nothing to willpower, still less to artifice. For this reason, organic self-repair is not understood as a technique but as a (biological) *disposition*. There is nothing specifically human in this natural function.

It is with other-repair[3] that the human factor truly comes into play, when self-repair alone is powerless to treat the lesions and remedy the privations of the body. Other-repair takes a strictly human turn with the introduction of biotechniques and biotechnologies, from the most simple to the most sophisticated, aimed at restoring the body to health, despite the irreducible marks of the flesh. The problem is not only one of progress, and the limits to the ability of science and technology to repair living things. The problem is also expressed in normative terms, around the dividing line between the "normal" and the "pathological."

Other-repair moves us away from repair as a (spontaneous) *disposition*. It brings in intention, will, and a set of techniques that we might call *"reparatio."* *Reparatio* employ material and symbolic objects (the surgeon's scalpel, the handyman's screwdriver, the lawyer's legal text, speech acts such as apologies, memorials, etc.) in different arrangements and configurations, as well as knowhow, practical routines, sequential acts, procedures and other mechanisms.[4]

This point is essential for precluding any attempt to naturalize repair. Between the living world and the world of culture, there is enough *same* and enough *other* for us to speak of an analogical relationship between the different models of repair. The scarring of damaged skin both is, and is not, like the patching-up of a broken object, is and is not like the work of mourning a loved one, is and is not like a public apology for an offense, is and is not like the mechanism for compensating the victims of past wrongs. To define the relationships between the different modes of repair, we can recall the dialectic of the "great kinds"—the Same, the Other and the Analogous—developed by Plato in the *Sophist* (254b–59d). It is the third kind, the Analogous, that acts as our guiding star in exploring the relationships between the modes of repair in each specific field. We might say, for instance, that scarring is to the physical as the work of mourning is to the psychological, or compensation to the legal, and so on. Analogy, as we know at least since Aristotle, captures likeness in the midst of contrast, "ordered relationships articulating similarity-in-difference."[5] It presupposes both imagination and interpretation to construct heuristic comparisons, developing a dynamic, creative meaning that reaches beyond univocality and false equivalences:

> An analogical hermeneutics is one that makes use of analogy to interpret, with the goal of producing a balanced or proportional interpretation but, at the same time, an analogy that is deliberately stretched, so as not to remain immobile or static. It is a lively, dynamic analogy that thrives on tension; it seeks to encompass opposites, up to their very limits; it lets them live; it sacrifices nothing for the sake of some spurious synthesis—which would simply be a return to univocality—but nor does it offer limitless openness to irreconcilable oppositions.[6]

The choice of an analogical hermeneutic method to outline the contours of repair is quite distinct from that of a structuralist method that analyzes, as does Claude Lévi-Strauss for example, abstract networks of binary relations within a society that form a system, that is, sets of correlating or opposing signs (such as raw vs. cooked).[7] The various forms of repair, due to their specific fields of application, cannot comprise a coherent system in which each of its expressions points correlatively to the others. But as we will see, this does not prevent them from borrowing ideal-type models of repair from each other, in certain cases. The structuralist method, though it may be eminently suited to analyzing certain social phenomena such as myths, is not equipped to grasp the multiplicity of models of repair. At another extreme, the analogical hermeneutic method stands in contrast to a pragmatic analytical method as practiced, for example, by Wittgenstein,[8] which would see acts of repair as language games and as forms of life that are irreducible to each other. A pragmatic analytical method is valuable for drawing attention to the uses of repair, in their particular expressions, but cannot scale up to the level of the common anthropological structures of repair as a general phenomenon. Only an analogical hermeneutic method can bring together the same and the other, the common and the different, and hold them together in a single chain of thought.

In support of such a method, this inquiry pursues three main objectives. Firstly, to clarify, describe and compare the different ideal-type models of repair by examining them in terms of their actual use and in terms of related or contrasting practices (repair/regeneration, repair/enhancement, repair/resilience, redress/restitution, reparation/retribution). Secondly, to historicize them by demonstrating, in each specific field, how the logic of repair has been substantially transformed by social change, legal innovations and technological advances. Thirdly, to evaluate them by subjecting the practices and uses of repair to normative examination, in each of their ideal-type models and in the ways they might intermesh. The ultimate aim is to establish not only whether everything *can* be repaired, but whether everything *should* be repaired.

The question of the irreparable runs like a thread throughout this analysis, but it is particularly salient in the final section on reparations policies as a response to exceptional crimes. Can history be repaired?[9] Are the nature and magnitude of crimes against humanity ever reparable? Here, the reparable comes face to face with the incommensurable. To repair, one must be able to measure. But how do we establish equivalences between exceptional crimes and potential compensation? How do we evaluate the impact of historical trauma on one person's lifetime, let alone on several generations? Does the recourse to money, and to material compensation, not betray the very nature of the crime and the memory of the victims? Must we therefore accept the "non-redeemable" (and therefore non-repairable) character of certain historical wrongs? Rather than a lack of redress, rather than a denial of the victims, the part of history that remains irreparable is, perhaps, a recognition of the radical nature of historical evil.

NOTES

1. B. Karsenti, *L'homme total–Sociologie, anthropologie et philosophie chez Marcel Mauss*. Paris: PUF, 2011.

2. A. Damasio, *Self Comes to Mind*. New York: Pantheon Books, 2010, p. 220.

3. The notion of other-repair originates from linguistics, where it refers to the correction of a speaker's utterance by another person. I borrow this concept and apply it more broadly to any form of repair (of living organisms, of the psyche, etc.) that relies on intervention from another quarter.

4. See, for example, the '*dispositifs* of redress' posited by J. Barbot & N. Dodier ("La force des dispositifs," *Annales. Histoire, Sciences Sociales*, vol. 71, no. 2, 2016, pp. 421–50).

5. D. Tracy, *The Analogical Imagination*. New York: Crossroad, 1991, p. 408.

6. M. Beuchot & J. Gonzalez, *Diversité et dialogue interculturel*. Paris: Editions des archives contemporaines, 2018.
7. C. Lévi-Strauss, *Mythologiques. Le cru et le cuit*, tome 1. Paris: Plon, 1978.
8. L. Wittgenstein, *Philosophical Investigations*. Englewood Cliffs, NJ: Prentice Hall, 1973.
9. A. Garapon, *Peut-on réparer l'histoire* ? Paris: Odile Jacob, 2008.

Chapter One

This Vulnerable Flesh

Inert matter can decompose, and be recomposed with something else, but it cannot repair itself. There is no internal mechanism that enables it to reconstitute a part of itself that has been destroyed. Only living organic matter, as Canguilhem reminds us,[1] is capable of self-repair. This observable fact leads on to a broader question: why and how do living organisms, including humans, repair themselves?

Living organisms are constantly subjected to disruption, to internal transformation and to attack from the outside, which demand suitable responses to ensure self-preservation. If we define life as, in Bichat's famous formula,[2] the set of functions that resist death, then repair is undoubtedly one of the core functions. Without a process of self-repair, especially of the vital organs, death would be imminent. And yet self-repair is but a partial and limited response to the finitude of living things, whose irremediable destiny is mortality. The resistance of which Bichat speaks is always temporary. The process of self-repair that maintains the integrity of the organism coexists, barring irreversible accidents, with a programmed obsolescence that prefigures its decline and ultimate end. Not everything in the living world can be repaired.

Humans, as living beings, are no exception to this state of affairs, save perhaps for the anguish generated by their own finitude. One can justifiably see this sentiment as being at the origin of the myths and religions that promise immortality, if not of the body, then at least of the soul, usually in another world. The myth of the immortality of the soul is a way of extirpating humanity from its mortal condition as a living entity. In addition to this imaginative projection, human societies have called upon reason, science and technology to stave off the specter of death when self-repair alone proves difficult or is powerless to save an organism. All such artifices, from the most rudimentary to the most sophisticated, which seek to prolong or substitute for our flagging capacity for self-repair, come under the category of "other-repair." Such is the progress of "enhancement technologies" that they are now redrawing the boundary between repair and performance and pushing the envelope of what it means to be human. The goal of the biotechnological transformation of humankind is on the way to joining, by another route, the myth of human immortality. This dream of transhumanity—imagining a form of human life freed from its finitude—is a theme we will be returning to.

Meanwhile, the very survival of humanity in the here-and-now is threatened by other phenomena far more harmful than technoscience to the global equilibria of our planet. The ethical concerns no longer center on the limits to the repair of human life, but on the preservation of any kind of life and—by extension—of nature itself, on which the possibility of future human life depends.

SELF-REPAIR AND REGENERATION

The Prometheus myth is not only rich in lessons about human overreach, when we seek to acquire powers that rival the prerogatives of the gods. The myth also tells us about the knowledge of the Ancients, who were aware of the body's ability to rebuild itself naturally after partial deterioration. For having stolen the sacred fire and given it to humanity, Prometheus provokes the wrath of Zeus, who inflicts a terrible punishment on him: Hephaestus chains him naked to a rock in the mountains of the Caucasus, where an eagle comes every day to peck out and devour his liver, which then grows back again. The endless torture of Prometheus attests, at the same time, to a resource specific to living organisms: the ability of an organ to self-repair after injury. In the myth, this characteristic, necessary to the preservation of life, is turned against the Titan to inflict hellish suffering.

The Prometheus story also raises questions about the science, beyond the myth, around the biological mechanisms at work in this reconstitutive process. More generally, the specifically scientific question, which applies to any organ, any tissue, indeed any living matter, concerns the distinction between self-repair and regeneration, terms that are sometimes conflated both in common parlance and in the life sciences. It depends on whether, after injury or amputation, the organ reconstitutes itself entirely until it is practically restored to its initial state or, alternatively, something remains that is irreparable and irreversible in the process of biological reconstitution, so that the organism is forever *other*. And do these mechanisms differ from one species to another? Do humans enjoy any special privilege in this respect?

Regeneration, in its narrow meaning, is the ability of a living entity (genome, cell, organ, organism, etc.) to reconstitute itself after its partial or even total destruction.[3] The lizard, if caught by a predator, can lose its tail and grow it back almost identically (a phenomenon known as autotomy). This well-known example continues to intrigue researchers keen to probe the mechanisms at work in what is seen as an archetypical form of regeneration. A team of scientists from the University of Arizona has taken a specific interest in a species of green lizard known as *Anolis carolinensis,* studying the mechanisms and genes involved in the process of reconstituting its tail.[4] No fewer than 326 genes are activated, to control the hormonal response, heal the wound, and manage the reptile's muscular-skeletal development. Confronted with a predator, the reptile can even cut off its own tail to save its life. This vital sacrifice is made possible by the presence of tiny cracks in certain vertebrae and a muscle structure made up of cones embedded inside other cones, so that when a predator seizes the animal's tail, its muscles contract and the cones come apart cleanly, snapping the vertebral column. The tail grows back thanks to cells that are capable of proliferating to form new tissues, in the manner of a regenerative bud. This phenomenon does not apply to all organs. Among cold-blooded animals, it is often the limbs or tail that can regenerate, but not vital organs such as the brain, heart or lungs.

Regeneration occurs not only as a functional response to aggression, amputation, or injury. It is also manifested in the ability of certain tissues affected by ageing to reconstitute themselves. Far from being inexorable for every species, cell death can sometimes be offset—as in the case of sea urchins, which can live up to one hundred years—by mechanisms that regenerate appendices such as feet and spines. This extraordinary resource, which counteracts the ageing of the organism, is linked to the presence of "multipotent" stem cells, capable of dividing and differentiating into several different types of cell.

A more general distinction can be drawn between three main operations by which regeneration can occur.[5] In the first, known as epimorphosis, the tissues in adult structures de-differentiate to form an undifferentiated mass of cells.[6] In the second, morphallaxis, existing tissues are rearranged, as can be seen in hydras. In the third, intermediate, type—a kind of compensatory regeneration—the cells divide but retain their differentiated functions.

The phenomenon of regeneration in certain animal species has always been a source of astonishment for humankind, even before the birth of biological science. Why does the lizard's tail grow back when our arms and legs are unable to? Is regeneration limited to a few species, and unknown to the higher vertebrates and humans? In reality, in birds and mammals, regeneration is not altogether absent, but it is limited to a small number of tissues, such as bone marrow, bone, the liver, and the outer layer of the skin. Our bones, for example, undergo a constant process of renewal, replacing old tissue with new. Bones are made up of cells (osteocytes) surrounded by an extracellular matrix. This matrix is renewed through an equilibrium between the action of two different cell types: osteoblasts, which synthetize the bone matrix, and osteoclasts, which eliminate ageing bone tissues.

In humans, it is the liver that possesses the greatest capacity to regenerate by renewing ageing cell tissue. As hepatic cells have a limited life span (300 to 500 days), they are constantly replaced by cell division. Regeneration also comes into play if part of the liver is destroyed, although never in the case of total loss:

> If 75 percent of the liver mass is removed, the organ recovers its full weight within 8 weeks in dogs, 3 weeks in rats, and 4 months in humans. No other organ displays such a power of regeneration: the proliferation potential of the liver is greater than that of extremely malignant cancers or that of embryo tissues. Once regenerated, the new liver weighs the same as at the outset (its growth is "organism-dependent") and this anatomical regeneration is mirrored by an equally rapid functional regeneration.[7]

The liver's exceptional propensity for regeneration, with such horrific consequences for poor old Prometheus, should not, however, blind us to the wider reality. In all the other organs that make up the human body and that of most mammals, regeneration is only very partial or is altogether nonexistent, especially in the wake of destruction.

The weakness of regeneration is partly offset by the mechanism of self-repair. What is the precise distinction between these two processes? In the case of regeneration, the *form* and the *function* of the affected organ or tissue are reconstituted almost identically to before. After losing its tail, the lizard recovers both the form of its tail and, conjointly, the same functions (e.g., in terms of mobility). In reality, the form is virtually identical but never exactly the same: the vertebrae are replaced by a cartilaginous tube, but the lizard's reconstituted tail is often shorter and paler.

In the case of self-repair, the form of the damaged organ will never return to its previous state; only the function can be restored, at least in part. Human skin cells offer a classic illustration that draws at the same time on the processes of regeneration and of self-repair. The outer layer of the epidermis consists of dead cells that are constantly being renewed thanks to the proliferation of cells in the basal layer. This is regeneration at work. If, due to an accident, such as a minor burn, the upper parts of the epidermis are affected, the destroyed part can still be regenerated through accelerated proliferation of the epidermal basal cells. The skin recovers its previous form and function. When the damage is deeper, such as in serious burns, the main part of the epidermis and the dermis is irreversibly affected. Here, regeneration gives way to self-repair, in this case in the form of scarring: "This complex physiological process, involving a large number of different cell types, results in the destruction of necrotic tissues and repair of substance losses. In this case, the damaged dermis is first replaced by a temporary fibrous connective tissue, which is later in turn replaced by a neodermis."[8] The damaged tissue that could not be regenerated is replaced by scar tissue. Astonishingly, there is a kind of competition between the two processes: "the regeneration of the specialized and functional cells of the damaged tissue is hampered by the presence of the faster-growing fibrous scar tissue. From this, we posit that the absence of regeneration power among a large number of vertebrates is due to the early formation of scar tissue."[9] Paradoxically, repair is not necessarily a second-best option compared to regeneration. The fact is that mammals regenerate less widely, and less well, than other groups such as reptiles, or simpler organisms that usually regenerate with ease such as anemones, starfish or hydras. The relative disadvantage of repair is the irreversible change in the form of the tissue or the damaged organ, whereas it is on the whole restored in the case of regeneration. But repair may offer a comparative advantage in natural selection if one considers the time factor, on which the preservation of an individual or a species depends: regeneration takes several weeks, even months (it takes more than sixty days for the lizard's tail to grow back), whereas self-repair, in the case of scarring, can be achieved much more quickly. This is why in the event of a deep burn, where the injury directly threatens the integrity of an organ, or the very survival of the organism, speedier repair takes precedence over slower regeneration.

For a long time, the preferred hypothesis to account for the difference between species where self-repair is the norm and those where regeneration takes precedence was that the first did not possess stem cells in sufficient quantity and quality.[10] More recent research[11] on the neoformation of hair follicles in mice after a wound tends instead to confirm the scenario of competition between the two processes. The correct explanation is not that regeneration is naturally absent in mammals (for lack of stem cells or a failure to recognize signs of regeneration) but that it is largely inhibited by the mechanism of repair: "the vital threat represented by large wounds undoubtedly amplified the imbalance between repair and regeneration."[12] These discoveries have been decisive in orienting clinical applications towards, in certain cases, disinhibiting the regenerative process in order to favor the restoration of the initial form of the damaged tissue (e.g., promoting hair regrowth rather than scarring). This phenomenon has been a popular theme in science fiction: the X-Men hero Wolverine, for example, has a power of regeneration that enables him to recover very quickly from all his wounds. In this fantasy scenario, the relative disadvantage of the usual kind of regeneration (its slowness) is entirely offset by its lightning-speed acceleration, restoring the hero to his initial state. Here, it is self-repair that is deactivated. That is why Wolverine emerges unscarred but regenerated.

From fiction to reality, there remains a difference of kind between the original tissue and the reconstituted tissue (for example, that of a major burn victim), a difference that resides in the scar: the scar is the indelible mark of the irreparable on the skin. The affected tissue will never return to its initial form, unlike that of the Marvel hero. Admittedly, the scar fulfills a similar function, namely of protection, to that of the original dermis. But only in part. For example, cutaneous scars are more sensitive to ultraviolet radiation and hair follicles do not develop under a scar. Where scars form following a myocardial infarct, one also finds a weakening of the heart muscle, which increases the risk of cardiovascular accident.

The fact remains that natural repair may, in the case of deep and lasting injuries, prove powerless to restore the earlier function (of mobility, digestion, protection, immunity, etc.). It is here that culture must take over from nature, where societies invent, construct and mobilize reparative techniques to supplement or substitute for self-repair.

MEDICINE, MAGIC AND BODILY REPAIR

Before constituting a body of biotechnological knowledge and knowhow, *other-repair* presents as a set of ordinary techniques and practices designed to compensate for the shortfalls of organic self-repair. It comes into play, of course, when an individual, such as a sorcerer or a doctor, acts directly on the body of another person; it is also evident in the way an individual might intentionally act on his or her own body. Self-medication is the prime example: it is, paradoxically, a form of other-repair in as much as the individual seeks to repair his or her own body as if it were an *other*. The body is at the same time objectivized and transformed by the subject into a body as a thing among other things, such as when one applies a dressing to a wound on one's own leg that is slow to heal.

It would be a mistake, however, to reduce the animal world to the realm of natural self-repair alone, while elevating humanity as the sole practitioners of other-repair. The Ancients were already aware that certain species are capable of a form of self-medication. In his *History of Animals*,[13] particularly Book IX, Aristotle gives several examples, such as that of the deer that, after giving birth, eats a plant of the genus *seseli*. Admittedly, Aristotle does not really describe the effects of this plant, but he does see it as a sort of medicine that represents a sign of intelligence in the animal (by comparison with women who also consumed *seseli* after childbirth). Despite recognizing this intelligence, Aristotle stops short of claiming that animals self-medicate; rather, they act in a spirit of self-preservation, without understanding the relations of cause and effect by which the substance works on the organism. It was left to later authors, such as Cicero and Plutarch[14]—sometimes citing the same examples—to acknowledge that animals had a real capacity for self-medication through the use of medicinal plants (for example, oregano for tortoises) and even for self-surgery (for example, elephants extracting spears from their bodies without tearing their flesh).

The issue, for them, was not whether animals could use expedients to relieve their suffering, but rather what caused such practices (i.e., whether to attribute intelligence or reason to an animal). The Stoics, in particular Seneca, contested this idea: animal behaviors, however ingenious they may appear, are in reality governed by the instincts with which Providence has equipped them to ensure their preservation. The opponents of this thesis, such as Plutarch or Porphyry, use:

> the theme of animal intelligence above all to show that man is not the purpose of the universe and that he has duties towards animals. Both the advocates and the opponents of the theory of animal intelligence can accept the idea of man adopting animal remedies; the debate does not deny the existence of animal self-medication, rather, it is about what causes this type of animal behavior.[15]

The problem raised by the Ancients is still keenly relevant to contemporary science, or it would be if it were not for the undeniable progress made in the observation of animal behavior, thanks to rigorous research protocols. The recent field of zoopharmacognosy[16] has refined our understanding of how animals self-medicate both for therapeutic and, indeed, prophylactic purposes. Even insects, such as ants and bees, are known to carry pieces of conifer resin with antifungal qualities back to their nests, where the resin will inhibit the growth of mold and bacteria. The remarkable thing here is that zoopharmacognosy works not for the sole benefit of the individual but for the colony as a whole. Such behaviors in insects are, however, the product of exclusively instinctive processes. The situation is different with birds and mammals, especially primates, where the pharmacognosic process is directly influenced by intelligence and by culture. Primatologists[17] have observed a female capuchin monkey in captivity salving her wounds with the aid of tools dipped in syrup (the same technique is sometimes used to treat wounds on her offspring). The preparation involved, and the use of plant material, demonstrate such skill that the research team compare this technique with the prehistoric development of human medicine.

Do all of these techniques of animal self-medication, whether instinctive or cultural, point to reparative practices? Not when they are purely preventive. Prophylaxis is not a reparative act, but pre-reparative: aimed at preventing a wound or other organic disorder and avoiding the need for repair. When primates rub millipedes on their skin to repel insects, they do so not to repair the wound caused by an insect bite, but to prevent it. Preventing damage is not about repairing, but about anticipating the risk of damage so as not to have to repair.[18] In other words, only therapeutic acts that presuppose existing damage, damage that was not avoided, can be assimilated to reparative acts. In some cases, however, the same process can serve both purposes (prevent and heal). When the North American brown bear makes a paste from saliva and roots to apply it to her fur, she does so both to repel insects (prevent) and to treat wounds (repair).[19]

The distinction between prevent and repair, between prophylaxis and therapy, applies equally to the human species, save perhaps for the degree of complexity. A finer distinction needs to be drawn, among prophylactic interventions, between primary prevention, intended to prevent the emergence of disease (e.g., vaccination), secondary prevention, which seeks to contain a health problem mainly by means of screening techniques, tertiary prevention, to avoid complications in existing conditions, and quaternary prevention, which relates to palliative care. In the last three levels, we find a sort of mixture between prevention and repair in as much as the interventions take place once the disease has already been contracted (with or without manifest symptoms). Tertiary preventive treatments, for example, are not designed to heal the disease directly by addressing its root causes, but they do seek to prevent the emergence of new symptoms and secondary diseases caused by the first. Hence the importance of distinguishing between *ex ante* prevention and *ex post* or *ad hoc* prevention. The same patient may of course, as part of a global treatment package, receive interventions in parallel that are directly reparative, as well as prophylactic.

Before crystallizing into technoscientific knowledge, prophylaxis developed historically in the form of magical practice. Whether to prevent the emergence of disease or the spread of epidemics, the act is performed to address supernatural causes. Chapels at the entrance into villages, amulets over fireplaces, rings on fingers, statues by the roadside, all such objects, endowed with supernatural powers, serve to prevent and protect against dangers, be they diseases or evil spirits. In the Christian West, venerating Saint Roch or Saint Anthony was thought to help prevent the plague, much as the protective eye painted on the prow of Greek boats was believed to safeguard sailors from epidemics and the hazards of the sea. Ancient Egypt, like other cultures, had its fetish objects such as the "magical intaglios," amulets designed to protect the bearer from evil and disease. The Egyptians sometimes wore intaglios on rings or embroidered onto a garment close to an organ they sought to protect.[20]

These magical and religious practices precede, but also foreshadow, the partition in Western scientific medicine between prophylactic and reparative interventions. Once the illness has been contracted, other objects and other rituals come into play to eradicate the source of the problem and repair the body. An anthropology of repair, even if it has a medical focus, must here step aside from the logocentrism of Western scientific rationality and open up to cultural worlds—including in the West—where intensity of belief matters more than experimental protocols. A cultural anthropology of bodily repair must begin by suspending, or at least placing brackets around, ideas about the rational scientific validity of causality relations between repair and healing. Its main purpose must be limited to describing and interpreting the collective beliefs that shape the course of reparative acts.

The anthropologist Sir James Frazer, in his famous study on the magical origins of kingship in Tonga, observed that certain kings were thought to have the gift of healing people through touch alone.[21] A Western doctor may of course question the efficacy of any such act of healing and demonstrate that this belief is false. But the anthropologist would be making a methodological error (known indeed, following Wittgenstein's critique, as "Frazer's error")[22] if he were to correct his informants' beliefs about their practices, or dismiss them simply as irrational and unfounded. In one sense, for the anthropologist, beliefs in magical powers of repair are neither true nor false: they are part of a symbolic world that must be described scrupulously. For cultural anthropology, the administration of an antibiotic to treat tuberculosis and the touch of a king to treat scrofula are merely two different modes of medical repair.

The historian Marc Bloch, in his pioneering study of historical anthropology,[23] may to some extent share Frazer's rationalism when he describes the belief in the healing power of the kings of England and France as a "collective error." But the core of his investigation probes the phenomenon of collective belief itself. What are the historical origins of this magical reparation of afflicted bodies? Why were kings thought to have the power to heal scrofula simply through the laying on of hands? Because, Bloch tells us, this supposedly supernatural power emanates from a being that is itself sacred and outside the common realm, a power that sets the King above other kings and lords; the oil with which he is anointed is of supernatural origin:[24] "The French and English kings were able to become miraculous physicians because they had already long been considered sacred persons: 'He is holy and the Anointed of the Lord,' as Pierre de Blois said of his master Henry II, in order to justify his wonder-working powers."[25]

This collective belief must be placed in its political context: the dramatization of this miraculous power was one of the ways by which the Kings of France could assert or reinforce their domination over their vassals, and over the feudal lords. The miraculous power to repair diseased bodies is, at the same time, presented as a political act. The ability to heal exceptional illnesses is not only a physical power over a few individuals afflicted with scrofula, it is a symbolic power over the entire body of society. The miraculous touch of the healer-kings must be understood as the instrument of an authority in search of legitimation, in other words, as a means of consolidating the collective belief in its domination.

The second methodological error, following "Frazer's error," would be to reduce the medical act of repairing the body in Ancient or non-Western societies to magical practices alone, in other words to the power of faith. Among many examples, we have the ayahuasca or cleansing rituals practiced by Amazonian communities. Ayahuasca is a vine which, when transformed with another plant, forms a beverage (of which the active ingredients are similar to neuromediators secreted naturally by the human body) that can be used to cleanse and detoxify. Far from being left to chance, the constitution and administration of this beverage rely on knowhow and a rationality that Western medicine can easily recognize. Ayahuasca rituals:

> always follow the same procedure and adopt a strictly methodical approach. They take this particular form not to "please" the participants or to try to give meaning to something that is *a priori* meaningless, but simply because they work best this way. They therefore correspond to a transmission of empirical and deductive knowledge, passed on by the healers from generation to generation.[26]

Ethnomedicine reveals the extraordinary variety and cultural diversity of curative practices, therapeutic rituals and botanical knowledge to be found in human societies. The medical act of bodily repair is never an isolated act (even in secular societies): it is packaged in a body of knowledge and knowhow, embedded in symbolic—sometimes mythological and sacred—worlds that define the relationship between human and non-human,[27] profane and sacred, feminine and masculine, mind and body.

Another illustration of this cultural diversity is provided by the Kallawayas of the Andes, whose culture even predates the colonization of the Inca Empire. The Kallawayas possess ancestral knowledge, kept alive despite Spanish colonization, of hundreds of medicinal plants (roots, leaves and grains), techniques for selecting, preserving and macerating them, and recipes for applying and administering them.[28] They travel from village to village offering treatment, particularly to combat malaria. Western science would have no difficulty in recognizing the efficacy, by its own criteria, of this ancestral plant-based medicine, and in using it for pharmaceutical and commercial purposes. From an anthropological standpoint, the essential point is that these preventive, therapeutic and curative acts depend on a whole set of incantations and rituals (for example, groups of musicians play drums and flutes to enter into contact with the spirits), and on particular symbols and visions of the world (the harmony of Mankind with Nature, notably Mother Earth or "Pachamama" in Andean cosmology). The therapeutic separation between scientific and magical repair, between natural and supernatural causes, is meaningless to the Kallawayas.[29] The ailments and diseases that affect an organism are not consigned to an afflicted part of a bodily entity; they threaten a wider social, natural and cosmic whole. Repairing is not only about healing a diseased body; it is about restoring it to an active place within a network of forces and a global cosmology.

The third anthropological error would be to unthinkingly accept the thesis of the "Great Divide" or "Grand Dichotomy," in Jack Goody's phrase,[30] between primitive and civilized societies, between the *bricoleur* and the engineer, between logical and prelogical thought, between the rational and the irrational. This is not to deny the difference in symbolic worlds and reparative practices between human societies or seek to downplay the mechanistic revolution of Western medicine, which is determined to expunge any vestige of vitalism, metaphysics or magic from its founding principles. The "grand dichotomy" thesis must be investigated, as we have seen, due to the coexistence in traditional societies of magical practices alongside scientific methods of classification and sophisticated medical techniques. This investigation is also retroactive when it comes to our own societies which, despite secularization and the autonomization of the life sciences, have by no means left behind magic and other modes of bodily repair that are irreducible to mechanistic medicine: "The very existence of these two trends, both expressed in the work of Lévi-Strauss, points to the inadequacy of the notion of two different modes of thought, approaches to knowledge, or forms of science, since both are present not only in the same societies but in the same individuals."[31] To say nothing of the development in our societies, over recent decades, of non-Western (and especially Chinese) medicines, some of which have even been integrated into the corpus of Western medicine, other very ancient practices of magical bodily repair still persist.[32]

Jeanne Favret-Saada produced an edifying case study during her "participant observation" of witchcraft practices in rural Mayenne in France. Not only because the ethnographer found herself "caught up" in a network of magical relations, but also because she so clearly highlights the often-conflictual coexistence—within a family, within a village and even within the same individual—between "official" medicine and "popular" medicine, with its faith-healers, *rebouteux* (bonesetters) and casters of spells.

This is the story of the Fourmond family. The father is suffering from late-stage cancer. The mother brings in the family doctor, but the sedatives prove largely inadequate to relieve the pain. At this point the uncle (Lenain) enters the scene. He attributes the ailment afflicting Monsieur Fourmond to witchcraft, and calls in his own brother, Jean Lenain, known in the village as *"the man from Quelaines,"* who has become a healer, a *"toucheur,"* after having himself been stricken by misfortune. As it happens, both the patient and his wife *believe* in the magical repair of the body by "touching," when official medicine proves insufficient or powerless. Exactly what form does this magical touching take? This mode of healing, the ethnographer writes, usually involves touching affected areas of the skin or the abdomen while at the same time performing rituals (for example, pronouncing spells or magical formulae, tracing a circle around a burn with one's fingers) and is an ability transmitted, often by a parent, in the form of a secret:

> more or less independent of the particular "gift" of this or that *"toucheur,"* the magical effect of these cures is supposed to be due exclusively to the hermetic nature of their transmission: the man who tells the *"secret"* (because, for example, he feels he is going to die and the time has come to pass it on) loses his *"force"*: however hard he tries to perform the ritual gestures and say the incantation, *"it no longer works."*[33]

Although in principle this "laying on of hands (*toucher*)" and "unwitching (*désensorceler*)" follow different rituals, they always converge on the action of a magical force that seeks to repair a stricken body.

Witchcraft, in the proper sense, depends on a triadic structure (witch, bewitched, unwitcher) and brings into play power relationships (magical powers) and relations of meaning (always conveyed by words):

> The witch's aim is to attract, by means of magic, the *"power"* or *vital* energy of a being totally lacking in magic means of defending himself. The bewitched, on the other hand, tries to avoid death or total loss of his *vital* force by calling on someone with magic power. Lastly, the unwitcher hopes he will be able to mobilize enough *magic* force against the witch to oblige him to return the *vital* force he stole from the bewitched.[34]

What, in other words, does the magical repair of the body consist of? Unlike mechanistic biomedical repair, the illness is not attributed (or not only) to natural causes, but to supernatural forces. While there may be physical acts of healing (such as touching), they are always accompanied by meta-physical effects such as the restoration of a life force that had been lost through the action of a malevolent being (the witch). The life force is always mediated through magical force, the first being restored by acting upon the second, in a struggle between witch and unwitcher.

Why are we faced here with a typical process of repair; at least, without judging its efficacy, at the level of belief? Because it is all about restoring, through a series of acts—in this case magical acts—the previous state of a being affected by a wound, an amputation, or a privation (of the life force). It is a play in three acts: the time of loss (affliction by misfortune), the time of intervention (the reparative act), and the time of reversal (the act of healing). However, the "unbewitched" person will never again be the same after this "witchcraft crisis," even if he has rid himself of the "curse." Bodily repair, even when magical, always leaves a residue and a mark (physical, moral or symbolic) of what can only be called the irreparable. Rarely are witches ever reconciled with the bewitched, even after the curse has been lifted. In some cases, such as in the French Antilles, the bewitched are sent to a region far away from their persecutor; in others, the bewitched seek directly or indirectly to take revenge, up to and including the physical destruction of the witch.[35]

This questioning of the thesis of the "great divide" aims not only to demonstrate the coexistence within our societies of medico-rational and medico-magical practices of repair. The very sources of Western medicine go back to the magical practices and religious rituals of Antiquity.[36] Of course, medicine, notably under the aegis of Claude Bernard,[37] has not escaped the vast process of rationalization of the sciences, rooting out the irrational, of which magic is the most extreme example. And yet, official scientific medicine has not entirely eradicated every irrational practice. Beside the traditional "relationship of trust" between doctor and patient, which sometimes has a direct (and not only psychological) impact on the improvement of a health condition, the prime illustration of this persistence is the placebo effect:

> As soon as patients find themselves in the medical social paradigm, their state of health already begins to improve. That being the case, how can we not make the connection with traditional medicines, in which the understanding of an illness and its treatment are interpreted through a cosmogony? The placebo effect clearly operates by the same logic. Patients, convinced that they have been taken in hand by a legitimate and legitimated institution, start to turn the corner towards an improvement in their condition. Proof—without having to invoke magical effects—of the charismatic domination of the medical institution.[38]

Questioning the thesis of the "great divide" should not imply that we fall back, conversely, on a superficial relativism in which all medical practices, Western and non-Western, "official" and "popular," are seen as equally rational and irrational, equally scientific and magical . . . It simply means demonstrating that rationality, experimentation and efficacy can be found, independently of the effects of belief, in practices and rituals that lie outside the domain of official Western medical treatments and, reciprocally, that some traces of magic may persist in the practices affiliated with Western scientific medicine.

REPAIRING OR ENHANCING BODIES

One marked difference, beyond their degree of efficacy, between magical and scientific repair of the body, lies in the propensity of the latter to bring in an endless flow of biotechnological innovations capable of modifying living matter. Such is the impact of past, present and future technoscientific revolutions that they are clearly redrawing the boundary between the repair and the enhancement of human organisms, even to the extent that the scientific and philosophical debate has crystalized around the possibility of creating a "post-humanity." Would a posthuman still need to be repaired? Can the posthuman defy the limits of finitude?

At face value, the dividing line between *repaired humanity* and *enhanced humanity* seems relatively clear, as does the frontier between reparative surgery and cosmetic surgery. Reparative surgery (rhinoplasty, blepharoplasty, mammoplasty, etc.), which in France is reimbursed by health insurance, is performed for medical purposes, to restore the body to an appearance closer to the patient's previous state (after suffering the consequences of a serious accident, trauma, cancer, etc.) or to a "norm" of physical integrity (if the subject has a congenital malformation, for example). "Cosmetic" surgery, by contrast, is performed solely with the aim of enhancing the physical well-being, perfecting the appearance, or addressing a psychological complex of the person requesting it. At the strictly medical level, cosmetic surgery interventions are never deemed "medically" necessary and, with very few exceptions, are not reimbursed by health insurance.

More generally, repair (whether self-repair or other-repair) aims to restore one or more functions of a damaged organism (following an accident or illness),[39] while enhancement aims to increase, by means of specific technologies, the appearance or performance of a living organism so as to make it superior to the standard for its species. The distinction starts to become porous and more problematic if, following Gilbert Hottois,[40] we view the human species as a sort of "natural cyborg." It is the nature of mankind, paradoxically, not to have a nature, or at least to be infinitely transformable: the human species, throughout its evolution, has sought to not only maintain but also increase its own potential, by a cumulative process. From this viewpoint, posthumanism is simply the rationalization of a process already at work at the heart of human evolution, except for the fact that the new "converging technologies" of nanotechnology, biotechnology, IT and cognitive science (NBIC)[41] are now capable of going well beyond; capable, indeed, of producing *Homo novus*.

In this respect, posthumanism enjoys a paradoxical relationship with modern humanism.[42] On the one hand, it shares with the Moderns the firm belief, found for example in Sartre, that Man is an infinitely perfectible being, a being-in-becoming destined to tear itself away from a static nature and onwards to *progress* through education, science and technology. On the other, it distances itself from that position, rejecting any form of essentialization of the human condition. Where the modern humanist might still ask, after Kant, "What is Man?," the posthumanist rejects this reification, preferring to ask "What new humanity do we want to construct?":

> The distinction between this antisubstantialist humanism and posthumanism is apparently just a matter of degree: once it falls within the reach of science and technology, the construction of man would no longer be limited to the spiritual project inspired, for example, by educational ideals. It would become a program for its material realization, aimed at creating a new man: no longer merely one who thinks and lives by breaking free of tradition (the humanist version), but one whose behavior, moods and faculties could be technically modified, to the point of undoing the identity ascribed to him until now (the posthumanist version). While it was about building on human plasticity at the level of intellectual virtualities, there was no real cause for concern. But if we have now got it into our heads to experiment with our bodily dispositions, then our most definitional markers are under threat.[43]

It is in response to these threats and the loss of these "definitional markers" (*repères structurants*), for example the threat posed by reproductive cloning to the principle of identity, that contemporary humanists like Jürgen Habermas[44] or Luc Ferry[45] join forces against posthumanism. The difference is therefore more than one of degree; there is a difference of nature between the two projects. What would remain that was *specifically* human to someone dispossessed of their birth, their singularity, their responsibility, their mortality? The project of Modernity, though unfinished, clearly has *limits* as far as the humanists are concerned; the very same limits that the transhumanists seek to escape. We are left with a conflicting moral imperative: for one side, it would be a crime against humanity to seek to eradicate the limits and, in a sense, eradicate what it means to be human; for the other, the crime would be to hold back from constantly and endlessly improving human performance and the human condition, even if it means creating some other kind of being.

There is in fact a dual movement within post/trans-humanism, contradictory only in appearance. On the one hand there is a fundamentally pessimistic movement, reflecting a kind of humanity-fatigue, weary of a species prone to suffering and illness, limited in its cognitive faculties and ultimately destined to die. This is not the pessimism of Adorno, who saw the dialectic of modern reason as a perversion of modernity. What the posthumanist wants is to give even more power to instrumental reason, without the limits of moral or communicative reason (at least in as far as it gets in the way of the first) in order to release humanity from its limitations. The message is clear: the time has come to turn the page on modern humanism and the old human species. On the other hand, the optimistic counterpart to this movement lies in the future vision of a species freed from bodily constraints, old age, and the likelihood of suffering and ageing. The disappearance of humanity is therefore the best possible news for humans themselves. The future belongs to posthumanity, and a glorious future it will be. After the age of consolation[46] of a humanity mired in its own finitude, vulnerability and fallibility will come the age of renewal of a reconstituted humanity, which will never have pushed its own boundaries so far. And will no longer be itself. After the pessimism of post-modernity, which, post-Auschwitz, no longer finds "a future with a *human face* desirable,"[47] we are promised, as Jean-Michel Truong puts it, a "totally inhuman expectancy," which will no longer need to console a fallen humanity, because that humanity is on its way out.

This is not the place to examine all the—absolutely essential—ethical questions raised by trans- or post-humanism, especially as it is not always easy to unravel what pertains, on the one hand, to the real and unprecedented scientific and technological advances that are already transforming humans into hybrid beings and, on the other, to the futuristic prophesies of the likes of Ray Kurzweil[48] or Max More, one of the founders of "extropianism" (a philosophy that advocates for unrestricted progress in science and technology).[49] Our problem is to establish whether the posthumanist hypothesis makes any form of repair meaningless. Does the posthuman still need to be repaired? Has the posthuman left behind any form of human finitude?

These questions reflect back on the status of the frontier between repair and performance, which directly affects the thresholds of human finitude: birth, disease and disability, intelligence, old age and death. The headline-making case of the South-African athlete Oscar Pistorius provides an excellent illustration. Pistorius was born with a disability that affected his lower limbs (no tibias, and deformities of the knees). A prosthesis was designed for him, so that he could use his legs. Thanks to this prosthesis, Pistorius is already more than a man, or at least a different kind of man. Medicine intervened initially to repair an organism deprived at birth of certain functions and organs. Nonetheless, Pistorius took gold in the 200 meters at the Paralympic Games in Athens in 2004. Furthermore, for the Beijing Olympics in 2008, the athlete submitted a request to the IOC Ethics Commission to be allowed to take part in the standard games (rather than the Paralympics): the Commission eventually turned down his request on the grounds that his carbon fiber prosthesis was more of an advantage than a handicap. From its response, it seems clear that the Commission feared a biotechnological arms race in the sporting arena that would undermine the principle of equality between competitors. Initially a being "diminished" by a handicap, Oscar Pistorius became an "enhanced being"[50] elevated to the rank of cyborg. The cursor has clearly moved from repair toward performance, on a scale that is more fluid than ever before.

On this scale, the very meaning of repair is no longer self-evident, well beyond the Pistorius example. More generally, a distinction can be drawn between three ways of enhancing humanity through the converging NBIC technologies:

> The first correspond to external devices that provide access to more information at any time, through computers and connected objects, for example. The second category corresponds to prostheses integrated into the body to restore a function lost or damaged by accident, to replace tissues or even whole organs, or to enhance a function, for example with cognitive implants. The third, and most worrying, concerns the enhancement of human capabilities that can be passed on to future generations. Some of these could significantly modify the human species, as would be the case with the use of CRISPR-Cas9[51] on human stem cells.[52]

Regardless of this legitimate concern about the future of the human species, posthumanity will continue to invoke ever more complex reparative techniques, if only with the aim of increasing human performance. This is something of a paradox: the more (post)-humanity is connected (to artificial devices) and biotechnologically sophisticated, the more it will need to be repaired. The posthuman may well, as the posthumanist prophecy goes, be exempted from birth, suffering and death, but only at the price of an extraordinary technological arsenal that will be constantly susceptible to internal malfunctions (there is a striking parallel here with modern cars, jam-packed with electronics, that spend more time in the repair workshop than more basic models). Incorporating nano-technological self-repair devices will not alter the problem; indeed, it may only make it worse: it will still be necessary to repair devices that are supposed to repair other mechanisms. The more sophisticated these new technologically remodeled bodies become, the more they will need to be repaired. Whether we are talking about reproductive cloning or ectogenesis to avoid the need for childbirth, about the prospects opened up by nanomedicine to put an end to all disease, or about techniques for uploading consciousness onto microchips to ensure immortality, in each case we will need to repair the nano-technologies, the microchips, the computers, the robots. . . . The posthuman world promised by the transhumanists will be one in which the dividing line between living things and matter, human and technological, repair and performance has been definitively blurred. But it is, paradoxically, a world of hyper-repair that looms on the horizon. Kurzweil may well predict the advent of the human body version 3.0, a body that is less and less biological, transplanted with microchips that will capture the signs of the outside world, a body that everyone will be able to change as and when they wish. But even if it performs ever more efficiently, this cyborg, this body version 3.0, half-body/half-machine will constantly be in for repair.

Without a doubt, posthumanism as a utopia, and indeed posthumanity as an incipient reality, are pushing back the limits of human finitude (birth, old age, death, etc.), but still remain within its boundaries. Cyborgs are not gods. The long-prophesized immortality will never be a posthuman state; rather—assuming that the fantasy becomes reality—it will be a process that needs to be endlessly constructed, modeled and perfected, a biological machine that needs endless repairs (due to mechanical wear, malfunctions, and the replacement of spares). However much the artificial world replaces the imperfection of living things, it will still be subject to the law of entropy. As Henri Atlan and Jean-Claude Ameisen have shown, all living organisms and all physical systems alike are destined to undergo degradation, obsolescence and, finally, death. Death or destruction is, as part of a dialectic relationship, necessary to the production of new life through the process that Ameisen calls "creative death."[53] The novel by Maylis de Kerangal *The Heart*,[54] on which the movie *Heal the Living* directed by Katell Quilleveré was based, is a vibrant illustration of what "creative death" can mean at the interhuman scale: the death of one person (the young Simon, left brain-dead after an accident) enables, through organ donation, the life of one or more others to continue (including Claire, who suffers from myocarditis and has been waiting for a transplant for months). The transplant, in this case, is more than a medical and biological operation, it is a physical, symbolic and ethical passage from one body to the other: the presence in the recipient of something other than herself, something necessary to remain alive.

In this sense, death is not a pathology. The same could be said of ageing. The posthumanist, as well as questioning the boundary between repair and performance, at the same time challenges the dividing line between the normal and the pathological. The aim is ultimately normative: to establish what deserves to be repaired and, where applicable, enhanced. For the transhumanist, it could be said, the entire human organism is pathological because it is imperfect, finite, and prone to *suffering* (from illness, negative moods, limited cognitive faculties, old age, and so on). Which is why it must be technically superseded. Even in the "normal" state, without observed clinical pathologies, there is something fundamentally pathological about human beings for the transhumanist. And it is this presupposition, with its far-reaching medical, ethical and political implications, that needs to be examined. Would a humanity stripped of all defects and pathologies—

a posthumanity, in other words—be preferable, more desirable, than a humanity condemned to a finite existence?

To answer this question, we can count on useful guidance from Canguilhem, who explores the frontier between the normal and the pathological in his famous essay.[55] Of course, science and technology have moved on since its publication, particularly as regards the barrier he erects between machines and living things, now that the NBIC technologies are conceiving and enacting their convergence and even unification. By playing off Bichat against Bernard, contesting the application of mechanistic models to living things, but without giving in to the temptation of naive vitalism, Canguilhem opens the way, if not to a rehabilitation of the pathological—that would hardly make sense—then at least to a different way of looking at it. The philosopher of science starts by underlining the ambivalence of the term "normal" or "normality," which refers sometimes to a fact that corresponds to a statistically observable norm (with certain divergences considered insignificant), and sometimes to an ideal, a perfect form. In other words, "normal" may be either descriptive or normative, and the two senses are often conflated in actual usage, including scientific usage: that which is statistically dominant tends to be valued as the ideal norm. Conversely, the pathological, as a deviation from the norm, is *de facto* devalued, and therefore deserves to be repaired and corrected to bring it back within the confines of the instituted ideal. That, at least, is the tendency that predominates in the mechanistic philosophy that assimilates living things with the physical properties of matter. From this angle, any deviation, variance or irregularity is a failure, a defect, an impurity that must be remedied. This is paradoxical: if living things do indeed obey the laws of mechanics, how could such irregularities come into existence?

To escape this dead end, Canguilhem is happy to invoke Bichat's "Research on Life and Death," which contrasts the instability and irregularity of vital forces with the uniformity of physical phenomena. Canguilhem subsequently rethinks deviations and irregularities entirely, not necessarily as abnormalities or pathologies, but as anomalies:

> In short, individual singularity can be interpreted either as a failure or as an attempt, as a fault or as an adventure. In the latter hypothesis, the human mind makes no negative value judgment, precisely because, as attempts or adventures, living forms are considered not beings referable to a real, pre-established type but organizations whose validity (that is, value) must be referred to the eventual success of their life. . . . At this point the term anomaly takes back the same, nonpejorative meaning as the corresponding (and no longer in use) adjective *anomal*. . . . Etymologically, an anomaly is an inequality, a difference in degree. The anomal is simply the different.[56]

In the same register, it is worth recalling that new species always emerge first as mutant species, including *Homo sapiens*, initially assimilated to a sort of monster compared to the species from which it immediately derives. And there is not an individual alive that does not display biological singularities (i.e., anomalies) to some degree. This is not to sing the praises of the anomalous, which might border on certain fundamentalist religious conceptions of living matter (such as the ban on the therapeutic abortion on the grounds that all human life is worth living, however serious and invalidating the embryo's disability might be); Canguilhem is careful not to do that. There are some anomalies, starting of course with illnesses and disabilities, which deserve to be repaired when they can be, or can reasonably hope to be.

The positive acknowledgement of anomalous difference should not lead to an inverse attitude that sees disability as an irreversible mark of destiny, thereby renouncing any recourse to scientific and technological innovations. The decision on whether or not to repair, based mainly on the surgical risk, implies a choice that is in no way systematic and which should take the form of a situational judgment of prudence (in the sense of Aristotle's *phronesis*), through discussion (with the patient, the family, the medical team), in which the norm is put to the test at the same time as the context, the patient's life history, the parties' considered convictions, the therapeutic opportunities, and so on.

The "anomal" becomes pathological, and genuinely abnormal, when situated in a complex of norms, power relations and socially defined meanings. The lesson to be drawn from Canguilhem's analysis is that the anomalous, though it might initially be seen as pathological by a transhumanist, and even by a humanist, can be, as he puts it, an "adventure in living." Even if it seems imperfect at first sight, a living form can turn out to be fruitful, creative, opening up new possibilities of life, thought and being. A mutant carrying anomalies that fails to conform to a specific statistical type can become, in the right context and the right environment, an accepted and perhaps even invasive variant, so much so that it subsequently becomes a new statistical norm. In this respect, repairing the anomaly is by no means an *a priori* necessity. Not every anomaly calls for repair. It all depends on how an organism interacts with and adapts to environments that are themselves changing. By making an *a priori* principle out of repairing any anomaly (in this case assimilated with pathology and abnormality) we would deprive ourselves of the life force in all its diversity and creativity. By seeking to repair all the supposed irregularities of nature, which would mean going against nature itself, we might nip in the bud new forms of life that could invent new ways of living. Even beyond living things: "If, then, it is true that anomaly, an individual variation on a specific theme, becomes pathological only in relation to a milieu of life and a kind of life, then the problem of the pathological in man cannot remain strictly biological, for human activity, work, and culture have the immediate effect of constantly altering the milieu of human life."[57]

The transition from the anomalous to the pathological—because, as Canguilhem reminds us, biology is not the only factor that affects humanity—depends not only on adaptation to the environment or 'milieu,' but also on collective representations. How and when does a society decide that an individual has gone from anomalous to pathological, from harmonious to monstrous, from fat to thin, from little to big, from sick to healthy? The question of the reparable and the irreparable is embedded within a wider issue: what place, and what form of representation, does a society offer those (the mentally ill, the disabled, the foreign, etc.) who lie outside the dominant norm?

In another essay, "Monstrosity and the Monstrous," Canguilhem surveys cultural and historical differences in the way societies, science, and the arts represent and objectivize the eccentricity of living things relative to the supposed regularity of nature. The depiction of monsters is a particularly telling indicator, almost a symptom. Whereas the Ancient Orient, where metempsychosis and metamorphosis were accepted beliefs, might see monsters as divine, Athens and Rome preferred to sacrifice them, or to reintegrate them into the city after purification. Monsters had to undergo magical repair in as much as they transgress the order of Nature, defined by its perfection. The monster is seen as an anti-cosmos, a cosmos gone astray. The Christian Middle Ages took inspiration from this view, turning the monster into an avatar of the devil, when teratology rhymes with demonology, when the monster is perceived as an offense to divine creation. Monsters could be exhibited as morbidly fascinating fairground attractions, just as they could be burned in the village square as witches. The work of the devil cannot be repaired (though it can be expelled) unless some rite of purification restores order to Creation. Whether the monster is on ostentatious display, for example in the bas-reliefs of churches or in illuminated manuscripts, or is disguised on the façades of gothic cathedrals, it is as a warning against evil spirits, against the risk of temptation. The monster is not only a real being, an impious birth that does violence to Creation; it is also a work of fiction. Imagination turns the monster into something monstrous, sometimes mixing up the real with the fabulous: monsters exist by the power of imagination.

The exhibition of the monstrous is therefore paradoxical: it is displayed so as to be better able to combat it, to attest to the superiority of the forces of good over the forces of evil, such as the gargoyle that still adorns the roofs of churches, a once-terrifying creature which, the legend goes, was neutralized by the Bishop of Rouen in the seventh century making the sign of the cross.

The work of Hieronymus Bosch bears striking witness to this fascination for monsters, a fascination that is at the same time a repulsion. While subverting the esthetic codes of his day, the very Christian Bosch seeks, by conjuring up a magical and monstrous bestiary, to denounce the moral failings (greed, lust, etc.) of his contemporaries. He who came to be nicknamed the "devil maker" sought to bring hearts and minds perverted by wrongdoing back to the straight and narrow path of the *spiritus sanctus* (Holy Spirit)—or by default, perhaps, a *spiritus sanus* (sound mind).

Behold the hybrid beings that emerge from his triptych *The Last Judgment*: in the central panel, Christ passes judgment on souls, while, below his halo, lies a world where misery, chaos and lust reign. Monstrous beings such as grylles (the "heads on legs" at the foot of the picture) mingle with men and women destined for damnation. Not only do the monsters move among the humans, but they can also at any moment penetrate them, contaminate them and transform them into repulsive half-animal, half-human hybrids. The monster is the reflection of our own moral monstrosity if we stray from the path of the Lord; the deregulation of nature that generates deformity is merely the woeful mirror image of the moral perversion of human nature, which Bosch, with his cathartic logic, holds up for us to see.

The fact that the Middle Ages and the Renaissance allowed the mad and the monstrous to coexist with the normal does not indicate—contrary to the hypothesis mooted by Canguilhem and by Foucault—that they were accepted as *anomal*, in all their diversity. The celebration of the monstrous during the Renaissance, as discussed by Canguilhem, is largely an illusion, just as the figure of the village idiot in the Middle Ages (before he was locked away in an asylum) can easily conjure up a false and clichéd pastoral image. Modernity, starting from the eighteenth century and especially from the emergence of mechanistic biology, has striven (not altogether successfully) to expel the imaginary from the scientific study of monsters, reducing them to their monstrosity, without the fantastical dimension of the monstrous. As Canguilhem puts it, the monster is shut away "in the embryologist's glass jar, where it serves to teach the norm."[58]

What does the new mechanistic norm tell us? That there are no exceptions to the rules and regularities of nature. Monstrosity is when the development of an organ is arrested at a stage that the other organs have left behind: "From then on, monstrosity appears to have revealed the secret of its causes and laws, while anomaly appears called upon to explicate the formation of the normal, not because the normal is an attenuated form of the pathological, but because the pathological is the normal impeded or deviated. Remove the impediment and you obtain the norm."[59] The monster may be rendered back to nature, at least in the laboratory,[60] but always with a form of retardation, impediment, or deviance. A few vitalists, however, have ventured to imagine life in all its possible forms, without submitting them to some higher law. In a sense, for the vitalists, there is nothing to repair, nothing to reject, and nothing to expunge from living things: living things, by opposition to matter, are the space where new forms are created. For a vitalist, there are no more monsters: monstrosity has metamorphosed into creativity.

The real revolution is the one dreamed of by the transhumanists: whereas the vitalists believe that all forms of life merit equal consideration because there are merely differential variations between beings, and no requirement to repair any lack of normality or legality, the transhumanists hold that everything in mankind is amenable to repair or enhancement, and that the envelope is constantly being pushed outwards. In the posthumanist promise, there is no longer any higher law in a venerated Cosmos, a deified Nature or an objective Natural Order: nature is *de facto* imperfect and defective, and so merits unlimited transformation. All that lives can potentially be repaired and improved. That which appears monstrous in today's human world will be tomorrow's posthumanity: when living things and matter, machine and human, are entirely indistinguishable, the cyborg will be the new normal. The monstrous as depicted by Bosch—a hybrid not only of man and animal, but also of man and machine—will become the new normative reality, minus the Last Judgment. Reality will be updated to align with fiction.

As we wait for this posthuman fiction to become reality, humanity must face up to the effects of *normalization* on the anomalous, and the correlative difficulty of accepting one's anomaly, one's difference, when it is socially pathologized and abnormalized. The question here is no longer to what extent the reparable is haunted by the irreparable, but whether all anomalies should be repaired. And the answer, as we saw, is far from being unilateral and unambiguous, including in strictly medical terms: deviation from a physiological constant (blood pressure, body temperature, pulse, etc.) is not in itself a pathology; it all depends on the patient as a whole, their history and antecedents, their life context, as well as the prevailing social and medical norms, and the ways in which these evolve.

The answer is not only medical. Canguilhem's reflections on abnormality, anomaly, and monstrosity have long enriched the purely medical or biological approach to disability by factoring in social and historical discourse. The history of the representation of the "deaf" is a good illustration. Until very recently, the deaf were only objectivized as deficient, physically if not mentally. The deaf were either excluded, or simply eliminated, as the Nazis did, or alternatively enjoined, via medical techniques, to find the path of hearing/speaking normality. The dominant medical discourse on the deaf is still one of disability and the need to repair deafness, making sign language a default language, and the world of the deaf a lesser world. Medically, the deaf count among the reparable, or more precisely among those to be repaired, thanks to recent progress in biotechnology (such as cochlear implants). It is only since the 1970s in the USA and Europe[61] that we have seen the emergence of a different sociological discourse on the deaf world, on Deaf identity, Deaf culture even, no longer perceived as an identity "by default" that needs to be repaired for the sake of the dominant norm, but recognized, starting with Sign, as a language in its own right: different—*anomal*, perhaps—but by no means abnormal. Like other minority cultures, the Deaf demand equal recognition:

> The discourse that considers the deaf as marked by difference rather than by deficiency can be said to have emerged when it turned away from the obsession with what was missing and began to highlight a way of living and of being-in-the-world. As deaf people came to occupy new positions in society and in the public space, they became beings endowed with rights (e.g. to education) and as research into sign language demonstrated that it is, in fact, just another language, the movement for the recognition of the existence of the Deaf cast a new light on their singularity.[62]

This social and historical detour through disability casts a new light on the very nature of the reparable. The reparable is not only a set of biological, technological and medical processes; it is also a set of social, historical and cultural norms and discourses. In this respect, it is expressed as an injunction, often presented as necessary and natural. By moving on from the question "what can we repair?" to "what must we repair?" or even "do we have the right to repair?" we can probe what is taken as self-evident. The social and medical discourse about repair clearly has the ability to open up extraordinary opportunities for those who see themselves as patients and who experience their disability through the filter of absence and suffering. It is quite another matter when the social and medical discourse on repair automatically associates any anomaly with a pathology and a deficient mode of existence, disregarding those who, instead, want their anomaly to be recognized through the register of *difference*.

We need to forge a new concept to categorize a mode of being that eludes the correlated registers of the reparable and the irreparable: the *a-reparable* might be a good choice of wording, due to its similarity to Canguilhem's *a-nomal*. The a-reparable, with its privative prefix, implies that the injunction to repair is neutralized, by virtue of a positive recognition of anomaly. Compared to the irreparable, the a-reparable is not non-reparable for any lack of options, it is arguably non-reparable because we have so many options: if we don't repair, it is not because we *can't* (technically, medically, etc.), but because we don't *want* to: the anomaly deserves to be experienced "as is" in a world shared by those who carry the anomaly and those who don't.

Where the posthumanists fall short is ultimately in their refusal to contemplate the wealth of human possibilities and the relative power that can be found in what they assume to be disabilities, defects or weaknesses that make up the human condition. Simone Korff-Sausse, among others, drawing on her experience as a therapist working with disabled children, calls for a radical change of perspective:

> Do these deformed or deficient children, then, have something to teach us? Rather then seeing them inevitably as beings to be repaired, marked by an incompleteness that needs to be compensated for or hidden, they could share with us their particular existential experience and get us to think about humanity's core questions: about origin, filiation, sexuality, and death.[63]

Ironically, what needs to be repaired, or at least transformed, is not so much the anomalous itself as social attitudes to disability and more generally to any form of anomaly, beyond outright rejection, voyeuristic curiosity, simple compassion or manifest indifference. What disability fundamentally challenges is the "sense of being at home," the unquestioning certainty of those who believe they live their lives without anomalies. With good reason, Korff-Sausse points to the parallel between the figure of the foreigner and that of the disabled: "I would like to take Edmond Jabès' words: 'What is a foreigner? Someone who makes you think you are at home' and paraphrase them by saying: 'What is a disabled person? Someone who makes you think you are normal.'"[64]

This change of attitude must begin from the first moments in the life of a child, particularly if the disability was not diagnosed *in utero*. Korff-Sausse recounts, from her experience as a therapist, the suffering of many mothers (and fathers) who sometimes don't dare to look at their disability-affected child, so wide is the chasm between the child of their dreams and the child they actually have. The shock is such that it has immediate and lasting effects on the way the child sees him or herself, especially if we posit, with Winnicott, that the mother's face acts as a mirror for the child, both in the way the child becomes conscious of him/herself, and as a refection of the mother's feelings towards him/her. It is in this broken mirror in that the child sees an image of abnormality, if not of monstrosity, as if the child were constantly reduced to his/her disability (especially if it is easily visible), undermining the whole basis of self-confidence necessary for self-construction. Some children with disabilities occasionally "play" with their handicap socially, paradoxically forefronting it, like the young girl approaching adults in the waiting room and asking: "I've got Downs; what about you?"[65] Rather than try to hide her difference, this young girl wears it, not as a pathology, but as a sign of diversity that calls for dialogue and mutual recognition.

This change of collective attitude must apply not only to anomalies that are automatically associated with abnormalities to be corrected and repaired. It also applies to structural features of human finitude such as old age and death, whose inevitability the posthumanists seek to eradicate. Old age, a very relative concept, has not only the aspect of incapacity, wrinkles and infirmity, or that of regret, fear of death and the realm of loneliness. It can also, conversely, be associated with experience, memory and transmission, and with the examined life extolled by Socrates, to say nothing of the vocation for wisdom commonly attributed to elders in traditional societies. The French TV series *Ad Vitam* (2018), co-directed by Thomas Cailley and Sébastien Mounier, is an excellent fictional illustration of what might happen to humanity after vanquishing death (humans can regenerate at will and stop the ageing process). In this society of immortals, the very "fact of being born," as Arendt calls it and, more crucially still, the succession of generations, are stripped of their foundations. Bringing up a new generation becomes superfluous for adults who can look forward to eternal youth. In the world of *Ad Vitam*, growing old and dying become a demand, a life choice, an act of resistance for a militant minority.

There are two extreme positions that need to be ruled out at this point. The first consists in thinking that all anomalies—and even the human body as a whole, being imperfect—are pathological and must therefore be repaired. The second consists in glorifying anomalies or in considering them to be irreversible, thereby excluding any recourse to repair and to technoscientific innovations. Between everything-is-reparable and nothing-is-reparable, a whole range of possibilities can unfold, depending on the desires of those with the anomaly (their history, their present, their hopes), their family and friends, the medical and therapeutic opportunities, and the social and legal norms.

By touching on the concepts of anomaly and the a-reparable we have moved forward in our exploration in that we have encountered, for the first time in this analysis, a negative function or usage of repair, as an attempt at *normalization*, whereas repair is spontaneously associated with a positive function: that of restoring or compensating for an absence or a loss.

RESTORING ECOSYSTEMS IN THE ANTHROPOCENE

It is the scientific and technological paradox of our time: while the transhumanists herald the advent of posthumanity, the climatologists (save of course for the skeptics) place mankind at the center of a new geohistorical era that bears its name: the Anthropocene. At the center, and at the origin. The Anthropocene, which follows on from the climatic era of the Holocene, is the period, starting from the beginning of the industrial era, in which human influence on the biosphere has reached such a level that it has become a geological force capable of modifying all of the planet's ecosystems. Human activity, its products, and its waste already form a new geological layer. At the very moment when biotechnology is becoming able to transform humans into another—hybrid—being, the planet is reminding us of our human, all-too-human, power to transform ecosystems. But this paradox may nonetheless lead to a shared goal: the transformation, if not of mankind's biological nature, then at least of its relationship with nature, a relationship inherited from modernity.

But what has this got to do with the question of repair? Everything, and on three different levels. Firstly, are ecosystems, or even the planet itself, actually capable of self-regulation and self-repair (and if so, to what extent)? Secondly, what if anything can human societies do (or what must they do) to repair the damage caused to ecological and climatic equilibria by industrial activity? Thirdly, is the ascendancy of the Anthropocene marked by irreversible and irreparable damage that directly threatens not only the reproduction of entire species but also the survival of human societies, and even the very existence of humans as a species?

The first problem arises in part independently of the harmful effects of human conduct on the major ecological equilibria. The epistemological question, which continues to stoke scientific, philosophical and even theological controversies, is whether we can view ecosystems, and the Earth itself, as living organisms. That ecosystems are made up of living beings, from micro-organisms to multicellular macro-organisms, goes without saying. What is open to debate, however, is whether ecosystems themselves can be assimilated to a kind of superorganism endowed, like all living beings, with mechanisms of self-regulation and self-repair. This controversy was indisputably initiated by the work of the iconoclastic climatologist James Lovelock, in collaboration with the biologist Lynn Margulis.[66] The Gaia hypothesis, as it was named, is one that is not unanimously accepted, starting with its status: is it a new multidisciplinary program in the Earth sciences (chemistry, biology, climatology, evolutionary theory, geology, etc.)? Is it a new philosophy of nature, or even a new political philosophy that seeks to prescribe a new way for mankind to live on Earth? Or is it no more than a folklore hypothesis for the New Age generation?

It must be said that in resuscitating the Greek name of the Earth goddess, who features largely in Hesiod's *Theogony*, Lovelock did little to facilitate the scientific reception of a hypothesis that seeks to revolutionize both the earth sciences and the life sciences by outlining an all-embracing theory. The core of Lovelock's hypothesis, of which the earliest formulations date back to the late 1960s and early 1970s,[67] is the quest to understand why our planet has remained viable since the appearance of the first living micro-organisms. How can we account for the fact that planet Earth—despite the existence of a structural thermodynamic imbalance (the coexistence of oxygen and methane in the atmosphere), despite major changes in the climate, despite the extinction of many species—has remained inhabitable? The key to explaining it, Lovelock tells us, is to hypothesize that "life" does not only react passively to an environment by adapting to it; rather, life directly influences it, or *bends* it, as Latour would later say. This talk of "life," with its tinge of vitalism, for which the British climatologist came in for plenty of stick, refers not only to all the living things that inhabit the Earth's ecosystems, but also to something *extra* that regulates the entire terrestrial system to maintain inhabitable conditions. That something—about with much has since been said and written—is supposed to regulate, at the global scale, the conditions of possibility for maintaining life on Earth. That something is Gaia: "Gaia is the planetary life system that includes everything influenced by and influencing the biota. The Gaia system shares with all living organisms the capacity for *homeostasis*—the regulation of the physical and chemical environment at a level that is favourable for life."[68]

By representing the Earth as an animated (or even "overanimated")[69] being, Lovelock not only undermines modern physics and metaphysics (which take the soul out of nature (*res extensa*) the better to invest it in the mind (*res cogitans*)), but also blurs the frontier between matter and life, not to mention the principles of the theory of evolution. It is no accident if some of the most radical criticisms came from evolutionary biologists such as Richard Dawkins.[70] Assimilating the Earth to a superorganism is scientifically untenable because all living beings are uniquely subject to natural selection and reproduction. The system that is Earth is a stranger to these laws of evolution, and so cannot be compared to an organism. The Gaia hypothesis is consequently dismissed as teleological illusion and mythological sleight-of-hand.[71] The criticism is unyielding and precludes any extension of the hypothesis of self-regulation and self-repair in nature, beyond living organisms *stricto sensu*.

Except that Lovelock's formulations of the Gaia hypothesis are far from unambiguous and can vary from one text to another. Some of them are clearly problematic, such as when Lovelock treats Gaia as a hypostatic entity ("The Revenge of Gaia") capable of acting on the stage of terrestrial history. Other propositions are not without ambiguity: "When I talk of Gaia as a superorganism, I do not for a moment have in mind a goddess or some sentient being. I am expressing my intuition that the Earth behaves as a self-regulating system, and that the proper science for its study is physiology."[72] It all hangs, as Latour rightly says, on the weight Lovelock places on the conjunction "as" to convey the comparison of Gaia to a superorganism: Gaia both *is* and *is not* a superorganism. Lovelock struggles with the endemic problem of holism that plagues the natural and social sciences when they attempt to conceptualize organisms in terms of the relationship between the whole and the parts. When the focus is on asserting a simple equivalence between Gaia and a superorganism, without further qualification, then the Earth is seen as a sort of unified whole regulating and bringing order to all of its parts, like a great clockmaker, to maintain global homeostasis. This line leads us straight into teleological and hypostatic dead ends: Gaia becomes a quasi-person. But another reading is possible: the one proposed by Latour in his critical but charitable commentary on the Gaia hypothesis. If Gaia cannot be seen as a great order-giving whole, it is because there is no plan, no grand engineer, no God capable of arranging, regulating and repairing all of its components. Gaia cannot be to ecosystems what the brain is to the rest of the body.

How is it possible to conceive of regulation at the global scale without presupposing an already constituted and unified whole? Latour himself wrestles with this difficulty and nudges the Gaia hypothesis towards the notion of immanence, of generalized interconnection between different forms of "agency." Rather than the vertical holistic model of the superorganism, he prefers a horizontal relationist model of agents constantly influencing each other, in a tradition that owes as much to Gabriel Tarde as to Louis Pasteur. Like Lovelock, Latour seeks to conceptualize a dynamic plane of immanence, at the planetary scale, without resorting to a transcendant whole:

> The whole originality—and it's true, I recognize it—the whole difficulty—of Lovelock's enterprise is that he plunges head first into an impossible question: how to obtain effects of *connection* among agencies without relying on an untenable conception of *the whole*. He sensed that extending the metaphor of organism to the Earth was senseless, and that micro-organisms were nevertheless indeed *conspiring* by sustaining the long-term existence of this critical zone within which all living entities are combined.[73]

The unsettled question is this: how do all these agencies (biotic and abiotic) on our planet manage to collaborate, despite endless disruption, without being unified and controlled by an all-encompassing organism? The only tenable proposition, which in no way resolves the underlying ontological problem, is to say that all these agencies constantly act and retroact "as if" the whole thing were regulated by a superorganism, but that this homeostasis cannot be attributed to some super-subject that acts as a grand ordering epicenter. By exercising this extreme methodological caution we can extend self-regulation and self-repair to groups of entities far larger than living organisms.

Though we speak—with all due caution—of self-regulation, self-repair, even of resilience, this in no way implies that ecosystems, once disrupted, are able to return to exactly the way they were before. The massive injection of oxygen into the atmosphere two billion years ago proved toxic to many microorganisms, and they won't be coming back. After a major disruption, the ecosystem becomes *other*. The resilience of ecosystems refers to their ability to absorb shocks and disruptions by reconfiguring the whole to maintain, functionally speaking, the overall conditions for some kind of life on earth:

> Analysis of ecological networks shows that ecosystems are resilient. They preserve their overall functionality when some of their links are deleted, but only up to a certain threshold, beyond which they become dislocated. Some 'cornerstone' species possess a very large number of links, which guarantee the stability of the ecosystem. The reintroduction of wolves into Yellowstone Park, for example, led to the reappearance of plants that had been over-consumed by elk, as well as several animal species associated with these plants.[74]

When just such a disruption threshold is reached, and certain key species no longer play their regulatory function, the ecosystem is threatened with disappearance.[75] This is when Gaia is supposed to step in as if, despite the imminent destruction of an ecosystem, her duty is to offset this loss in order to maintain the possibility of life. It is as if ecosystems themselves behaved like interconnected agencies.

The Earth, as a network of interconnected forces, has clearly sustained life through a succession of climatic regimes. The unnerving question is, of course, will it continue to do so in future, given the past and ongoing transformations that have triggered the Anthropocene? To put it starkly, will Gaia survive the Anthropocene, and, if so, at what cost? Is the Anthropocene just another climatic regime like those of the past (which the planet can therefore regulate) or is such a particular climatic regime that it threatens the fundamental parameters that make life on Earth, and especially human life, possible? And if there is regulation, might it not be at the cost, if not of human survival, then at least of human lives . . . ? These questions have opened up new controversies and rekindled old ones about the Gaia hypothesis. Even the theory of the Anthropocene, though currently dominant in the scientific community, particularly in the IPCC (Intergovernmental Panel on Climate Change), is not unanimously accepted: climate skeptics such as the climatologist Richard Lindzen and the geophysicist Vincent Courtillot have expressed doubts about the scientific foundations of theories that ascribe the cause of global warming to human activity.

It is worth following Lovelock further in his thoughts about the Anthropocene, if only because of his considerable influence on contemporary environmental and ecological movements (Deep Ecology in particular). Much has been made of his recent alarmist calls for a general awareness-raising campaign to "save the planet," advocating neo-Malthusian policies.[76] Under this hypothesis, Gaia is clearly threatened by the Anthropocene and mankind is called upon to react or feel the brunt of Gaia's "vengeance." This view is a fairly radical break from Lovelock's earlier ideas about the effects of human activity on the Earth-system. The surprise lies in the relatively relaxed attitude of the former Shell engineer to the effects of industrial pollution on the biosphere, and in particular on climate change. Lovelock's argument merits close attention: "Man's present activity as a polluter is trivial by comparison and he cannot thereby seriously change the present state of Gaia, let alone hazard her existence."[77]

This argument is based on the hypothesis that the human species is a species like any other. In other words, since pollution is the product of a living creature (the human species), it should be seen as an integral part of how Gaia works. Industrial pollution is "natural" because it is produced by a "natural" being. Gaia can therefore handle its regulation:

> If organisms produce a compound that impacts the environment, this output could then be interpreted functionally: the partial depletion of the ozone layer (potentially offsetting other mechanisms that increase ozone production) might not be entirely harmful. It could play an important role in Gaia for maintaining certain equilibria. And surely living entities are capable, in turn, of *adapting* to these episodes of pollution, just as the peppered moth has adapted to the consequences of the industrial activity of the 19th century? In the same way that living things adapted to an oxygen-rich atmosphere, likewise, for Lovelock, humans could adapt to an increase in the intensity of UV light resulting from the thinning of the ozone layer, so long as racial taboos do not prevent gene flow between UV-sensitive populations and those who are better adapted.[78]

Not only is industrial pollution "naturalized," it can even have "positive" effects on other living organisms that can benefit from it (in much the same way as grass benefits from cow pats). As a result, policies aimed at regulating the impact of industrial pollution, in the name of ecological transition, to limit global warming, begin to seem irrelevant and aimless . . .

This argument, though coherent, is to say the least disconcerting, and could give ammunition to the more liberal "laissez-faire" climate skeptics, despite the fact that Lovelock is strongly committed to the deep ecology movement! What then is most likely to disturb Gaia? Lovelock's answer, at least up until the 1980s, was to blame overpopulation and intensive agriculture. Whereas industrial pollution is "naturalized," agriculture is "artificialized." Again, a surprising argument. Not only, as Dutreuil points out, are Lovelock's statements about agriculture weakly supported by experimental observation, they also jeopardize the consistency of the model. After all, if mankind is to be seen as a natural species, then its agricultural activities, even if intensive, must be viewed through the same "Gaian" lens. Gaia should be able to regulate them. Through the importance he places on agriculture, Lovelock on the one hand paradoxically puts mankind back at the "center" of the system by singling it out, albeit negatively, as a species unlike any other, and on the other hand invites doubts as to Gaia's capacity for self-regulation and self-repair.

How do these controversies have a direct bearing on our topic? If we suppose that Gaia is able to regulate the harmful effects of human activity (such as massive greenhouse gas emissions), then the question of repair no longer arises. Reciprocally, the question of self-repair in the ecological domain cannot arise, either because we assume that the unprecedented intensity of the effects of human activity overwhelms Gaia's power to regulate the maintenance of life on earth, directly threatening the survival of the human species, or because we purely and simply deny the existence of anything assimilable to Gaia and that, without a "pilot," the planet really is in danger, and the future of the human species hangs in the balance. The question of regulation and ecological repair would in this case be in the hands of mankind alone, putting mankind back "at the center" of the system, implementing a reparative ecology to meet the challenge of the Anthropocene. And yet this imperative of ecological repair is far from self-evident, even though not a day goes by without politicians, the media, and intellectuals sounding the alarm about the urgent need to take action for the planet (and it may already be too late).

What should we repair? To speak of Nature as an object of repair can easily be confusing. Since the advent of the Anthropocene, the effects of human activity have spread to every surface of the planet. The water in the rivers, seas and oceans, the forest ecosystems, the air, the soil and the living species are all, to various degrees and depending on their geography, impacted by human activity. If the Anthropocene radically challenges the great divide between Man and Nature, it is because, in a way dear to Latour, it sustains a kind of *anthropomorphism*: Man forms and informs Nature with his powers and his actions. If we must repair, then we must repair a Nature that is, in part, "human."

To what end should we repair? This is a deeply divisive question for ecological movements themselves and for the policies they advocate. Ecological repair may be aimed primarily at preserving the human species within an environment that is advantageous to humans (to the possible detriment of the survival of certain species or the maintenance of certain ecosystems).

If so, then ecological repair is still enmeshed in the anthropocentrism of the Moderns. Alternatively, ecological repair (as professed, for example, by deep ecology) can be aimed at every form of life on Earth, with no special privileges for the human species (which could, moreover, be classed as a nuisance species). In practice, despite incessant calls from ecological groups to preserve all ecosystems and save species threatened with disappearance, the dominant tendency in ecological and energy policies is indisputably anthropocentric. Their main goal is to guarantee the living conditions of future human generations.

Who should repair? We need to distinguish here between different scales and modalities of responsibility. On one side is a moral responsibility which, following Hans Jonas, we might define as a new categorical imperative: ensuring that the effects of our actions are compatible with the permanence of an authentically human life on earth.[79] Note that the attribution of responsibility in Jonas remains very largely anthropocentric: it is above all about guaranteeing the conditions for future human life. The idea of a moral responsibility for there to be a future humanity contains nothing that is binding, nor does it allow us to impute real environmental damage in accordance with the degree of involvement and destructiveness of natural and legal persons. Certain societies, certain governments, certain businesses are clearly more responsible than others for systemic environmental degradation. The idea of a moral responsibility based on a "heuristic of fear" may have some utility in promoting a more universal awareness, but it might at the same time have the effect of diluting the responsibilities and imperatives for repair. Asking traditional societies, still living in the preindustrial age, to "repair" the consequences of pollution caused by industrialized countries would be philosophically unjust. It is, however, undeniable—and this is what Jonas was getting at—that the negative global effects of the destruction of ecosystems far exceed the scope of action of any particular individual or collective entity. This is why engagement is required from the international community to mitigate the damage, along the lines of the COP international climate conferences, which commit the signatory states to transform their economies in order to limit global warming. But without a legally binding authority and a legally equitable principle to determine the responsibilities of each party (for example, the polluter-pays principle), ecological repair will remain at the stage of wishful thinking.

How can we repair the environment? It has to be said that, over the last twenty years, governments have put in place increasingly binding legal instruments, even if limitations and loopholes persist. A distinction must be made between measures of repair and measures of avoidance, mitigation and compensation. Avoidance measures are designed to prevent the implementation of development projects that are expected to have negative environmental impacts. Avoidance, in other words, involves preventive or prophylactic practices that aim to create conditions where repair will be unnecessary. For example:

> in the marine environment, many port projects were blocked in the Mediterranean after a marine plant, Neptune grass (*Posidonia oceanica*), was granted legal protection. This phanerogam, whose ancestors returned to the marine environment, forms vast meadows of huge ecological significance on the Mediterranean seabed. Found anywhere from the surface down to a depth of some forty meters, Neptune grass is very sensitive to any coastal development. Since it became legally protected in 1988, its mere presence is sufficient to block any maritime construction project that might threaten it.[80]

Mitigation measures, by contrast, intervene once a project has been built or is being built. They are not, strictly speaking, a form of repair, in as much as the aim is not to restore the site to its state prior to the execution of the project but rather to limit the negative effects of artificialization on an ecosystem (for example by modifying the initial project to diminish habitat loss for a directly impacted species). In environmental law, such repair or restitution is known as "primary reparation" (or "primary remediation"). More often than not, primary reparation is impossible and "complementary reparation" (or remediation) will be required. Reparation, though it seeks to compensate for a loss, is not *stricto sensu* a form of compensation. Reparation takes place when the damage caused can easily be observed, whereas compensation intervenes when a development project has been given administrative clearance, the aim being to "compensate" for damage that could not be avoided: "If this distinction between reparation and compensation were not clearly established, there would be a significant risk of seeing development projects authorized that endanger the environment, on the pretext that the 'future' damage could be 'repaired,' even if it were irreversible."[81]

While the concept of reparation is clearly established in civil liability litigation, as we will see in chapter 4, its usage in environmental law is less evident, even though it is enshrined in French constitutional law, in the Charter for the Environment.[82] Article 4 of the Charter states explicitly that "Everyone shall be required, in the conditions provided for by law, to contribute to the making good of any damage he or she may have caused to the environment."[83] Article 5 defines more specifically the scope and modalities of government intervention:

> When the occurrence of any damage, albeit unpredictable in the current state of scientific knowledge, may seriously and irreversibly harm the environment, public authorities shall, with due respect for the principle of precaution and the areas within their jurisdiction, ensure the implementation of procedures for risk

assessment and the adoption of temporary measures commensurate with the risk involved in order to preclude the occurrence of such damage.[84]

The innovation lies in the extension of the notion of reparation to cover damages that do not directly affect persons. French judges have two legal tools at their disposal for assessing reparations when damage has been proven. Either *reparation in kind*—which consists in restoring something to a state close to its previous condition (for example asking the offender to erase graffiti on someone's property)—or *reparation by equivalence*, itself subdivided into pecuniary and non-pecuniary or "equivalent in-kind" reparations. Pecuniary reparation essentially entails the payment of compensation when restitution to the initial state is manifestly impossible (as in the case of irreparable destruction). Equivalent in-kind reparations, similarly, apply only when reparation in kind is deemed impossible or inappropriate: the objective is to compensate for the original loss by obtaining (non-pecuniary) measures that restore the rights of the victim (for example the obligation for a newspaper found guilty of libel to publish the court's findings).

The main difficulty of extending the legal principle and modalities of reparation from civil law to environmental law resides in the fact that Nature is not a person. Nature is an object, never a subject, of law, despite attempts to modify her status.[85] Gaia doesn't sue . . . How can reparation be made to an entity that cannot ask for reparation? How can reparation be legally instituted in a system that is above all designed to repair the damage caused by one person to another? If we see the environment as a *res communis*, an inappropriable common good, then, since Nature cannot speak for herself, it is surely up to the state, as the guarantor of the public interest, to ensure the protection of the environment and, where necessary, demand reparation for damage caused. The problem is that the state may be both judge and party, may itself be the cause of environmental damage, and may prioritize economic, political or military interests over those of the environment. States are rarely good advocates for Gaia. One way around this loophole is to grant accredited status to environmental defense organizations "approved by the administration to act for the reparation of environmental damage under Article L 142-2 of the Environmental Code. The advantage of this strategy is that it highlights the ability and capacity of such organizations to take action to protect the collective interests that they defend by virtue of their status."[86]

However, this solution is far from resolving all the difficulties involved in the reparation of the environment. Quite apart from the fact that we are dealing with individual non-profit organizations that are supposed to defend collective (human and non-human) interests, the question is: on which criteria, on the basis of which priorities, on the grounds of which scientific principles are we to determine the damage caused to the environment by human activity? If we can't get Nature to tell us what "reparations" are required, then it will always be up to us humans to plead in her place. To speak in legal terms about the reparation of the environment (as the shared legacy of all human beings) rather than the reparation of Nature is already significant: the damage caused is measured primarily in terms of the harm done to humanity. The Charter for the Environment is, in letter and in spirit, anthropocentric.[87] It is not the damage done to Nature as such that counts; it is the damage to the "natural" environment insofar as it restricts the range of human habitability.

On top of the problem of the legal status of nature *vs.* the environment comes the problem of the modalities of reparation. European Community law,[88] like French law,[89] tends to prefer reparation in kind overcompensation (which is resorted to only when the first is impossible).[90] In environmental law, reparation in kind can take three forms. Primary reparation is aimed at restoring a given environment to its original state after destruction or significant loss (for example by planting a tree of the same species as the tree that was destroyed).[91] Secondary (or complementary) reparation is invoked when restoration to the initial state is compromised. Complementary measures are then supposed to "compensate for this shortfall and provide natural resources or a level of ecological services comparable to what would have been the case if the original state of the site had been restored."[92] If, for example, it is not possible to reintroduce a species, due to irreversible damage, a complementary measure might consist, where possible, in introducing a closely related species capable of adapting to the modified environment. Because primary and complementary reparation generate "intermediate losses" between the moment when the damage is attested and the moment when remedial action is initiated, some legal statutes, such as European Directive 2004/35/EC provide for compensatory measures.

As well as the difficulties of identifying the agencies responsible for damage and for taking reparative measures,[93] ecological repair poses an even tougher challenge. Primary reparation, in particular, is aimed at restoring an ecosystem to its state prior to the damage. But is such an objective possible, or even desirable? Even the "compensatory" measures can never return it to its earlier condition;[94] at best it might be a similar condition, or perhaps an idealized one. To deny this fact is to deny the operation of time and the transformations inherent in all ecosystems. Expressions such as "returning an environment to its natural state," "restoring an ecological niche" that prevail in environmental law are by no means unproblematic.

Independently of the type of damage involved, the problem of a putative return to the earlier state of nature keeps questioning and at the same time shifting the dividing line between humans and non-humans.[95] Since the Neolithic Revolution and the invention of agriculture, if not before, mankind has constantly modified its environment and has been transformed by it in return. Anthropomorphism, although it has taken an unprecedented turn since the Industrial Revolution, is not an invention of Modernity. When the law speaks of restoring something to its original state, does that mean before all human intervention? That would be to forget that ecological systems are dynamic: returning something to its original state would mean ignoring the possible evolutions that an ecosystem might have undergone in the absence of human intervention. Once again, time is overlooked:

> Ecological systems are not fixed: while they present a very great stability over a short time scale, they are the product of a history and are intrinsically liable to evolve over long time scales. There is therefore no "natural" reason to want to preserve one state rather than another. The disappearance of systems, of population groups, or of species is a "normal" phenomenon that allows new forms of life and organization to emerge. Striving to safeguard what exists at any cost ultimately denies a fundamental reality that is consubstantial with all living systems: they evolve because they are mortal.[96]

This argument ties up with our prudent plea, with Canguilhem, for the diversity of life and touches directly on the issue of the *duty*—as opposed to the *power*—to repair nature. Nor is it far removed from Lovelock's early writings on the power of Gaia to regulate industrial pollution. The most disconcerting thing is that the "anthropo-reparation" of nature could, by postulating a return to a pre-anthropic state, generate harmful effects for nature itself. In seeking to repair the damages he himself has inflicted on Nature, Man—still all too Promethean—generates unintended consequences (as, for example, when the introduction of a replacement species disrupts the natural balance of an ecosystem).

So should we forget the whole project of repairing nature and adopt a *laissez-faire* approach? The alternative put forward by Badot and Richard, which they judge to be under-exploited, despite being less costly and supposedly more effective, is to "leverage the natural spontaneity of environments or, more prosaically, *to leave Nature the heck alone to let her find her own new state of equilibrium.*"[97] In other words, instead of making "artificial" repairs in the name of a largely imaginary initial state of nature, it is preferable to let nature self-regulate and self-repair. Note that the authors are in no way opposed to the idea of limiting man-made disturbance to ecosystems; they do not go along with Lovelock's supposition that all human activities, including those that pollute, are "natural" or "Gaian." The objective, at the same time, is to limit the eco-reparative power of humans so as to allow nature to find its own states of equilibrium.

The problem, which the authors do not directly address, is the impossibility for ecological systems to attain or recover any form of equilibrium, due to the systematic destruction of any form of life. Must we allow non-life to reign supreme? In as much as mankind is directly responsible for this damage, surely reparative action is justified, to compensate for the impossibility of natural self-repair? The objection becomes more radical when extended to the prospects for future human life. It is by no means certain that mankind itself will ultimately survive the Anthropocene. Promoting the capacity of ecosystems for resilience and self-repair ("leaving Nature the heck alone") does not imply that we should renounce ecological repair measures, when life is no longer able to regenerate equilibria "naturally."

The fact remains that ecological repair, however carefully implemented, will never achieve a pure and simple return to the ecological situation prior to the damage. The ecological reparable leaves behind, to varying degrees, a "relative irreparable" which is the mark of time on the transformation of ecosystems. Even when "repaired," an ecosystem will always be different to what it was before its man-made disturbance. This is just as true when humans deliberately intervene in the reparative process as when nature repairs itself. The meaning of ecological repair, due to this irreducible element of the irreparable, is the possibility for life, not to return to its prior state, but to produce life anew and to generate new spectra of equilibrium, often at the cost of modifying some species, and even of allowing others to go extinct. There is not in itself anything dramatic or catastrophic about this "relative irreparable," even if the disappearance of certain species or ecosystems is potentially tragic, for themselves and for the human populations that depend on them. There is nothing alarming about the relative irreparable, because ecosystems are dynamic and have been constantly evolving, even in the absence of man-made disturbance, ever since the first life forms appeared on Earth. It is not only civilizations that are mortal, to paraphrase the poet Paul Valéry, it is every form of life. The relative irreparable, though it prevents return to the life-that-was, in no way inhibits the possibility of new forms of life, including by adapting and transforming existing forms to the Age of the Anthropocene (due to poaching, elephants born *without* tusks now tend to reproduce and multiply faster than those *with* tusks).

The worrying scenario is that of an "absolute irreparable," synonymous with the irreversibility of the ongoing process, with the Anthropocene threatening all ecosystemic equilibria to the point, if not of making all future life impossible, then at least of making the preservation of human life problematic. The most disturbing scenarios, some of which warn us that "it is already too late," clearly remain within an anthropocentric narrative. It is first and foremost mankind that is imperiled by the climate regime of the Anthropocene. Unlike the relative ecological irreparable, the absolute ecological irreparable implies not only that there is no return to a pre-traumatic situation (for example before the time of global warming), but, more seriously still, that the change is irreversible, and will make it impossible, for at least part of humanity, to preserve itself and to reproduce, that is, to reconstitute ecosystemic equilibria that will support human habitation, failing some sort of new natural selection . . . The notion of the absolute ecological irreparable should, however, be handled with care insofar as the Earth has already experienced major disruption events in the past (albeit accompanied by mass extinctions) while continuing to produce life. As for what new place mankind will occupy in the planet's future, that remains to be seen.

This final digression confirms our starting hypothesis and takes us back to the title of this chapter: repair is only an issue because living entities are easily wounded. Spontaneous repair (self-repair) and artificial repair (other-repair) are responses inherent in living beings, designed to defer their mortality and, more generally, to restore homeostasis when vital equilibria are jeopardized by significant losses. When repair takes place, it never amounts to a return to the *status quo ante*, as in the case of regeneration: rather, it signifies the possibility of recovering a vital capacity and a functional equilibrium necessary for the maintenance of the organism. There is nothing specifically human in the spontaneous mechanism of self-repair found across a broad swathe of living entities. Human living entities are distinct only in their unrivaled propensity for constructing artifices (*reparatio*) to compensate for defective self-repair. It is as *techné* that human repair stands out from the rest of the natural order. This scientific and technological power has reached such a threshold of innovation and sophistication that it has begun to blur the boundary between the living and the machine. Humanity no longer demands only to be repaired, but to be enhanced. The dream of immortality promised by the transhumanists will change nothing, however, about the ontological fact of repair, even for bionic beings. Pushing back the limits of human finitude will require ever more repairs, whether to living machines or to machine-like living entities. Even enhanced with electrodes and augmented with microchips, mankind will be more reparable than ever . . . The limits of finitude may be transgressed, but they will not be abolished.

The controversies surrounding transhumanism have enabled us to shift the question of repair from what might be called the descriptive level to the prescriptive level. The problem is no longer whether we can (technically) repair whatever remains unrepaired, but manifestly what we *must* repair. Knowing what must be repaired entails a whole set of norms (social, political, medical, etc.) and injunctions to repair, all of them relative, which may run contrary to the diversity of life and the right to recognize and lay claim to a-nomality. This is why it seemed opportune to posit a third value—the a-reparable—in counterpoint to the defining binary of the reparable and the irreparable. The a-reparable is not an absence or a lack of reparability (as might be the case with the irreparable); if anything it points to an excess of reparability, in that it runs counter to the dominant norm by asserting the right not to be repaired. The reparable is bounded by a lower limit (the irreparable) and an upper limit (the a-reparable).

The last, and by no means the least, of the challenges that punctuate this chapter directly questions our starting hypothesis that only living beings are capable of self-repair. The challenge comes directly from climatology, under the initial impulse of Lovelock, who took the bold step of comparing the planet and its ecosystems with living organisms. It is only under the prudent methodological banner of metaphor that it makes sense to extend homeostatic and self-reparative properties to ecosystems. Its implications, however, are far from metaphorical: does the new climate regime of the Anthropocene not fundamentally negate the possibility for ecosystems to generate new forms of equilibrium that will ensure continued habitability for life in general, and human life in particular? It is only in the eventuality that the planet is no longer able to guarantee these equilibria that measures of ecological repair become meaningful. Not in the vain hope of returning to a pre-anthropic state, but of restoring—when nature is clearly powerless to do so—the possibility of life moving forward.

NOTES

1. G. Canguilhem, *Knowledge of Life*, ed. P. Marrati, T. Meyers, trans S. Geroulanos, D. Ginsburg. New York: Fordham University Press, 2008.

2. Xavier Bichat, 1771–1802, pioneering French pathologist.

3. The thoughts developed here were enriched by discussions with the biologists Pascal Sommer and Louis Casteilla, specialists in regeneration and repair.

4. E. Hutchins, G-L Markov, W-L, Eckalbar, R-M. George, J-M. King, et al., "Transcriptomic Analysis of Tail Regeneration in the Lizard *Anolis carolinensis* Reveals Activation of Conserved Vertebrate Developmental and Repair Mechanisms," *PLOS ONE* 9(8), e105004, 2014.

5. S.F. Gilbert, *Developmental Biology*, Sunderland: Sinauer Associates Inc., 2000.

6. For example, when a limb of an adult salamander is amputated, the remaining cells can rebuild the complete limb. The new cells only reconstruct the missing structures, without generating additional growth.

7. J. Caroli, Y. Hecht, J. André, "Foie," *Encyclopædia Universalis* [online, in French], accessed on April 5, 2018. http://www.universalis.fr/encyclopedie/foie//.

8. Michel Démarchez, "Régénération et cicatrisation de la peau," https://biologidelapeau.fr/spip.php?rubrique42.
9. C. Ziller, A. Paraf, A. Cruickshank, "Régénération et cicatrisation," *Encyclopædia Universalis* [online, in French], accessed on April 5, 2018. http://www.universalis.fr/encyclopedie/regeneration-et-cicatrisation.
10. Aberdam Daniel, "Réparer ou régénérer, il faut choisir," *Médecine/Sciences*, 23, pp. 783–807, 2007.
11. G. Cotsarelis, "Epithelial stem cells: a folliculocentric view," *J Invest Dermatol*, 126, pp. 1459–68, 2006.
12. D. Aberdam, "Réparer ou régénérer, il faut choisir," *op. cit.*
13. Aristotle, *History of Animals*. London: Bell, 1887. See also J. Bouffartigue "L'automédication des animaux chez les auteurrs antiques" in Isabelle Boehm & Pascal Luccioni (eds.), *Le médecin initié par l'animal*, Lyon, Maison de l'Orient et de la Méditerranée, 2008, pp. 79–96.
14. Plutarch, *On the Intelligence of Animals*. Cambridge, MA: Loeb Classical Library, 1957.
15. P. Gaillard-Seux, "L'automédication animale: le serpent et le fenouil, l'hirondelle et la chélidoine. Du mythe à l'indication médicale," *Histoire, médecine et santé* [online, in French], 8 | Winter 2015, posted July 3, 2017, accessed April 20, 2018. http://journals.openedition.org/hms/862; DOI : 10.4000/hms.862.
16. E. Rodriguez & R. Wrangham, "Zoopharmacognosy: The use of medicinal plants by animals," *Phytochemical Potential of Tropical Plants*, vol. 27, 1993, pp. 89–105.
17. B.G. Ritchie & D.M. Fragaszy, "Capuchin monkey (*Cebus apella*) grooms her infant's wound with tools," *American Journal of Primatology*, vol. 16, no. 4, 1988, pp. 345–48.
18. Analogously, as we will see, social interactions are also governed by a whole palette of techniques (such as maintaining appropriate distance) to avoid giving offense in face-to-face interactions and therefore having to make reparation. This "face-saving" knowhow is also prophylactic in nature.
19. E.M. Costa-Neto, "Zoopharmacognosy, the self-medication behavior of animals," *Interfaces Científicas—Saúde e Ambiente*, vol. 1, no. 1, 2012, pp. 61–72.
20. E. Zwierlein-Diehl, "Les intailles magiques," *Pallas*, 2007, vol. 75, pp. 249–62.
21. J. Frazer, *The Golden Bough*. New York: Oxford University Press, 1998.
22. L. Wittgenstein, *Remarks on Frazer's Golden Bough*. Brynmill: Humanities, 1983.
23. M. Bloch, *The Royal Touch*, trans. J.E. Anderson. London: Routledge, 2015.
24. According to legend, this oil comes from the Holy Ampulla carried to Reims by a dove, symbolizing the Holy Spirit, for the baptism of Clovis, France's first Christian king.
25. M. Bloch, *op. cit.*, p. 54.
26. E. Gondard, "Visages de la médecine," *Sociétés*, 2013/3 (n° 121), pp. 127–35.
27. Philippe Descola, *Par-delà nature et culture*. Paris: Gallimard, 2005.

28. Joseph W. Bastien, *Healers of the Andes: Kallawaya Herbalists and Their Medicinal Plants*. Salt Lake City: University of Utah Press, 1988.

29. This is true, historically, for all Andean cultures, where medical acts, such as applying medicinal plants or performing surgical operations, have always been accompanied by magic, religious incantations and prayers (Jan G. R. Elferink, "The Inca healer: empirical medical knowledge and magic in pre-Columbian Peru," *Revista de Indias*, 2015, vol. LXXV, n. 264, pp. 323–50).

30. J. Goody, *The Domestication of the Savage Mind*. Cambridge: Cambridge University Press, 1977, pp. 245–46.

31. *Ibid.*, p. 148.

32. More radically still than Goody, Bruno Latour, in his essay *Nous n'avons jamais été modernes* (Paris: La découverte, 1991), clearly challenges the "great divide" thesis and, correlatively, the modern project of conceptual and rational purity which is supposed to guarantee our superiority over primitives. We have never been modern, claims the philosopher, because "scientific objects," far from having an autonomous existence, are in fact "hybrid objets" embedded in a grid of social, cultural and political symbols and techniques.

33. J. Favret-Saada, Deadly Words, trans. Catherine Cullen, Cambridge University Press, 2010, pp. 45–46.

34. *Ibid.*, p. 70.

35. Ch. Bougerol, "La sorcellerie aux Antilles : Interactions et malheurs," *Socio-anthropologie* [online], 5 | 1999, posted January 15, 2003, accessed April 25, 2018.

36. F. Olmer, "La médecine dans l'Antiquité : professionnels et pratiques," *Sociétés & Représentations*, vol. 28, no. 2, 2009, pp. 153–72.

37. Cl. Bernard, *Principes de médecine expérimentale*. Paris: PUF, 2008.

38. E. Gondard, "Visages de la médecine," *op. cit.*

39. In the case of a congenital disability or birth defect, it is difficult to speak of repair as the restoration of organic functions. It is more to do with implementing organs and functions that were initially missing from an organism. This makes it a paradoxical form of repair, which can only have meaning—and a problematic meaning at that—if we assume that the repair is justified to correct the formation and development of an organism that has not developed "normally," and which should have developed towards a "statistical norm" characteristic of its species. In other cases, repair is conceived of in imaginary mode. Some children born with disabilities, in the struggle to come to terms with the loss of the "dreamt-of child," imagine a magical time when they had no disability, from which springs hope of a possible return to that lost state: "Evoking a magical time before the handicap makes it possible at the same time to imagine that there will be a time after, when the handicap will disappear; an illusion maintained by a range of medical interventions. Deep down, all handicapped children hold on to this belief in healing or repair" (S. Korff-Sausse, *Le miroir brisé*. Paris: Calmann-Lévy, 1996). What Korff-Sausse calls an illusion can, however, if not become reality, then at least help to transform reality, when medicine partly repairs a disability that was previously thought to be irreversible.

40. G. Hottois, *Philosophie et idéologies trans/posthumanistes*, foreword by Jean-Yves Goffi. Paris: Vrin, coll. "Pour demain," 2017.

41. The NBIC technologies represent a multidisciplinary field of scientific investigation and experimentation, at the crossroads between nanotechnology (the exploration of the infinitely small), biotechnology (the manipulation of living organisms) information technology (notably artificial intelligence), and the cognitive sciences (the study of brain function). The convergence of these research areas is redrawing the boundaries between the physical sciences and the life sciences, and even the human sciences. Due to their economic and medical implications, the "NBICs" have attracted considerable investment in recent years from companies and governments, ranging from Silicon Valley start-ups to Google-Apple-Facebook-Amazon-Microsoft (GAHAM) to the EU's "Human Brain Project (HBP)" which seeks to reconstitute the human brain from computer simulation models (see for example Thierry Magnin, *Penser l'humain au temps de l'homme augmenté*. Paris: Albin Michel, 2017, pp. 40–44).

42. J-M. Besnier, *Demain, les posthumains*. Paris: Fayard, 2012.

43. *Ibid.*, p. 58.

44. J. Habermas, *The Future of Human Nature*. Cambridge: Polity, 2003.

45. L. Ferry, *La révolution transhumaniste*. Paris: Plon, 2016.

46. M. Foessel, *Le temps de la consolation*. Paris: Seuil, 2015.

47. J-M. Truong, *Totalement inhumaine*. Paris: Les empêcheurs de tourner en rond, 2003, p. 18.

48. R. Kurzweil, *The Singularity is Near: When Humans Transcend Biology*. New York: Penguin, 2005. To further muddy the waters, Kurzweil is not only the prophet of a future humanity and a science-fiction author, but also a brilliant MIT-trained engineer, one of the first designers of reading machines for the visually impaired, and currently heads an initiative on machine learning for natural language processing at Google.

49. "We challenge the inevitability of aging and death, and we seek continuing enhancements to our intellectual abilities, our physical capacities, and our emotional development. . . . We champion the use of science and technology to eradicate constraints on lifespan, intelligence, personal vitality, and freedom" (M. More, *Extropian Principles v3.0*, https://extropynow.weebly.com/extropianism.html) accessed April 13, 2022.

50. Jean-Michel Besnier, *Demain, les post-humains, op. cit.*, p. 92.

51. Cas9 is an enzyme used in genetic engineering to modify the genomes of plant and animal cells.

52. Thierry Magnin, *Penser l'humain au temps de l'Homme augmenté*. Paris: Albin Michel, 2017, p. 62.

53. J-C. Ameisen, *La sculpture du vivant. Le suicide cellulaire ou la mort créatrice*. Paris: Seuil, 1999.

54. Maylis de Kerangal, *The Heart*, trans. S. Taylor. New York: Picador, 2017.

55. G. Canguilhem, *The Normal and the Pathological*, trans. C.R. Fawcett. New York: Zone Books, 1991.

56. G. Canguilhem, *Knowledge of Life, op. cit.*, p. 125.

57. *Ibid.*, p. 209.

58. G. Canguilhem, *Knowledge of Life, op. cit.*, p. 140.

59. *Ibid.*, p. 231.

60. As recently as the first half of the last century, at colonial exhibitions in Europe and the USA, non-Western "specimens" were exhibited in veritable human zoos. The "natives" were not far from having the status of fairground freaks, in particular the women, often kept near naked and objectivized as "sexual monsters." Abdellatif Kechiche's remarkable movie *Black Venus* tells the story of the "Hottentot Venus" from South Africa, one of the victims of the colonial construction of indigenous abnormality.

61. The sociological and anthropological work of Bernard Mottez has played a key role in France for the recognition of a Deaf identity (see B. Mottez, *Les sourds existent-ils ?* (texts collected by Andréa Benvenuto). Paris: L'Harmattan, 2006).

62. A. Benvenuto, "De quoi parlons-nous quand nous parlons de 'sourds?'" *Télémaque*, 25, pp. 73–86, 2004/1.

63. S. Korff-Sausse, *Le miroir brisé, op. cit.*, p. 18.

64. *Ibid.*, p. 70.

65. *Ibid.*, p. 55.

66. See in particular J. Lovelock, *Gaia: A New Look at Life on Earth*. Oxford: Oxford University Press, 2000.

67. J. Lovelock & L. Margulis, "Atmospheric homeostasis by and for the biosphere: the Gaia hypothesis." *Tellus*, 1974, 26(1–2), 2–10. Sébastien Dutreuil offers an excellent summary of the genealogy of the Gaia hypothesis: S. Dutreuil, "L'hypothèse Gaïa : pourquoi s'y intéresser même si l'on pense que la Terre n'est pas un organisme?," *Bulletin de la Société d'Histoire et d'Épistémologie des Sciences de la Vie* (SHESVIE), 19 (2): 229–41.

68. J. Lovelock, *Gaia, the Practical Science of Planetary Medicine*. Oxford: Oxford University Press, 2000, p. 56.

69. B. Latour, *Facing Gaia: Eight Lectures on the New Climatic Regime*, trans. C. Porter. Cambridge: Polity, 2017.

70. R. Dawkins, *The extended phenotype: The gene as the unit of selection*. Oxford: W.H. Freeman and Company, 1982.

71. Among many other criticisms, Toby Tyrrell seeks to disprove all the scientific underpinnings of the Gaia hypothesis by demonstrating that it doesn't pass Popper's refutability test: it is at best, he suggests, a pseudo-science (*On Gaia: A Critical Investigation of the Relationship Between Life and Earth*). Princeton: Princeton University Press, 2013).

72. J. Lovelock, *Gaia, the Practical Science of Planetary Medicine*, op. cit., p. 57.

73. B. Latour, *Facing Gaia: Eight Lectures on the New Climatic Regime, op. cit.,* p. 97.

74. S. Legendre, "La résilience des écosystèmes," *De la réparation* (Christophe Schaeffer, ed.). Paris: L'Harmattan, 2010, p. 46.

75. Ecosystems come in very different sizes and densities (e.g. marshland, forest) in constant interaction with each other, or even occupying the same geographic area.

76. This is especially true in *The Revenge of Gaia: Why the Earth is Fighting Back—and How We Can Still Save Humanity.* New York: Allen Lane, 2006. I particularly recommend another commentary by Sébastien Dutreuil on this question,

"Lovelock, Gaïa et la pollution : un scientifique entrepreneur à l'origine d'une nouvelle science et d'une philosophie politique de la nature," *Zilsel : science, technique, société*, Editions du Croquant, 2017, pp. 19–61.

77. James Lovelock & Sidney Epton, "The Quest for Gaia," *New Scientist*, February 6, 1975, p. 305.

78. Sébastien Dutreuil, "Lovelock, Gaïa et la pollution" *op. cit.*, p. 19.

79. H. Jonas, *The Imperative of Responsibility*. Chicago: Chicago University Press, 1984.

80. P. Francour, "Les mesures compensatoires permettent-elles une réelle réparation des milieux naturels?," *De la réparation, op. cit.*, p. 101.

81. M-P. Camproux-Duffrène, "La réparation du dommage environnemental," *De la réparation, ibid.*, p. 137.

82. The *Charte de l'environnement* or Charter for the Environment, a constitutional statute, was integrated into the corpus of French constitutional law in 2005. The charter sets out three basic principles: the principle of prevention, the principle of precaution, and the polluter-pays principle.

83. From the website of France's Constitutional Council, accessed April 23, 2022. URL: https://www.conseil-constitutionnel.fr/en/charter-for-the-environment.

84. *Ibid.*

85. M-A. Hermitte, "La nature, sujet de droit?," *Annales. Histoire, Sciences Sociales*, vol. 66e année, no. 1, 2011, pp. 173–212; V. David, "La lente consécration de la nature, sujet de droit: le monde est-il stone?," *Revue juridique de l'Environnement*, 3, 2012, pp. 469–85.

86. M-P. Camproux-Duffrène, "La réparation du dommage environnemental," *De la réparation, op. cit.,* p. 135.

87. As illustrated by the very first article of the Charter: "Everyone has the right to live in a balanced environment which shows due respect for health."

88. See for example Directive 2004/35/EC of the European Parliament and of the Council on environmental liability, in which Articles 6, 7 and 8 deal with remedial actions. More recently (February 2, 2018), the International Court of Justice (ICJ) ruled that a state was obliged to repair environmental damage caused to another state: Nicaragua was ordered to compensate Costa Rica for the environmental harm caused by cutting two canals through an area that turned out to be under Costa Rican sovereignty.

89. For example Decree no. 2009-468 of April 23, 2009, relating to the prevention and reparation of certain types of damage to the environment.

90. In practice, reparations in kind are almost impossible in many cases, such as those involving air pollution. The frequent recourse to compensation by the judiciary reinforces the anthropocentric dimension of environmental law: "Nature" receives no direct benefit from the fact that such-and-such an environmental non-profit association or some local authority is paid compensation.

91. Primary reparation can itself take different forms, such as the restoration or rehabilitation of a site of ecological interest, the preservation and enhancement of an ecosystem, or the creation of artificial habitats.

92. M-P. Camproux-Duffrène, "La réparation du dommage environnemental," *op. cit.*, p. 130.

93. France's Environmental Liability Act of August 1, 2008 (*la Loi LRE*), though ambitious in its goals, has resulted in very few penalties, due mainly to its limited scope of application. In practice, a significant number of environmental offences fall outside the framework established by this law.

94. L. Centemeri, "Reframing problems of incommensurability in environmental conflicts through pragmatic sociology. From value pluralism to the plurality of modes of engagement with the environment," *Environmental Values*, 24, (3), 299–320, 2015.

95. See the excellent contribution by Pierre-Marie Badot and Hervé Richard, "Est-il possible et loisible de 'réparer' la Nature?," *De la réparation, op. cit.*, pp. 75–77.

96. *Ibid.*, p. 78.

97. *Ibid.*, p. 79.

Chapter Two

The Fragmented Mind

Can minds be repaired? The question may seem rather incongruous. What does *repairing a mind* even mean? These questions touch on crucial debates currently raging in the cognitive sciences, psychology, and the philosophy of mind. If we reduce the mind to living matter, as the naturalists advocate,[1] the problem boils down to whether the brain can be repaired, and if so, how. In this case, if it were not for the particularity of the brain relative to the other organs, our reflections on repairing the mind would be a simple extension of our reflections on repairing anything living. The first line of inquiry would be a branch or offshoot of the second: repairing minds *just as* we repair any living entity, in this case a brain.

Without having to postulate "a ghost in the machine"[2] or an "additional fact,"[3] in other words without having to espouse a spiritualist (as opposed to naturalist) hypothesis or subscribe to the dualism of substance, it seems safe to suggest that there is a plurality of viewpoints and modes of action with regard to the mind.[4] Minds can be spoken, they can be perceived, and described either as brains and neural circuits, or as the psyche, "the mental" . . . without postulating that one is material, and the other immaterial. We could say, with Strawson,[5] that the mind, like the body, is prone to two types of predication and discourse, either as an object of observation and explanation (the brain), or in a relationship to experience marked by the use of possessives (*my* consciousness, *your* intentions, *her* feelings) and deictics (here, now, today). This duality of perspective can, without contradiction, be articulated with an ontological monism: there is only one entity (the mind), perceived through descriptive frameworks that are both irreducible and at the same time correlated (every thought must correspond to a neural connection).[6]

Naturalism becomes problematic (i.e., reductionist or "eliminativist") as professed for example by Patricia Churchland,[7] when it results in an epistemological and methodological monism: when it seeks to "eliminate" from the discourse on the mind anything that does not strictly relate to neuroscience (not only the humanities, but also other sub-branches of cognitive science such as experimental psychology). In other words, the only discourse authorized on the mind would be one based on the science of the brain. We can take arms against this reductionism and plead instead for multiperspectivism in the study of the mind.

It is within this epistemological framework that we can envisage reparative actions that do not act directly (but always mediately) on the brain and can examine mind-repair techniques (for psychic or mental issues) that are irreducible to those encountered in the modification of living matter such as the brain. These include both lay and professional therapeutic practices that claim to act upon mental dysfunctions: debilitating psychical transformations that impact people's relationships to others and to themselves. The problem is to define exactly what we are trying to repair: symptoms, traumas, life histories, the ability to cope with everyday life? In all likelihood, we will need once more to explore the frontier between the normal and the pathological and, by the same measure, the attempt at *normalization* that presides over any form of therapeutic repair of the human psyche.

REPAIRING AND REGENERATING THE HUMAN BRAIN

Can the brain self-repair? Until recently, scientists believed the contrary: after a lesion in the central nervous system, the brain is incapable, it was thought, of either regenerating or repairing itself.[8] In short, we have a stock of neurons at birth that progressively disappear without hope of regeneration, particularly if there is a lesion. This thesis was dented in the 1990s, however, by American researchers who showed that, in two areas of the brain at least—the subventricular zone, and especially the hippocampus—the creation of new neurons can be observed.[9] Furthermore, this neurogenesis can be reinforced by physical exercise and by taking certain medicines. The hopes raised by such a discovery are easy to imagine.

However, these hopes were, if not dashed, then at least seriously dampened by a recent research team from UCSF.[10] The previous results were based on experiments on species such as rats and mice. Experiments on the hippocampus of human embryos and adult subjects, however, showed a decline in neurogenesis as from the first years of life. The initial dogma (that regeneration of human neurons was impossible) is still somewhat shaken, but the hope that was aroused is far from bearing fruit (the observed regeneration was limited to certain areas of the brain and was, above all, very temporary). The scientific jury is still out on human neurogenesis, pending further research:

At the Pasteur Institute in Paris, in the Memory and Perception laboratory headed by leading neurogenesis specialist Pierre-Marie Lledo, there is praise for the quality of the UCSF study, while remaining extremely guarded about its conclusions. "In-depth analysis is now required on these results to understand why they totally contradict the earlier results, especially those of the Swedish team of Jonas Frisen (Institut Karolinska)," says Pasteur Institute researcher Mariana Alonso. "This raises questions about technique (the relevance of the markers) and sampling (which brains were studied). And we can't yet rule out the possibility that newly-formed neurons do not respond in the same way to the markers, in adults and in children." Alonso recognizes one crucial point, however: "The value of this study is to show that neurogenesis in human adults is not of the same magnitude as in mice; on this we are all agreed."[11]

What remains an established fact today, until proven to the contrary, is the brain's great plasticity, which enables it, in the absence of limited regeneration, to perform self-repair on lesions (without medical intervention). The key distinction between the two processes (regeneration and self-repair) that we analyzed for living entities in general remains every bit as relevant for the brain.[12] Though limited to action on certain lesions, while others remain irreversible and irreparable, self-repair is indeed a characteristic of the brain and operates discreetly and spontaneously, without external intervention. In this case it does not involve the creation of new neurons (as in neurogenesis), but rather a rearrangement of, and collaboration between, neurons confronted with a lesion. Neural and cerebral plasticity are expressed in the brain's capacity to create, undo, or reorganize networks of neurons and the connections between them; a process which, unlike human neurogenesis, intervenes in every phase of development.

Neural plasticity acts on "normal" (lesion-free) subjects at every stage in the learning, organization and reorganization of knowledge and skills. It is more active, however, during the first years of life due to the larger stock of neurons (neurons not used in one brain area are assigned to cover shortfalls in another). Plasticity diminishes over time, but without altogether disappearing. A study conducted by a team from Inserm[13] demonstrated what happens with people afflicted by unilateral spatial negligence, a neurological disorder that emerges as the result of a lesion arising in one hemisphere of the brain, typically after a stroke. These patients behave as if part of the world did not exist (they may, for example, only eat the food on the left-hand side of a plate). What do we find in the best cases (i.e., where self-repair is successful)? We observe, due to the plasticity of the brain, a reorganization of neural networks. In effect, the neural network of the right hemisphere begins to repair, by means of intermediate networks, the damaged neurons of the left hemisphere (and reciprocally when it is the right hemisphere that is affected).

Cerebral self-repair comes across here as a hidden talent from the depths of the human brain, without the conscious, intentional, deliberate intervention of the subject (only an outside observer can objectify it, for example by taking brain scans). Strictly speaking, the subject's brain "gets repaired" without the subject doing anything. Repairer and repaired act as biologically autonomous beings that intervene without any deliberate conscious action on the part of the subject (just as the neural networks of the left and right hemispheres can act reciprocally, through synaptic communication, either as repairer or as repaired). There is no "ghost in the machine," but a whole series of processes and operations of unparalleled complexity (with billions of synaptic connections) that make it possible, thanks to the plasticity of the brain, to gradually restore basic functions. By repairing itself at the neural scale, the brain "repairs me" to my functional and vital capacities.

The proportion of self-repair in the brain is considerable, and clearly performs a homeostatic function, constantly rebalancing in response to disruptions that affect not only the brain itself but also the organism as a whole. The distinction between self-regulation and self-repair is strongly maintained here, the latter being in one sense a subfunction or a special case of the former. To regulate all the imbalances that beset the organism from day to day, even in the absence of significant accidents, the (non-conscious) brain proceeds with constant micro-repairs on all the vital systems, usually without this ever emerging into consciousness. Lesion or no lesion, the non-conscious part of the brain, using its map of the body, continually makes corrections in response to chemical signals received from the organism. On the basis of what Damasio calls "homeostatic ranges," which represent a measurement of the distance between the current state and the desired state, the brain performs adjustments when a physical state threatens to go off the scale necessary to the equilibrium and maintenance of the organism. All these mechanisms usually come into play without any deliberate input from consciousness: repair and regulation are coordinated by another me within myself, which does not take the form of a "subject":

> The entire operation is as blind and "subject-less" as gene networks themselves are. Absence of mind and of self is perfectly compatible with spontaneous and implicit "intention" and "purpose." The basic "intention" of the design is to maintain structure and state, but a larger "purpose" can be construed from such multiple intentions: to survive.[14]

It would clearly be impossible, due to the sheer quantity of systems (immune, digestive, circulatory, respiratory) and the complexity of the operations, for the conscious part of the brain to constantly perform all of the maintenance, correction and repair operations at every level of the organism. The conscious self, with different degrees of intensity,[15] intervenes precisely when the non-conscious brain can no longer make the vital adjustments by itself, when it can no longer keep everything within the homeostatic ranges. It is mainly by means of the emotions that the non-conscious brain "informs" the conscious self, using neurotransmitters, either of an optimal range (pleasures and rewards) or of a dangerous range (unpleasurable feelings, pain, and punishment). Nor is this information model limited to the present state of the organism: the non-conscious brain, with a wealth of experience stored in memory, can pick up on clues to predict and advise[16] the conscious brain either of "good things" (for example by releasing dopamine or oxytocin), or of a manifest hazard (by releasing prolactin). This is where the conscious brain (in particular the "core self") steps in to restore the threatened equilibria intentionally and artificially:

> Brains expanded the possibilities of life management even when they did not produce minds, let alone conscious minds. For that reason they too prevailed. By the time minds and consciousness were added to the mix, the possibilities of regulation expanded even more and made way for the kind of management that occurs not just within one organism but across many organisms, in societies.[17]

It may be, however, that the brain itself is damaged or defective and unable to repair itself (and consequently the entire affected organism). When the brain no longer "gets repaired" naturally and spontaneously, external and artificial repair may be called for. This can be done directly and physically on the brain via neurosurgery, the branch of surgery that studies and treats disorders of the brain, the cerebellum and the medulla. If so, it is an "other," in this case a professional, who repairs the damaged part of the patient's brain: a typical instance of other-repair where self-repair is insufficient or deficient. From this point of view, there is no substantial difference, save perhaps for the complexity of the operation, between the other-repair of living matter in general and the other-repair of the mind (in the form of a brain). There is no analogy here between two modes of repair; there is a continuum, within the same operational and discursive register, from living matter to mind. We see this, for example, when a brain tumor develops in the meninges (a meningioma). Other-repair, among other possible practices (including chemotherapy), involves a surgical procedure for which an incision must be made in the skull. The aim of the operation is to remove as much cancerous tissue as possible without touching the healthy brain. Except in those cases where the locally anesthetized patient is able to guide the surgeon, surgical other-repair proceeds without any deliberate action by the patient, other than signing the informed consent form (when that is possible): another person repairs "my" brain in "my" place. The use of possessives here is problematic in as far as discourse on the brain is typically third-person discourse (that of an observer). When I speak of "my" brain: strictly speaking, I have no relationship with "my" brain, even though, in a sense, it belongs to me and provides the neural basis for all my thoughts. Whether it self-regulates, self-repairs, or is repaired by a surgeon, the brain has something paradoxical about it, something of the other-in-myself (even when I am shown a scanned image of "my" brain on a screen).

An equivalent, though not identical, process is observed in the pharmacological treatment of mental illnesses not ascribable to brain lesions. The term itself "mental illnesses" seems to belong to another register, another discourse on the mind, no longer directly about the brain, but about "the mental," the psyche. In this case, the patient might say "I suffer from anxiety," or "I suffer from hallucinations"; we would hardly expect them to say, "My brain hurts" (a very different predicate from "My head hurts"). In this register, the use of the possessive to describe experience can be fully justified, just as I might say "my psyche" or "my consciousness." There are, however, ways of repairing mental disorders that intervene directly on the functioning of the brain, without the patient intervening directly in the process, other than to agree to treatment and through the psychological effects of beliefs about the efficacy of a treatment. A case in point is that of pharmacological treatments, which can be assimilated to the chemical repair of mental dysfunctions, with synthetic chemistry modifying the natural chemistry of the brain. Unlike neurosurgery, there is no direct physical intervention on the brain (as when the surgeon extracts cancerous cells), but a chemical intervention, through the ingestion of substances (medicinal and psychotropic drugs) that, by modifying neural communication, act in return on the symptoms of an illness. More precisely, the different classes of substance (benzodiazepines, neuroleptics, antidepressants) act on the transmission of signals in the nervous system that rely on chemical compounds (neurotransmitters):

> Certain neurons in our brain liberate neurotransmitters that have an excitatory effect, as in the case of glutamate: they trigger or facilitate the production of electric impulses in the target neurons; other neurons liberate a neurotransmitter such as gammaaminobutyric acid (GABA), which reduces—indeed eliminates—excitation, on which account they are called inhibitory. All of them act on specific receptors, specialized molecular "locks" that recognize and translate the chemical signal into an electric signal.[18]

How exactly do these medicinal substances work? In the case of tranquilizers like the benzodiazepines, the substances amplify the effect of GABA on the receptors. In other words, they facilitate the inhibition of "overheating" cerebral activity by "helping" the inhibitory neurotransmitters whose interneural communication is impeded (by an anxiety disorder).

Whether by surgical act or by chemical action, in what sense can we speak about repairing the brain? We should start by saying that despite considerable advances in neurosurgery (increasingly computer and robot-assisted) we are still a long way from being able to repair all cerebral lesions. Some lesions are irreversible and strictly irreparable, leading to functional paralysis, if not physical or brain death. Even when the lesions are reparable, with all the risks inherent in an operation (in particular the risk of affecting healthy and vital areas of the brain, to say nothing of nosocomial infections), the subject will never be the same after surgery as before the disorder arose. For one thing, the nature and form of the damaged area will never return to the initial state (the patient will sometimes have to follow a lifelong course of treatment, as for example after a cerebrovascular accident). For another, the behavioral functions associated with the affected area, while they may to some extent—depending on the success of the operation—recover capacities close to the prior situation, will forever remain fragile. While the absolute irreparable of the brain reaches its limit in physical or brain death, there remains a relative irreparable in the functioning of the brain and of the organism as a whole.

The same conclusion applies to the chemical repair of mental illnesses. On what exactly do the drugs act? Clearly, they act on symptoms associated with a pathology (depression, anxiety, hallucinations, etc.), not necessarily eradicating them, but at least mitigating their intensity. These chemical substances do not act directly on the immediate causes of the illness and do not in themselves enable the patient to return to a pre-pathological situation. At best they will "stabilize" the subject's condition, except in those cases where the symptoms are aggravated by side effects. The inevitable presence of side effects (such as weight gain for neuroleptics and certain antidepressants) is already a sign of a more general transformation of the subject. The sad fact is that the chemical repair of mental disorders—necessary and sometimes vital as it is, particularly to mitigate the suffering of the patients—is quite limited and does not equate to repairing the actual illness. Not only can it, while addressing some symptoms, generate others by collateral effect; chemical repair can also play a role in masking the root causes of mental illness. The symptoms *reveal* the illness, but it would be illusory to think that because the symptoms have diminished, the causes of the pathology have been resolved. Chemical treatments cannot strictly repair mental pathologies; they may relieve and attenuate the symptoms, but not necessarily make them disappear.

REPAIR AS A WORK OF MOURNING

Acting not only on the symptoms of mental illness but on its causes; that is the mission to which clinical psychology lays claim, as do the many associated therapeutic practices (sophrology, hypnotherapy, etc.) that have blossomed in several decades, sometimes drawing their principles of action from very ancient medical traditions. There is also, except in cognitive psychology and neuropsychology, a shift of focus toward another discourse and another mode of intervention on the mind: no longer as a brain, but as a mentality or a psyche. It is no longer about acting directly, physically and chemically, on the cerebral system, but about acting *mediately* through psychological intervention on the patient's psychic experience.[19] In what sense can we still speak of repair? Can mental disorders be repaired by strictly psychotherapeutic means?

This is a good point to look back, through all the progress made by neuroscience, to the founding father of psychoanalysis, as Freud was one of the first to propose a discourse on the disorders of the psyche (the unconscious psyche in this case) that was not based on observable physical lesions.[20] Taking seriously those who were dismissed as "imaginary invalids": that was the substance of the Freudian revolution. A revolution which, I believe, has survived all the criticisms, sometimes well-founded, that later came to be leveled at the psychoanalytic model. Of the many writings Freud has left us—some of which may today leave us nonplussed, on account of certain underlying assumptions—there is one, one of the best, *Mourning and Melancholia*,[21] which is of particular relevance to us. The notion of repair is admittedly absent from the semantic field that permeates the essay, but the arguments deployed tell us about an essential facet of repair. Repair, in its psychological variant, is a response to the primordial experience of *loss*. Even beyond psychology, in analogical terms, in all of its manifestations (biological, social, legal, historical, etc.), repair is generally a *response* to a *loss* (of an organ, of an ability, of a right, of self-esteem, etc.), except in the case of birth disabilities. To repair is to seek to compensate for the loss of something or someone; not of just any thing, but of a thing that is valued or deemed necessary for the maintenance of life, or of one's physical or moral integrity. Repair represents the set of processes (biological, psychological, social, legal, etc.), of efforts, and of work required to compensate for a *loss*.

In his essay, Freud does not expand further; he remains focused on a particular psychological experience of loss, the loss of the *love-object* (whether a real being or a symbolic entity, such as an ideal). Mourning is the first reaction to the loss of the beloved being or thing. And though mourning brings its share of suffering, there is nothing pathological about it, Freud tells us, in the clinical meaning of the term (to suffer from the absence of a loved one is a "normal" reaction). Especially as it gives rise to work, the famous *work of mourning*: the effort that must be made by the subject to come to terms with its loss, an effort of symbolic and libidinal disinvestment (from the lost object) which generally involves displacing the investment onto another loved and valued being. The work of mourning is in many respects one of displacement and substitution. Psychological repair could be conceived of more generally along the lines of the work of mourning: letting go of one object by investing in another, even when there is no physical disappearance of a loved one (for example, in the context of the Oedipus complex, relinquishing the child's libidinal investment in one of its parents by sublimating it into play, by investing love in other beings, and so on). It might be said that the work of mourning, once completed, is a psychological repair that has overcome the initial ordeal.

But if this is repair, what exactly is being repaired? It is not about restoring the previous state of the subject (the loss is irremediable, especially with the physical disappearance of a loved one); there is no going back. Is it a question of erasing the memory of trauma? Not at all. Repairing is not a way of recovering the lost being, even subliminally, unlike scarring, which makes it possible to recover, at least in part, the previous state of dermal function after a wound. Psychological repair does not operate in the same way as biological repair. While there is a fundamental continuity from repairing living organisms to repairing the mind, in the form of the brain, there is undeniably a discontinuity with repairing the mind in the form of the psyche (even if there is still a neural correlation in the repair of the psyche). Only by analogy can we perceive a kinship between the two modes of repair. Only by analogy—or indeed by metaphor, to resist the temptation of naturalization—can we comprehend the work of mourning as a form of psychic scarring to seal up a narcissistic and libidinal wound. Analogy is a way of apprehending a resemblance (*seeing as*, Ricœur would say) through a four-term expression without having to assume an exact equivalence between the terms: scarring is to the repair of living matter as the work of mourning is to the repair of the psyche. While it might be said that scarring, as a form of self-repair after a wound, enables a new (if more fragile) dermis to appear, the work of mourning does not make the lost object reappear. Skin reappears after a wound; the love-object does not reappear after mourning. The work of mourning, if it succeeds, helps instead to make it disappear as a symptom. A more accurate analog equivalent of the scar would be the substitute onto whom the subject's feelings are displaced.

The work of mourning enables the subject to retrieve, not the prior state, not even partially, but the possibility of being and acting in the present once again, and projecting into the future: "when the work of mourning is completed," writes Freud, "the ego becomes free and uninhibited again."[22] We might say, drawing inspiration from Ricœur,[23] that the work of mourning, as a mode of psychological repair, restores the subject's ability to say, to tell, to act and to take moral responsibility for its action. The work of mourning, in other words, through the relinquishment of the lost object (the reality-test) and, correlatively, the symbolic substitution of the lost object, brings about a gradual (and sometimes only partial) restoration of the subject's capacity for desire and love. Repair, then, is the work and the process that can be thought of, in Spinozan terms, as *conatus* (our desire to be and effort to exist), making it possible for the subject to be, act, desire and love again.

It is this process that is missing in melancholia. Melancholia shares similar symptoms with mourning but differs fundamentally by the subject's inability to come to terms with the loss of the loved one and to commence an operation of substitution. The pathology of the melancholic lies in an excessive identification with the lost love-object, which translates into a severe loss of self-esteem, i.e. into a narcissistic regression associated with clinical signs of depression (insomnia, loss of appetite, loss of libido, persistent sense of guilt, etc.). The loss of the love-object is converted into regression inside the ego itself. In a striking passage, Freud explains the pathogenic process involved:

> An object-choice, an attachment of the libido to a particular person, had at one time existed; then, owing to a real slight or disappointment coming from this loved person, the object-relationship was shattered. The result was not the normal one of a withdrawal of the libido from this object and a displacement of it on to a new one, but something different, for whose coming about various conditions seem to be necessary. The object-cathexis proved to have little power of resistance and was brought to an end. But the free libido was not displaced on to another object; it was withdrawn into the ego. There, however, it was not employed in any unspecified way, but served to establish an *identification* of the ego with the abandoned object.[24]

The melancholic state is set apart from the work of mourning by the impossibility of undertaking the gradual operation of displacement and substitution of the love-object, falling back instead on an operation of pathological identification with the ego. The challenge for melancholia is to consent to loss and separation: the absent one is constantly present as a specter that haunts the psyche. The absent Other keeps being *re-presented* as a ghost: "At the slightest hint of its presence, the pain can be reopened. This nostalgia—in the strict sense of the word, the pain of return, of *nostos*—plunges us into weariness and longing for the homeland."[25] The experience of loss manifests itself as an irreparable that afflicts the subject's most basic capacity to be, speak and act. In melancholia, as Spinoza might have said, the *conatus* is depleted.

While we could hold up the work of mourning as a paradigm example of the psychological repair of the psyche, we should remind ourselves that the notion of repair was not a cardinal concept in the Freudian lexicon. It was to become one, however—in the specific sense of making repair or reparation—in the writings of some of his successors, particularly Melanie Klein (and, later, Donald Winnicott), in a legacy that owes much to *Mourning and Melancholia*. In her essay *Love, Hate and Reparation*[26] Klein lays down the foundations for the analysis of the process of reparation, a theory derived from her experience in pediatrics. It is in childhood, in infancy even, that the need for reparation emerges and crystalizes. Of primary interest to us is the way reparation refers to the ordeal of *loss*, at least as a form of compensatory response. Reparation, in the Kleinian model, in many respects fulfills the function of the work of mourning in the Freudian model. Reparation is presented as one of several possible responses (such as manic defense) to what Klein calls, in memory of Freud, "the depressive position." In contrast, however, to the Freudian concept of melancholia, Klein's "depressive position"[27] follows a normal process in the development of the child, only becoming pathological in the absence, precisely, of reparation. The "depressive position" is the direct consequence of the child's renouncing something of the mother (the source of nourishing satisfaction and erotic desire). "Depressive anxiety" centers on the imagined danger of destroying and losing the mother due to the child's sadism.

Where does the child's need for reparation come from? From an ambivalence between the love (the good breast) and the hate (the bad breast) that the child feels for its mother:

> The baby, to whom his mother is primarily only an object which satisfies all his desires—a good breast, as it were—soon begins to respond to these gratifications and to her care by developing feelings of love towards her as a person. But this first love is already disturbed at its roots by destructive impulses. Love and hate are struggling together in the baby's mind; and this struggle to a certain extent persists throughout life and is liable to become a source of danger in human relationships.[28]

And where do these destructive impulses come from? Essentially from a state of lack or frustration when the mother fails to respond to the child's needs and, by extension, from the child's feeling of emotional dependency on the mother. Hate, in other words, stems from the child's overly exclusive love for its mother. The result is a sense of intense guilt within the child for feeling these destructive impulses.

And what, then, is reparation? In the child, the process is aimed at "making reparation" for the hate that it feels toward its mother, for example offering a smile by way of symbolic reparation. The process of reparation is necessary to prevent guilt transforming into despair, and a "depressive position" into lasting melancholic depression. What is remarkable is that this need for reparation will, says Klein, persist throughout life through a symbolic displacement of the mother-figure onto other figures likely to be affected by mixed feelings of love and hate:

> Our grievances against our parents for having frustrated us, together with the feelings of hate and revenge to which these have given rise in us, and again, the feelings of guilt and despair arising out of this hate and revenge because we have injured the parents whom at the same time we loved—all these, in phantasy, we may undo in retrospect (taking away some of the grounds for hatred), by playing at the same time the parts of loving parents and loving children. At the same time, in our unconscious phantasy we make good the injuries which we did in phantasy, and for which we still unconsciously feel very guilty. This *making reparation* is, in my view, a fundamental element in love and in all human relationships.[29]

This is a crucial point: by bringing in what she calls "phantasy," Klein shows that the sense of guilt does not necessarily stem from anything the child actually did to harm its mother (such as biting her nipple), but from an imaginary projection of simply feeling hate for her and the correlative fear of destroying, losing and abandoning the love-object. The extra step that Klein takes is in indexing any subsequent form of impulse-to-repair in human relations against what might be termed an "archaic" impulse-to-repair within the narrow framework of the ambivalent love-hate relationship of the child toward its mother.

That is a step that I personally would be hesitant to take, especially when Klein makes it into a monocausal explanatory factor that might reasonably leave us a little perplexed, as when she ascribes the gratification a man derives from giving his wife a baby to his need to atone for his sadistic wishes towards his mother. The Kleinian framework does, however, enrich the Freudian model by making reparation a structural component (among others) of human psychic development since early childhood. Like the work of mourning, reparation plays a positive, self-therapeutic role in overcoming the depressive position and, at the same time, the anxiety drive and the sense of guilt. As Winnicott, following on from Klein, writes: "it is not possible for a human being to stand the destructiveness that is basic in human relationships, that is to say, in instinctual loving, except by a gradual development associated with the experience of reparation and restitution."[30]

Reparation at the same time allows the individual to recognize the other, and above all the mother, as a being separate from itself, without being in a position of omnipresent control over the love- (and hate-) object. Reparation, in other words, contributes to the process of subjectivation and autonomization of the self, even if the "depressive position" is liable to resurface throughout life, when the subject is once again faced with loss and bereavement. The gradual separation from the mother (assuming she herself relinquishes a position of total power over her child) acts in this sense as a primitive work of mourning, with reparation invoked as a response to feelings of guilt for wanting to destroy, abandon and ultimately lose the love-object.

This constructive function of reparation can, however, be double-sided. One could speak of it as a negative function of psychological repair when it develops into a quasi-compulsion along pathological lines, when the reparative impulse is so strong that it can drive the subject to keep hurting others. As if the disposition to repair somehow became autonomous, stagnating in the psyche to the point where it constantly and perversely generates sadistic impulses. The causal relationship is inverted: instead of making reparation for having harmed (or fantasizing about harming) the love-object, the subject harms in order to have to make reparation. This is the hypothesis sometimes put forward to explain certain acts of abuse where the abuser, after the act of violence, is seen to be eager to console and care for the victim. It is as though the root cause of the act was not the sadistic impulse (which is perhaps only the effect) but rather the reparative impulse, acting as a veritable compulsion to repair (and as the cause of the sadistic process).

This pathogenic framework of psychological repair can take a still more perverse turn when the love-object derives sadistic pleasure from putting the subject in a constant position of guilt, so that he or she must systematically make reparation for wrongs and failings that are usually non-existent or imaginary (or by blaming the victim for wrongs that were actually committed by the accuser). This is exactly the *modus operandi* of coercive control: the victim of coercive control is accused and blamed for every possible ill. The coercive controller seeks to destroy every last residue of narcissism in his (or her) prey: manipulative guilt-tripping is one of the controller's most devious weapons, especially when deployed through insinuation. The sense of guilt affects the primordial structures of the victim, causing him or her to regress to an archaic "depressive position" that usually culminates in depression pure and simple. Here, reparation no longer fulfills its therapeutic function; it becomes caught up in a pathological circle, especially when the victim's own life history makes them more susceptible than others to guilt and reparation.[31]

The structure awaiting reparation is lodged in the psyche of the victim and ensnared in the perversion of the tormentor, who directly derives sadistic pleasure from it. Rather than bringing an end to the victim's sense of indebtedness and guilt, reparation calls for further reparations, which will never satisfy the demand of the controller (who will demand ever more apologies, gifts, and sacrifices). As the constant reproach of the coercive controller goes: *How are you going to make up for it this time?* Reparation is lost in an infinite regression of guilt. Victims go so far as to divest themselves of all their possessions, to give up the time they used to devote to their children, their friends or their job: to make reparation, the victim is belittled until she (the majority, but not all, are women) is ready to sacrifice herself for her tormentor. The risk, unless a third party intervenes—a "meta-gaze," as Korff-Sausse calls it—is that the victim will be cut off from all her friends and family. As a permanent scapegoat (it is always her fault, never that of the controller), the victim must give herself body and soul to her tormentor. Reparation is perverted into a logic of sacrifice: the constant duty of reparation becomes the hell of daily life. Given the state of emotional dependency of the victims of coercive control, instead of abandoning the love-object (and the object of suffering), we see them undergo a narcissistic loss of the ego (self-incrimination and low self-esteem). Instead of resembling the work of mourning, the infernal reparation in which the victim is enclosed leads straight to melancholia. Instead of leading to separation from the loved one from whom they should be fleeing, reparation reinforces their emotional dependency on the controller. Instead of repairing oneself by repairing the other, reparation culminates in the destruction of the self by the other. In a mechanism of regression, the victim finds herself placed in a situation of emotional dependency that mirrors that of a young child with an all-powerful mother (or father) who heaps guilt upon her child.

This detour via Kleinian theory enriches the initial Freudian model in another respect. The work of mourning is primarily about repairing oneself, with the accent on the *oneself* when the subject ceases to invest in the love-object. It is, in other words, a form of therapeutic self-repair. In the Kleinian theoretical framework, it is primarily about repairing the *other* and, at source, the real or imaginary wrong committed against the mother. This model highlights the function and the intersubjective use of reparation, whose decisive consequences for social relations we will examine later. But is it really only about repairing the *other*? In reality, the process is more complex. On first analysis, the imperative of reparation is indeed directed toward the other and aims to compensate for a dissymmetry (the wrong committed has caused another person to *lose* something), and reestablish reciprocity in an intersubjective relationship. On closer inspection, however, this psychological disposition to repair the other is indeed aimed at *repairing oneself* (alleviating the burden of guilt and escaping from depressive anxiety: repairing the other (morally) in order to repair oneself (psychologically). In a sense, the primary intention is not other-repair but self-repair. The former is a means to attaining the latter, which is at the same time the root cause (the reason why the act of making reparation is undertaken). To return to Winnicott's example, the symbolic gift that the child offers the mother is above all a way for the child to relieve its feelings of guilt.

SELF-REPAIR AS SELF-CARE

The association of the word *self* with *repair* can be highly misleading. Does the use of a reflexive pronoun imply a reflexive, and indeed reflective, act? That is far from being systematically the case. Repair and reparation may take place independently of the will or even the consciousness of the subject. Particularly during the infantile phases of reparation, where it tends to be experienced passively, without reflective mediation. The use of this pronominal form in the context of psychological repair, while different from the operation of cerebral self-repair, is paradoxically closer to "something is repairing inside of me."

This is true even for the work of mourning in adult life. In *Mourning and Melancholia*, Freud observes that we do not have all the elements at our disposal to explain how the withdrawal of the libido (from the lost object) actually operates, a process he compares to a veritable death struggle, albeit symbolic, between the ego and the love-object (the work of mourning is complete when the ego recognizes itself as stronger, as superior to the object). He observes that this "is not a process that can be accomplished in a moment," but must be "one in which progress is long-drawn-out and gradual. Whether it begins simultaneously at several points or follows some sort of fixed sequence is not easy to decide."[32] The popular saying "time is a great healer" has no scientific basis if we seek to reify time as an autonomous causal factor, but remains relevant if we take it to mean that the work of mourning *takes time*, time for the psyche to draw back from its investment in the love-object and to settle on objects of substitution. But this process largely takes place, like the self-repair of a wound, without our knowledge. Folk wisdom such as "time is a great healer" or "let time do its work" means not only that it takes time to let go of the lost object, but also that there are things independent of us (unconscious processes, fortuitous encounters, shifts of focus) that intervene in the process of repair. The work of mourning is a task that takes place partly *within* us, but also partly *without* us, or at least without an active, conscious and deliberate process. The impersonal form "something is repairing inside of me" coexists paradoxically with the pronominal form "I am repairing myself."

Not every loss triggers a work of mourning in the strong sense of the term. Daily life is peppered with micro-losses, usually symbolic, that dent our self-esteem to minor degrees. As Freud, again, notes in his study: "If the object does not possess this great significance for the ego—a significance reinforced by a thousand links—then, too, its loss will not be of a kind to cause either mourning or melancholia."[33] The loss is quickly offset by a plurality of other attachments that enable the subject to resist and to be only mildly affected. To speak of repair in such cases would be excessive; it would be more judicious to speak, at most, of daily micro-repairs that help maintain the subject in a state of relative affective and emotional stability. The little setbacks of daily life can take a more dramatic turn, however, when an already fragile subject is confronted with a real bereavement. For there to be any psychological repair, in the strict sense, the experience of loss and, correlatively, the love-object itself, must be "of great significance." It is, then, a matter of degree: the stronger the emotional dependency on the love-object, the harder will be the work of self-repair demanded of the grieving subject.

While psychological self-repair takes place largely without our knowledge, we also need to take account of active processes of repair that can be grouped together, following Pierre Hadot and Michel Foucault, around the notion of *souci de soi* or self-care. It is in this register that the "self" in "self-repair" becomes truly reflexive, which can be reinforced by using the personal pronoun as a grammatical object: *repairing oneself*. Hence the need to distinguish between repairs that take place at a physiological or unconscious level (such as cerebral self-repair) and repairs that are made consciously, deliberately, and artificially. For the latter, we reserve the term *reparatio*. At the level of the individual self, the *reparatio* represent particular modalities of self-care and techniques of the self. Societies and cultures bestow upon individuals a whole palette of techniques of self-repair, both spiritual and corporeal, that can be practiced alone or as a group. Even without professional intervention, these ordinary *reparatio* are still nonetheless socialized, and are transmissible in the form of traditions: meditation, storytelling, self-writing, breathing techniques, relaxation exercises, sporting, artistic and musical practices, restorative baths and the like.

Walking, among other such techniques, offers a good illustration when it is disconnected from its purely utilitarian function. Not all walking is therapeutic. Walking becomes *reparatio* when the stroller or hiker leaves behind the space of daily preoccupations and lets go of the worries of the mind to open up to a landscape and make space in their thoughts.[34] In the landscape, the ever-receding horizon keeps pace with the walker who is unafraid of "wandering" paths that lead to nowhere. Walking is primarily a body technique, one that is socially marked, as Marcel Mauss observed, and at the same time an entirely personal way of moving forward. People can be recognized by their gait as easily as by their voice. But it is a body technique that produces effects on the mind when it modifies our relationship with time, especially in the slowness of the stroll, as a way of stretching out time. Walking almost literally outpaces the tumults of daily existence and the wounds of the mind: the walker's breathing affects their way of thinking. When a hike is spread over several days, the everyday is eroded away. The suspended time of walking, alone or in a group, at the same time frees up new spaces for thought, dialogue, dreaming, and the contemplation of unfamiliar landscapes, unless, in a return to the "natal home," as Deleuze calls it, it harks back to familiar scenes that simultaneously represent regeneration and projection toward an elsewhere. We all walk our own path, quickly or slowly, breathlessly or restfully, on familiar ground or in unknown territory, on the long road of pilgrimage, on marked trails, or on the well-trodden paths of our childhood. There is a type of posture and a way of stepping out, a bodily disposition to walking that makes it a "spiritual exercise."[35]

As well as a spiritual exercise, walking can become a therapeutic exercise, a *reparatio* of the mind, getting it to keep in step, as it were, and putting the aching soul on the path to recovery: "walking means having your feet on the earth both physically and morally, being rooted, from the feet up, in your own existence."[36] David Le Breton lists its therapeutic benefits: fewer worries, freer thoughts, escape from the circular time of rumination, a break from our sedentary lifestyle, a suspension of our modes of identity and identification. The pain of mourning and separation "loses its sting under the immensity of the sky or of the landscape. On learning of the death of Fernando Pessoa, Miguel Torga closed his medical practice and headed up into the mountains. 'There, with the pines and the rocks, I wept for the death of the greatest poet of our times.'"[37]

Among our contemporaries, Sylvain Tesson has turned walking into a veritable way of life, an art of writing, and a mode of self-repair, following a serious accident that literally shattered him:

> Physically, physiologically and morally, walking treated my wounds. I don't know much about psychology, so, to repair a broken body, I preferred to walk. I set out limping, and came back standing. I detached myself from all the darkness that was with me on the starting line. All the dross, the melancholy that resulted from my time in hospital, I shed it like unwanted clothes.[38]

The result is an admirable book written in the course of his long peregrination along the *chemins noirs* of rural France: the most remote, most overgrown, and least signposted "wandering paths."[39] His account can be read as a slow and gradual repair of the self, mind and body, struggling with his own fragility (paralyzed stomach, deformed features, spinal column bolted together), without the intervention of a therapist or any third party. Rather than the rehabilitation centers prescribed by his doctor, Tesson preferred to recover his strength by taking on steep footpaths. This almost initiatory voyage of repair is not entirely solitary, however: sometimes other walking friends come to share a stretch of road and a slice of life with him; at other times, chance meetings in remote villages provide an opportunity to escape the pain while pursuing his journey and his quest. At the end of his trek through the Norman *bocage*, Tesson does not recover his former face, nor his pin-free legs. After his accident, he will never be the same; the irreparable will remain engraved on his body and in his mind.

In what sense, then, was his walking adventure nonetheless reparative? In the sense of getting a new grip on life. Not a return to what he was before, but a restoration of his ability to be, and a reconfiguration of his ability to live:

> Walking was like fishing: hours would go by and then suddenly there would be a movement—a bite, maybe? I've hooked a thought! In the evenings, as I was falling asleep, the magic lantern images would flit through my mind. Was this a diminished life? Yes. But reduced to its most simple, and perhaps most beautiful, expression. The challenge was to make this sweet tension last.[40]

Walking, with Tesson, is more than a form of repair: it is an exercise in living. In the very process of repair, something *extraneous* is felt, something that goes beyond the renewal of the *conatus*: another mode of existence; life reduced to its most simple expression. Walking becomes a way of living.

Walking, like other ordinary techniques of the self, can be reparative, or can take the place of prophylactic interventions. What we saw earlier at the scale of life in general is valid here at the scale of the mind. The prophylactic techniques of the self are designed specifically to prevent mental pain and anguish, so as not to have to repair them. Whereas the *reparatio* come into play once the loss, trauma or injury has occurred, prophylactic techniques make sense only before reaching breaking point, before ordinary existence is interrupted. Prophylaxis, in other words, seeks to act in order to avoid repair. The old adage "prevention is better than cure" holds true well beyond the medical field. But while the goals of prevention and of repair are different, they sometimes adopt the same techniques. Meditation, walking, and writing, for example, can serve to repair the wounds of the mind after the experience of loss; but they can also serve to maintain a lifestyle, a preventive mode of existence, so as to maintain a psychic equilibrium, regenerate a *conatus*, bolster self-esteem and self-confidence to make the subject better able to cope with life's challenges. Each of us cultivates, throughout life, through our lived experiences, our lapses and relapses, a whole range of prophylactic techniques of self. For some it is walking alone and reading, for others sport and meditation. There is nothing mutually exclusive above these *reparatio*; they can perfectly well be mutually supportive in the process of self-reconstruction. The same is true of other techniques such as pharmacology or psychotherapy. It is frequently the combination of multiple *reparatio*, drawn from different registers and different practices, that enables the subject to overcome the trials of life.

Though they require learning, knowhow and a certain maturity, these reparative and prophylactic techniques are accessible to the ordinary subject. It is a very different matter with the *reparatio* theorized and practiced by self-repair professionals. Philosophers may not have a monopoly on this line of work, but they are clearly pioneers in the field. Not that they hesitate to repurpose practices found in the world of ordinary life: walking is a practice that unites centuries of philosophers, from the Peripatetics, who walked as they taught, to Nietzsche's hikes on the Engadin mountains, to Kant's daily constitutionals around the gardens of Königsberg. More than this art of walking, more even than repair, philosophers have invented innovative reparative techniques. Pierre Hadot and Michel Foucault made this a specific focus of research in their meticulous study of self-care (*epimeleia heautou*) in the cultures of Hellenistic Greece and Rome. It is very much a question of repair because the philosopher must take care of the soul, just as the doctor's vocation is to take care of the body.

However, "the maladies of the soul" that the philosophers seek to heal do not map neatly onto the "mental illnesses" treated by psychologists and psychiatrists. There is no easy correspondence, despite often similar symptoms, such as the notorious melancholia well-known to the Ancients, especially as subjects who may appear to be free from mental disorders in the psychiatric sense may nonetheless be considered "ill" by the philosophers. The ambitious politician hell-bent on glory, honors and wealth is, for the philosopher, a "troubled soul." "Diseased souls" are above all "immoral souls" that have strayed from the ways of wisdom and the path of virtue. The main purpose of *philosophia medicans* is to look after and take care of such lost souls.[41]

The notion of repair may not be part of the philosophical lexicon, but it is reflected in certain significant philosophical themes such as the healing and restoration of pure souls (for example in Plato's *Meno*[42] (80d)), more precisely in the soul's remembering of knowledge it acquired outside of the physical body and which it lost when it was re-embodied. Here, repair is expressed in the language of *anamnesis*. The soul, corrupted within the body, must *repair* itself, in other words correct itself, to be restored to its state prior to birth (the theory of reminiscence serves to demonstrate both the immortality of the soul and the existence of realities beyond human perception). Death is paradoxically the ultimate realm of repair, where the soul separates once again from the body and is literally reborn.

This explains the importance Plato places on the spiritual exercises on which he expounds in *Timaeus*[43] (exercising the superior part of the soul to harmonize it with the Cosmos) and above all in *Phaedo*[44] (philosophy as an exercise in death) and which he practiced with his disciples in the Academy: philosophy is "an exercise of death because death is the separation of the soul and the body, and the philosopher spends his time trying to detach his soul from his body. The body causes us no end of trouble, because of the passions which it engenders and the needs it imposes upon us."[45] The active reflexive form *repair oneself* is expressed, in Platonic theory and practice, by a set of *reparatio* designed to teach the body how to die in each of us. The medical discourse of healing is reinforced and augmented by the religious discourse of purification: "And doesn't this 'purification,'" asks Socrates, ". . . consist in separating the soul as much as possible from the body, and accustoming it to withdraw from its dispersal throughout the body and concentrate itself in isolation? And to have its dwelling, so far as it can, both now and in the future, alone by itself, freed from the chains of the body?"[46]

This separation, and this setting-free, are precisely related to what Plato, like Socrates, calls death.[47] Before it actually happens, death must be practiced, so that the soul has a little as possible to do with the body during its lifetime. This *reparatio* exceeds the lifetime of the philosopher: it takes the form of a patient preparation for the return to the pure soul when the end finally comes. The philosophical exercise of death is a promise of happiness in the celestial afterlife. The Platonic philosopher does not fear death, but, unlike the Epicurean philosopher, he most certainly fears the gods at the time of the Last Judgment. Plato warns against the "terrible danger" awaiting those who do not follow the strict path of philosophy: the "descent into Hades." Such negligence of the self would be irreversible and, consequently, irreparable.

The philosopher, in his quest for wisdom, must consent to the *loss* of his body in order to recover the virtue of his soul and the hope of happiness in Elysium. The work of mourning, to use a Freudian term anachronistically, must focus on abandoning the impure body: mourning the body (with its sensual pleasures and passions) is the condition for repairing the spirit in this world and preparing it patiently for the next.[48] This therapeutic function of philosophy has, at the same time, a political horizon, more precisely one of education (*paidagogia*) of a political order, which is especially in evidence in *Alcibiades*:[49] he who would govern others, he who would rule over the city, must first know how to govern himself (ridding himself of the passions in order to gain wisdom, knowledge and virtue).[50] The acquisition of knowledge is nothing, in Hellenistic culture, without the prospect of genuine self-transformation (self-care is the horizon of self-knowledge): a repair that is, at the same time, a conversion. If he aspires to *repair* the city (with its vices, its subterfuges and its corruption) and build a just Republic, the would-be ruler must first be able to *repair himself*, to mourn the separation from his body and his passions.

Until such time as this ideal city could be built, it was within his own Academy, at the limited scale of a small community, that Plato hoped to implement his precepts, based on an education that owed much both to Socratic dialectic teaching and to Pythagorean principles. Such is the importance of contradictory debate in the Platonic Academy: "From this perspective, the object of the discussion and its doctrinal content are of secondary importance. What counts is the practice of dialogue, and the transformation which it brings."[51] The injunction to take care of one's soul, to repair oneself and convert to the Good, which applies to every member of the Academy, is also realized through contact with others: the other disciples and the masters. The injunction to repair oneself is aimed at the individual, as the bearer and symbol of a philosophical and existential responsibility, but it is fulfilled in a shared world, in a constant dialogue: the living dialectic is an integral part of self-transformation. Repairing oneself is anything but an exclusively solitary exercise or solipsistic attitude by which repairer and repaired are brought together within the same subject. Others, starting with the masters, play a key role in repairing and elevating the individual self. In short, the goal is to *repair oneself with others*. In as far as each is invited at the same time to repair the others, to contribute to their own transformations, it would be judicious to speak of inter-repair or mutual repair. Repairer and repaired can be, in turn, oneself or another: *repairing oneself as another, with others*.

Meanwhile, without changing registers, the Epicurean schools propose another version of what might retrospectively be assimilated to a philosophy of repair. What are the troubles of the soul that need to be healed? The fear of the gods, the terror of death, the dissatisfaction of desire, the inability to endure suffering. The *reparatio* are no longer presented as an "exercise in death" or as *anamnesis*—remembering an original state marked by the purity of the soul (before its embodiment)—but as exercises designed to heal the mind (*ataraxia*, the tranquility of the soul) and the body. Here, repairing oneself does not mean seeking to return to an original state, but accepting the guidance of a norm inscribed in an ideal world. The norm by which we are to repair, correct and transform ourselves is not some lost origin, but the prospect of the wisdom of the gods: "The gods spend their lives enjoying their own perfection and the pure pleasure of existing, with no needs and no worries, in the most pleasant company."[52] Taking inspiration from the celestial life implies an effort of self-transformation toward an ascetic discipline of desires and pleasures: satisfying basic needs and enjoying simple things, while renouncing riches and whatever is superfluous. The quest for pleasure so extolled by the Epicureans is in fact the very antithesis of excess or abundance. There is no room for *hubris*. Happiness in this life is possible only through exercise, discipline and repair of the soul and the body. Epicurus sums up the four principles at the end of the *Epistle to Menoeceus* where he presents, in medical language, his "fourfold remedy":

> The gods are not to be feared,
> Death is not to be dreaded;
> What is good is easy to acquire,
> What is bad is easy to bear.[53]

The Epicureans, like most of the Hellenistic and Roman schools, share with the Platonic schools the idea that techniques of self-transformation, including in meditative and ascetic mode, depend on dialogue and encounter in a common world. Friendship is everywhere encouraged as a virtue and as a condition for the repair of the self. There is no self-repair, no self-transformation, no self-healing without the mediation of the Other. Particularly so with the philosophical exercise that consists in unburdening oneself of guilt, a form of talking therapy that would later be reconfigured by the Christian and psychoanalytic schools. It was mainly through the ritual of confession that the Epicureans practiced this exercise: "For the master, free self-expression meant not being afraid to hand out reproaches; for the disciple, it meant not hesitating to admit one's faults, and even not being afraid to tell friends about their own faults. One of the school's primary activities thus consisted in corrective and formative dialogue."[54]

These techniques of the self, though they differ in the way the underlying intersubjective dimension is expressed, point to the moral dimension of repair. Repair serves here to correct the thoughts and actions of oneself and others, raising them up toward the ideal norm. We saw the same supposition in the Kleinian model, from a psychoanalytic perspective, in which the movement of reparation stems from the desire to free oneself from the crushing weight of guilt and avoid sinking into a depressive position. Among the Epicureans, as indeed with the Stoics and later in the Christian traditions, guilt arises not only from the sense of having wanted to hurt another (i.e., the mother in Kleinian theory), but from straying from the path of philosophy and the rules laid down by the masters and "directors of conscience" (the portrait of Epicurus featured prominently on the walls of the schools to remind disciples of the permanent presence of the wise guide whose rules they must follow). Each time a disciple infringes a rule, and feels guilty, he is enjoined to correct his error and make reparation (examination of conscience, confession, etc.). Reparation, in this context, is a permanent exercise in moral correction. The "repaired," as the counterpart of the "repairer," cannot be reduced either to an intrasubjective relationship (repaired and repairer within the same subject), or to an intersubjective relationship (like the child (repairer) with regard to its mother (repaired)); it extends instead to a set of rules and precepts. Repairing oneself is about coming back into compliance with the rule and with the order of the community. The two processes are correlative: *repairing* (transitive) the act of deviance makes it possible to *repair oneself* (reflexive) in order to be released from guilt. By the examination of conscience and the practice of confession, the Epicurean philosopher unburdens his soul and thereby resumes his place in the community, while re-establishing his relationship to the norm.

REPAIR AND RESILIENCE

Since modern philosophy has taken refuge in doctrinal teaching, essentially behind university walls, and since the transmission of a body of knowledge no longer comes with an obligation of self-transformation, philosophy has lost much of its reparative function. In our time, the multiple variants of psychology and personal development have taken over philosophy's mission of repair. Therapeutic nature retreats, individual psychotherapies and fitness seminars have replaced philosophizing communities as the locus for dialogue between masters and disciples.

The *reparatio* techniques of the philosophers are, however, of a different nature: repairing lost souls is not like repairing mental disorders or restoring self-confidence; putting people on the path of virtue and truth is not the same as healing psychic trauma or restoring the vitality of the body; philosotherapy is not psychotherapy. But a crosscutting issue persists, which concerns the extent to which repair of the self calls for the intervention of another, or others. This ranges from the radical form in which repairer and repaired are merged within the same subject, when the repair of the self leaves no place for the other in the process of self-reconstruction, to the opposite form, in which the subject consents to be repaired very largely by another. We can distinguish between at least three modes of relationship on this self-repair/ other-repair continuum: repairing oneself without another, repairing oneself with another, and being repaired by another.

A number of debates (Freud and Ferenczi, Lacan and Green) on the optimal psychoanalytic approach seem to center on the degree and mode of intervention of the psychotherapist in the repair of psychic disorders. The rule of abstinence advocated by the orthodox Freudians, and indeed by the Lacanians, prohibits in principle any form of intervention in the patient's life by the psychotherapist, even in the form of advice or interpretation, let alone in the form of close relationships (friendly or erotic). The mechanism of the "talking cure," invented by Freud, is supposed to allow for the free association of ideas, which must in no way be impeded by the intervention of the analyst. To a large extent, especially when the analyst and the analysand are not physically face-to-face, this amounts to talking to oneself in front of someone else. Combined with talking therapy and the use of narrative, the goal of the cure is to enable the patient to retrieve unconscious associations through regression, and thereby undo the process of repression.

What role, then, does the psychotherapist play? Essentially that of a canvas for the projection of the love and hate felt by the analysand during childhood, a projection better known as transference. In the present of analysis, the subject reenacts childhood conflicts of the past. The patient invests the psychotherapist with instinctual feelings (the converse process of projection from the analyst onto the analysand is known as counter-transference). In this—the least interventionist—therapeutic approach, it is the patient who is more active in the endeavor to bring unconscious drives into consciousness. The question, as Jacques Robion underlines, is whether "alone, you can find this trace of the past just by talking about yourself to another person. To believe that talking without any answer can free you from your determinisms, is quite simply to deny the existence of the unconscious."[55] And, taking opposition to the rule of abstinence to extremes, "therapies have appeared specifically to repair frustration, administered by therapists dripping with benevolence, who take the place of the good parents, no less; the parents who are assumed to have frustrated the patients as children."[56]

In what sense can we speak of repair in the context of psychotherapy?[57] The notion of reparation, at least, is a central concept in psychoanalytic discourse since the work of Klein and Winnicott. However, as we saw, it is primarily thought of as a kind of disposition rather than as fixed part of a psychotherapeutic framework: the subject *repairs him or herself* (they relieve their sense of guilt) *by making reparation* to another (e.g., the mother). In the talking cure, we are dealing with another model of repair: not repairing oneself by repairing another, but repairing oneself *with* another, through the intervention, however discrete, of another, who takes the face of the therapist.

But what is it we are repairing, or think we are repairing? Sometimes the symptoms, but that is far from always the case: they may even worsen, at least to begin with, when analysis weakens the subject's defenses. Are we repairing the subject's history? No, in so far as therapy cannot aspire to return the subject to a pre-traumatic and pre-conflictual state, as if the event, real or imagined, had never occurred. Analytical other-repair does not erase history. The work of repair consists, instead, of making history conscious in a kind of *anamnesis*: bringing repressed traumatic memories and infantile conflicts to the surface of the psyche. Far from erasing the subject's history, which remains irreversible, the task of analysis is to give it another meaning, another destiny, to bring it to consciousness in order to prevent repressed feelings surfacing in the guise of symptoms. The end goal of the Freudian cure, though it is sometimes endless, is as modest as it is substantial: to be able to work and have a fulfilling sexuality.

If analysis is far from able to deliver on all its promises, that may be due as much to the relevance of the therapeutic mechanism itself as to the psychic structure of the subject, with its inherent resistance:

> It is that much harder for the patient to accept the other-repair of frustration as most of the time he unconsciously wishes it to be the *parental object* that repairs the harm it has done to him, before he *allows himself to be repaired* by the therapeutic third-party. The unconscious desire to obtain reparation for some parental injustice is, moreover, the underlying meaning of the *rumination* that we so often observe in our patients.[58]

The failure of therapeutic other-repair is ultimately down to the failure of the transference relationship, when the therapist does not act as a sufficient or appropriate canvas of projection and substitution to repair the patient's infantile trauma. The strict rule of abstinence may even reinforce the subject's sense of injustice when the approach requires the subject to find the path to self-repair on their own. Subjects are asked to repair themselves (psychologically), when in fact they want (moral) reparation for the injustice they suffered. The strict rule of abstinence, under this heterodox hypothesis, prevents the psychotherapist from assuming the position of a surrogate parental repairer.

There is a certain economy of debt at play here. How can such a long-standing debt be paid if the main people responsible for it are absent? The key question in therapy is whether the patient's desire to settle old debts (with his or her parents) can find a way, through the analytical cure, to draw a line under it all (the resentment, the frustration, the desire for revenge, and so on). Therapy seeks, in other words, to obtain justice for the subject in the absence of the accused. Repairing the subject psychologically is like restoring the subject to his or her rights. The analytical setting is transformed symbolically into a court of law in which the subject is suing for justice. Psychotherapeutic reparation is best seen not as Ancient theater but as courtroom drama; it seeks to remedy an injury and restore a right that was denied: "The parental object, which failed in its duties, *must* pay its debt, repair the *damage* done. This attempt to 'settle the accounts' is played out transferentially on the analytic stage, specifically in and through rumination. The analyst *will pay* for the patient."[59]

Looking beyond the analytic mode of *reparatio*, one can surmise that no form of psychotherapy ever directly repairs the history of the subject, in the sense of restoring a subject to a time before the psychological injury, real or imagined. Symbolically restoring a right or paying a debt is not the same as forgetting a wrong. The chains of debt can be broken, but not those of memory. What happened is, to that extent, irreparable. Whatever the operating procedure, whatever the therapeutic *reparatio* (talking cure, hypnotherapy, behaviorist therapy, sophrology), the subject will still be *other*. But this alteration will lead to a different outcome if psychotherapy manages, on the one hand, to relieve or even resolve disabling symptoms, and on the other, to retrospectively give new meaning to the subject's life by overcoming the frustration, resentment and rumination, finally giving the subject a projective handle on their own existence, and restoring, not an inaccessible lost state, but a renewed *conatus*. Such is the vocation of the psychotherapeutic other-repair of the self.

Can we go further than the psychotherapeutic repair of the self? Further, in the sense that overcoming trauma[60] might enable the subject to grow stronger in their present and future life? We are touching here on the concept of *resilience*, which once again brings up, this time at the psychological scale, the frontier between repair and performance that we investigated at the scale of living matter in our discussion of transhumanism. Resilience, an increasingly fashionable and sometimes contested notion, is polysemic. Derived from the Latin *resilientia* ("bouncing back"), resilience was initially used in mechanical physics to designate a material's shock-resistance (its capacity to absorb energy when deformed by an impact). By extension, it refers to the capacity of a body, an organism, a psyche, a species or a system to withstand sudden change.

The first experiments on resilience in the domain of psychology—before common usage redefined the term—date back to the Second World War, when American educational psychologists in Hawaii studied abused and abandoned children who presented with risks of psychopathology. Werner and Smith observed that some of them (a minority) presented no pathological disorders attributable to individual disposition or environmental factors.[61] Contrary to the received wisdom that children who had survived abuse, rape and other traumas had no hope of succeeding in life, that they were condemned to drifting, to madness, to social maladjustment, or to reproducing what they themselves had suffered, psychologists sought to understand why certain children managed to overcome their trauma. The problem of resilience stemmed from this question: why did a minority of children whose traumatic histories should, statistically, have led to social or behavioral disorders manage to develop in later life (learn a trade, start a family, etc.) without major pathologies, following a life journey similar to children not known to have suffered such traumas? These children were consequently labeled "resilient."

We owe it to John Bowlby, in the wake of Klein, Winnicott and Lorenz, to have outlined other contours of resilience in the field of child and adolescent psychiatry, based on a theory of attachment between the child and its mother or other caregiver.[62] When the child is threatened in its psychological security, literally separated from an attachment figure, it is in danger of developing psychopathological disorders. Here, resilience refers to all the processes that enable subjects to withstand this initial traumatic shock by investing emotionally in substitute persons. The more the social and cultural environment (family, clan, childcare structures, etc.) offers possibilities for affectional reattachment, the better the subject's chances of having a resilient trajectory. Building on this research, while pursuing his own work, based on his experience of the concentration camps and his experience as a psychiatrist, Boris Cyrulnik has done much to popularize the notion of resilience in France.[63]

The scientific controversies here center as much on the factors that supposedly intervene in the process of resilience as on what is meant by a "resilient subject." The debate in the first case concerns the demarcation between biological factors (genetic predispositions, sexual hormones, immune systems) and environmental factors (family, school, and "resilience tutors" who show empathy, affection and consideration for the subject).[64] In the second case, the debate reflects back directly on where to draw the border between resilience and self-repair. The two terms sometimes overlap: resilience can be seen as a modality of self-repair, in the same way as the work of mourning, for example. Resilience does not mean, therefore, that the subject can return to an earlier pre-traumatic state, as in the mechanical process of repair. The initial trauma is not erased from the psychic apparatus, but it is partially neutralized by "resilience factors." Piecing one's life back together in no way means that the traces of trauma have disappeared from the memory, or indeed from the brain. Instead of an ability to wind the clock back, resilience gives the subject the ability to move forward, a capacity for living, for loving, in short for restoring their *conatus*: their desire to be and effort to exist. In this sense, resilience is psychologically distinct from resistance, which is the process by which a person who has built up a degree of emotional protection deals, in the moment, with an ordeal or a trauma. Resilience comes into play retrospectively, in the way a person picks up their life after an emotional shock.

Resilience is more radically differentiated from self-repair, in our definition, when it presupposes a kind of invulnerability to trauma, especially as a result of biological factors. Further still, resilience is often used to describe not only the characteristics that enable a subject to cope with trauma, but that additional something that can transform the trials of life into opportunities to surpass oneself. "Bouncing back" for a new start after a setback is thought to increase and reinforce the power of the subject, echoing Nietzsche's "what doesn't kill me makes me stronger." It is not simply about reestablishing the *conatus*; it is about increasing its intensity and capability: "the concept of resilience implies a sort of specific added value signifying that, in certain cases, trauma will add something that the life of this or that subject might not have made possible, were it not for the encounter with this event."[65] This "additional something" is conceived of as a new lease of life, one that would never have been realized if the individual had not undergone the trauma. As Vincent de Gaulejac said, when looking back at the life of Boris Cyrulnik: "Had you been to school, you would have followed a conventional career path. Your marginality is a source of unexpected ideas."[66] In other words, Cyrulnik, by this account, not only absorbed the shocks in question (missing out on school because of the war, narrowly escaping deportation, although his parents died in the camps, becoming an orphan, etc.), he overcame them in a way that made him into a psychiatrist with innovative ideas. Where other individuals who suffered similar traumas fell prey to depression or suicide, certain resilience factors enabled Boris Cyrulnik to go further than self-repair, and to become a resilient being.

At this point we can distinguish between at least two variants of resilience. On the one hand, a Freudian-inspired variant, despite sometimes heated debates with psychoanalysts, which assimilates resilience to self-repair in the form of the work of mourning. Cyrulnik sometimes speaks of "repairing an emotional niche," or "coming back to life after a psychic trauma."[67] In the natural world, this might be symbolized by a tree that continuous to live and grow outwards even after its top has been cut off (or by land ravaged by fire, to which plant and animal life eventually return). On the other hand, a Nietzschean-inspired variant that assimilates resilience to self-enhancement in the form of an increased life-force after a traumatic ordeal. This might be symbolized by the Japanese art of *kintsugi*, which embellishes a previously broken object by coating it with lacquer mixed with powdered gold (making the object more beautiful than if it had never been damaged).

One way of reconciling or articulating these two distinct orientations might be to think in terms of variations. When, for example, the child's trauma (separation, abuse, abandonment, etc.) occurs at a very young age and the social environment offers few alternatives by way of affective tutors, repair will be very difficult and the legacy will be lasting. When, by contrast, the child has known affective security during the first years of life, the subsequent advent of trauma will be easier to overcome, especially if formative tutors are on hand to rebuild the child's emotional confidence. Repair becomes performance-based resilience (rather than simply reparative resilience) when, in addition to overcoming the trauma, the subject manages, with the help of their entourage, to develop capacities for life, thought and action that (one assumes) they would not have been able to draw upon had their life followed a path without that defining breakpoint.

Among many examples, the way the writers of the French Antilles, such as Edouard Glissant and Patrick Chamoiseau, reconstruct the slavery-tainted past and rethink Creole identity presents all the traits of resilience as the source of an increased life-force. On the one hand, they advocate for the recognition of the founding crime of the former slave-owning societies, a crime of which the Antilles still bears the scars and the stigmata. On the other, this collective trauma, this historical shock, is reconstructed as a watershed of encounters, cultural blending, and original creation that give post-slavery societies their particular genius. Resilience is to be found here, in as far as the crime has spawned some positivity:

> When I look back (says Chamoiseau) to the time of slavery, I see a multitude of agonies . . . much agony, much suffering, but also much rebirth, much germination and blossoming. This extraordinary process of death, symbolic death, concrete death, torture—this offense against humanity—quite unexpectedly produced new cultural propositions, new musical propositions, new identity propositions that make us much more adaptable and much more agile today, if we have to try and understand the world.[68]

In this process, we find once again the idea of an *addition*, a *supplement* of creativity, of capability, of understanding typical of the way resilience is supposed to operate on those who have increased their life-fund after sustaining trauma. The existence of this creativity, particularly in cultural domains (artistic, literary, culinary, linguistic, etc.), is an established characteristic of Creole societies. In his interview, however, Chamoiseau does not dwell on the fact that most people in the Antilles are a long way from any process of resilience. The suffering, alienation and pauperization that he mentions in the interview are not limited to their slave ancestors: they directly impact—on a different scale, of course—the descendants of slaves, who struggle to repair, psychologically and socially, the damage caused by slavery and its transgenerational legacy.[69] Resilience, in the Antilles, is the characteristic of a minority. But has this resilient minority truly overcome any vulnerability? Cultural creativity is no barrier against psychological fragility and social insecurity.

The concept of resilience, for all its fecundity, must therefore be handled with care. On the one hand, because the factors supposedly at work in resilience partly escape experimental observation. However enlightened and well-constructed it may be, the employment[70] of the self or of a group is only one element in a much wider set of determining factors, even if the construction of a narrative identity can itself be part of the resilience process. On the other hand, the idea of certain subjects having a natural invulnerability is empirically very doubtful. There is nothing to say that a subject who is resilient at one point in their existence is not liable to "lapse" when confronted with a new traumatic ordeal; clinical examples abound.

Finally, and this remark is just as valid for self-repair as for resilience, the way emotional shock is absorbed can involve "perverse" behaviors such as sado-masochism, assigning sexual significance to the scene of the original trauma. Self-repair can, in other words, generate other pathologies.[71] So much so that many practitioners are highly skeptical about complete self-repair, to say nothing of permanent resilience. Among the critics of the concept of resilience, Serge Tisseron speaks of "the love of trauma" when the individual is reluctant to heal, drawing sustenance from the intensity of the trauma, like Dostoevsky evoking the gratification of self-mortification. Something similar is found when trauma is transformed into creativity, in a process that could be compared to Freudian sublimation. This is, indeed, one of the paths that resilience can take, and perhaps a more promising one, in as much as it opens up to others, unlike a pure narcissistic regression into trauma. But this openness, if we bear in mind that all these modes of repair or resilience can coexist in the same subject, is not always exempt from destructive impulses. Witness, for example, the case of Picasso, as related by Tisseron. Afflicted by many traumas during his childhood (thought to be dead at birth, victim of an earthquake during his childhood), Picasso, it has been claimed, turned his art into a powerful instrument of resilience. But descriptions of the man himself tell of "a despot, a domestic manipulator":

> To speak of reconstruction after a trauma makes perfect sense. However, does it make sense to speak of a "resilient personality"? Picasso presented many personality traits, in particular with his successive women and children, that clash with the seductive pastels used to depict "resilience." Picasso undoubtedly "repaired himself" by creating his pictorial works, but he also did so by establishing a sadistic relationship with those close to him.[72]

Far from repairing the self with another, or as another, the subject here "repairs himself" to the detriment of another, by diminishing or dominating another person. As though repair (of the self) could only be achieved by destruction (of the other). Unlike the Kleinian model of repairing the self by repairing the other (reconstructive repair), repairing the self here depends on destroying the other (destructive repair).

The same phenomenon of destructive repair[73] is observed at the neurological scale in the case of lobotomies performed on schizophrenic patients, a practice frequent up until the 1950s: symptoms (delirium, hallucinations, etc.) were repaired at the cost of the destruction of a substantial part of the psychic life of the patients (such as making it impossible for them to construct a narrative, or to project themselves in time). So much so that some patients preferred not to be repaired, even if that meant continuing to suffer, rather than undergo the irremediable destruction of their subjectivity and what was left of their zest for life.

These clinical cases, and others, reframe the sensitive debate around the normalizing function of repair, which we have already encountered at the scale of living organisms. There is a historical, social, and socio-medical dimension in the norm that imposes modes of self-repair. And this norm can amount to a form of social control and political repression. The debate is already an old one, dating back notably to Michel Foucault and the antipsychiatry movement of the 1960s. Should we repair the mad?[74] How much mental a-reparability can a society tolerate? Just how far can a society go in making its subjects take responsibility for their own mental repair?

The choice made by some individuals not to be repaired, despite persistent suffering, is not always linked, as the analytical hypothesis would have it, to a perverse attachment to their own pain. The issue we touched on earlier about "deaf identity" laying claim to difference also applies to anomalies of the psyche relative to the dominant norm. We must of course distinguish between cases where the request for repair of the self comes directly from the subject and those where it is imposed by a medical, administrative or family authority. Not so very long ago, patient consent was not sought before sterilizing people with Down syndrome, lobotomizing schizophrenics or (even today) imposing a gender on hermaphrodites at birth, a measure of the considerable menace of medical and social violence that can be contained in the injunction to repair oneself—or get oneself repaired—mentally. Milos Forman subtly denounced the dangers in *One Flew Over the Cuckoo's Nest* (1975), where the most perverse aspect of the drama that plays out in a psychiatric hospital in Oregon is in fact the head nurse, who tyrannizes and punishes patients in the name of a social normality that has itself become perverse.[75] Electroconvulsive therapy and lobotomies are repressive responses to the anomalies of patients who are above all alienated by what Erving Goffman calls a *total institution*.[76] The experience of any mental anomaly highlights the relativity of the norms of totalitarian regimes, some of which have pursued the extermination of the supposedly mad, many of whom were merely opponents or dissidents.[77] It also questions the dominance of reparative mental norms in reputedly democratic regimes: until fairly recently in France, for example, homosexuality was classified as an illness or a perversion (to say nothing of those countries where this sexual orientation is violently repressed even today). The psychiatric institution can be presented both as an inventory of the medical symptoms of the patients and as an inventory of the social symptoms of a society. What needs to be repaired, the mentally ill, or society as a whole? This is not a provocative question: many pathologies classified as mental are directly engendered by the social, cultural and economic transformations of the contemporary world. The social norms and the medical norms around mental disorders need to be examined conjointly.

Canguilhem reminds us that the anomalies of living matter make up the diversity and the range of unprecedented possibilities of life. This observation also applies to mental anomalies, some of which undoubtedly represent untested possibilities of the psyche. It is with this in mind that philosophers such as Gilles Deleuze and Félix Guattari, sometimes accused of glorifying madness, chose to interpret limited states of the psyche as veritable experiments in living, for example in the form of schizo-analysis,[78] while others proposed creative art workshops (*art brut* or "raw art" in particular) for example at the Clinique de La Borde in Switzerland, at the initiative of Dr. Jean Oury. In place of the injunctive mode—to repair oneself (or have oneself repaired) mentally, redolent of repressive normalization—they proposed an incentive mode: encouraging people to experiment with and express their own mental difference. No longer seeing the unconscious as a stage on which the main character (the patient psychiatrized in an institution or analyzed on a couch) is to be repaired but, as Deleuze and Guattari put it, as a "factory," as a production system that creates affects and intensities. Although it was never really an argument in praise of folly, the call for schizo-analysis was far from addressing every problem, particularly for patients in distress who are resistant to any form of creative sublimation and who demand to be institutionalized, to say nothing of subjects who are actually or potentially dangerous. Mental self-repair is as relevant today as it was then. The antipsychiatry movement, though its influence has faded, still serves to unmask a function of mental repair that is, itself, pathological when it takes the form of an attempt at repressive normalization.

Even when the request for care comes from the actual subject, consciously and knowingly, the question of social and legal norms remains crucial, in that they tend to pre-format the subject's own decision. There are injunctive social modes that preside, implicitly and silently, over self-injunctions to seek psychological or psychiatric repair of oneself, with a form of symbolic violence. It is as though subjects do not have the impression of acting under an objective constraint when they decide to seek mental repair. Recognizing mental anomaly is not the same thing as glorifying madness and wanting to deprive mentally ill subjects of care, especially if they represent a clear danger to society. A treatment order pronounced by a judge, on the advice of a psychiatric expert, is above all issued to protect society and to prevent a possible recurrence. The injunction placed on the subject by the legal authority to allow themselves to be repaired (treated, corrected) is designed primarily to avoid the need to repair the social body.

THE AGE OF SELF-REPAIR

Every society has its mechanisms of repair, and mobilizes them in its own ways, with specific *reparatio* and in particular domains. Our own is paradoxically ever less reparative in its relationship to things, and ever more reparative in its relationship to itself, to law and to history. The neoliberal mode of capitalist production is such that it leaves increasingly less room for the possibility of repairing objects. Partly because the equipment we use has such a degree of technological sophistication that the everyday user does not have the required skills to get damaged objects back into shape and working order. Even repairers, when they can be found, tend increasingly to replace rather than repair parts in defective devices, due to a lack of specific skills. And partly because equipment, especially computer hardware and household appliances, is designed for a relatively short operating lifetime. The capitalist era of planned obsolescence makes it cheaper to buy new than to get a defective part repaired, a process reinforced by the capitalist mode of desire, with its premium on novelty, supposedly delivering ever more enjoyment and functionality to the consumer. The unrestrained accumulation of new things to consume, correlated with constant technological innovation, overshadows the repair of old things, which is so central to traditional societies. In the neoliberal world, we throw away, we reject, we sometimes replace, we buy more and more, but we patch up, we restore, we mend less and less.

The same observation is inescapable in the context of employment relations: the gradual decline of processes of repair in relations of production, combined with the increase in precarity, generates social costs as well as psychic costs for ever more atomized and isolated workers. While precarity directly affects the most fragile categories of the world of employment, the new neoliberal norms of management apply to all employees, and particularly to middle managers. The new spirit of capitalism, as it emerges for example from the management texts that have shaped corporate attitudes since the late 1970s,[79] seeks to replace the Fordist model of work with a new, networked organization, based on personal initiative and relative autonomy in one's job. The cost of this change is counted in terms of social, material and psychic insecurity. Worker autonomy comes at a price: the injunction to keep on achieving.[80] Knowing how to communicate, negotiate, motivate yourself, manage your time, rise to the challenge, push the envelope—these are the new slogans of neoliberal management, initially imposed on private sector workers and now being generalized across the public sector under the label *new public management*.[81] Economic competitiveness, modeled on sporting competition, demands that workers constantly outperform themselves.

The autonomy advocated by the Enlightenment philosophers sought, by opposition to heteronomy, to extirpate humanity from its state of dependency and emancipate it from its supervisory authorities (religious, political, or other). By a negative dialectic of neoliberal appropriation, the quest for autonomy has paradoxically become an instrument of alienation in the workplace. Whereas philosophical autonomy was supposed, in political terms, to guarantee the subject's sovereignty, autonomization in the work environment contributes to their fragility. The accountability that was once spread across the company now tends instead to filter down to individuals, placing an ever more pressing weight on each employee's shoulders.

The limitless quest for achievement clearly has its downside: "the weariness of the self," to borrow the title of Alain Ehrenberg's book.[82] A psychic symptom of something rotten in the world of work, this self-weariness refers to a new form of depression, a direct consequence of the cult of achievement. A depression that is less to do with a conflictual relationship with authority, or discipline, than with directives expressed in terms of flexibility, change, reactiveness, and constant innovation. When workers can no longer live up to these new norms, they fall into this self-weariness, the notorious "burnout" which affects a growing number of employees. This growth in depression corresponds to an "addictive explosion"—as Ehrenberg calls it—of drug use, both to boost performance and to stave off, and sometimes treat, depression.

The other manifestation of the quest for achievement is the need for self-repair, especially when the individual identifies as the main vector of whatever is going wrong with his or her job (rather than blaming the norms of the work organization or the company's own dysfunctions). Remotivation seminars, antidepressive or performance-enhancing pharmacology, psychotherapy or coaching sessions have become the *sine qua non* of self-repair in the psychic economy of post-industrial capitalism.[83] One remarkable achievement of this new mode of capitalist production is that it makes things ever less repairable, does ever less to repair strained work relationships, and yet at the same time demands self-repair (except from the marginalized and the excluded) when people can no longer keep up with the pace of performance.

It is by virtue of all these symptoms that we live in the age of self-repair. There is clearly, as we saw with the requirement for self-attentiveness and self-care in the Hellenistic cultures, a transhistorical and transcultural dimension to the repair of the subject. Self-repair is not an invention of the modern world. The work of mourning is timeless, though it has been expressed in profoundly different ways throughout time and across human societies. The possibility of constructing and mobilizing *reparatio* to overcome a misfortune, an emotional shock, or a bereavement, is written into the anthropological heart of every human being.

However, social, economic and cultural changes in Western societies, due to increasing individualization and precarization, have undoubtedly contributed to making repair more acute, and modifying the forms that it takes. The contemporary age of self-repair is strictly coterminous with a subjectivity that is as assertive as it is vulnerable. This transformation is the direct legacy of a modernity that Charles Taylor defines by "the primacy of self-fulfillment, particularly in its therapeutic variants."[84]

An excellent example of what Taylor calls our "expressivist" culture is to be found in the transformations of the literary field in the contemporary era. Of course, from an anthropological angle, it is easy to agree with Alexandre Gefen that there have always been literary forms designed to assuage a loss or an absence, to heal life's woes, and to answer the anguish of finitude. The recent contemporary era, however, is marked by a turn in the art of writing: "It is this collective imaginary where literature (with no distinction between 'high literature' and creative writing workshops for all)—in place of religion or some political project—seeks to repair our victimhood, to remedy these traumas of the individual memory or the social fabric."[85] Whereas a substantial part of twentieth-century literature turned it into an autonomized object, a gratuitous activity, absorbed in its own plays on words and forms, writing increasingly nourishes the project of accompanying the much-vaunted autonomization of subjects at the edge of the precipice, of salving the wounds of individual and collective existence, of repairing the sense of loss, of remedying absence, uncertainty and weariness of self. When Robbe-Grillet and Blanchot asserted that "the writer has nothing to say," when Derrida insisted that "there is nothing outside the text," echoing the "death of the author" announced by Barthes and Foucault, the idea of literature fulfilling a therapeutic purpose could hardly have seemed more remote. Only the text counted; in itself and for itself. Literature—even "minor" literature[86]—was primarily an exercise in style, not a flaunting of the author's subjectivity.

This heyday of literature for literature's sake was followed by the age of art therapy and "expressivist" literature. The text flies off the page to become a work of mourning when a writer confronts, for example, the death of someone close (Philippe Forest,[87] Camille Laurens,[88] Laure Adler,[89] Pierre Jourde[90], and others). As a technique of *reparatio*, the work of writing must enable the letting-go of the lost object: the text becomes a substitute for the absence of the loved one. In his diagnosis, Gefen underlines "the way writers set up their narrative as a kind of course of treatment for mourning, by verbalizing it and integrating it into an autobiographical journey through a problematic process of literary embodiment."[91] The same literary diagnosis applies when the writer is confronted with illness and, more generally, any biographical rupture in their existence. The literary autobiography becomes a psychotherapy in its own right, to triumph over shame (Christine Angot,[92] Annie Ernal[93]), to exorcize the memories of rape (Helene Duffau,[94] Edouard Louis[95]), or to heal the wounds of heartbreak (Yves Charnet[96]). Where trauma generates a void and a discontinuity in the biographical journey, where an event creates dissonance in the depth of the subject, that is where the emplotment of the self knits up the holes in continuity and distances the harrowing event by relocating it within a broader narrative structure. The literary value of the text is ultimately of little importance; all that counts is the authenticity-value attached to the author of the narrative. The text becomes a pretext for expressing suffering, for relieving a pain, for accompanying an illness along one of the paths explored by Fritz Zorn in an "autopathography" he wrote about his cancer, to ward off bodily pain and mental fragmentation. The therapeutic virtue of the text takes precedence over its literary quality: "To begin the healing process," writes Bernard Pingaud, "maybe all it takes is a sentence, just one. This one, for example."[97] It is in this new context that therapeutic writing workshops came to replace literary salons. The democratization of the literary field authorizes everyone to take up a pen and recount the wounds of their existence.[98]

The new expressivist norm of the literary world in return affects the status of the reader, when reading itself becomes a resource for self-understanding and self-repair. That which lies outside the text is now held sacred, and this is true as much of the author who re-emerges through the door of art-therapy as for the reader suddenly called upon, through contact with the literary text, to become a bibliotherapist. This self-transformation through reading goes far beyond the ancient *catharsis* that Aristotle saw in the tragic theater as a means of washing away harmful emotions: "Literature has become a treatment, and literary value is judged by its therapeutic efficacy, not only for the one who heals his or her traumas by verbalizing them, but also for the reader, who finds consolation in the book."[99] We are all invited, with the help of our doctor and our psychotherapist if so desired, to compile our own library, to bury ourselves in the book we need, when we need it, in order to construct or reconstruct ourselves. Every story becomes what Alain de Botton calls a "self-help manual."[100]

Like the act of writing, the act of reading, in its therapeutic aim, has a transhistorical dimension with models that reach far back into Antiquity.[101] An ordinary *reparatio*, though long reserved for the literate classes and restricted to societies with writing systems, reading, in its many different forms (public reading, quiet reading), has undergone—and continues to undergo in the digital era—a series of major transformations, until it has become a favorite therapeutic exercise of our contemporaries. The reading of stories, though a timeless pursuit, is a large component of the contemporary age of self-repair, in which it is both a social symptom and an individual therapy. The novel is no longer only an initiatory tale in the Goethean tradition of the *Bildungsroman*, but one of the ordinary ways of healing the wounds of life in a society that keeps piling more and more requirements and responsibilities onto individuals. Literature, Ricœur claimed, is a laboratory for experimenting with other possible selves. It has become more than that: a fictional clinic in which fragmented minds are pieced back together.

Beyond the historical diagnosis, it is of course difficult to measure the (biblio)-therapeutic efficacy of literary *reparatio*:

> Whether we are talking about Mithridatism, exorcism, transitional displacement or catharsis, the underlying mechanism remains opaque. Should we identify with the character of a novel, in the hope of coming out changed, healed by contact with a work of art? What are the requirements as regards the involvement of the reading subject, and his or her capacity for concentration, for empathy or, indeed, for self-detachment?[102]

The limits Gefen evokes are tighter still in the case of more serious mental disorders, in which the act of reading becomes at best a problematic exercise. It is usually in association with other *reparatio* that reading can have beneficial effects on the human psyche. The therapeutic mechanism may be opaque, but there seems little doubt that both the act of narrating (orally or in writing) and the act of reading have powers: not, of course, to clear up symptoms or to restore a pre-traumatic state, but to initiate work on the meaning of suffering, of biographical discontinuities, of tragic life events. Reading and writing in no way erase life's traumas, but they help to reconfigure them, by verbalizing them, by projecting them into fictional worlds, by comparing them with other stories. The construction of—or identification with—characters in a novel can provide a space for experimentation and repair of the self in the form of a narraive identity.

I called this chapter *The Fragmented Mind* to give an amplitude to the notion of repair that both attaches it to living organisms in general and also detaches it from them when it directly invokes techniques to reassemble the pieces of the human psyche. The mind as brain benefits, to some degree, from internal mechanisms of self-repair after certain types of lesion. This homeostatic function of the brain, to use Damasio's term, does not quite represent *oneself* (or paradoxically "another myself") so much as the non-conscious part of the brain that intervenes to regulate all the vital systems, keeping them within manageable "ranges." It is when the non-conscious brain is no longer able to self-repair and self-regulate, or only with great difficulty, that the conscious psyche—with its own specific tonalities—comes into play. Self-repair can then call upon its resources of *reparatio*, either to act directly on the brain, or to intervene on the psyche.

The repair of the self, whether with or without an other, whether lay or professional, extends as far in time and space as human beings have striven to *respond* to the experience of *loss* (of a loved one, of an ideal, of esteem, etc.). Stretching well beyond psychoanalysis, the work of mourning, as initially analyzed by Freud, appears to offer a suitable paradigm for understanding what self-repair means, at the psychological level, and also for understanding its failure when the subject cannot bring him or herself to consent to the loss. When it does succeed, it certainly does not signify a return to the situation before the harm was done, as if nothing had happened. The psychological repair of the self does not erase the trauma from the face of time. Something always remains, to varying degrees, depending on the intensity of the traumatic experience, something that is the stigmata of the irreparable and the sign of human fragility. When psychological repair of the self is possible, it can only be the result of a sometimes interminable process that leads toward the partial or complete restoration of the capacity to live and to love, a dynamic process that I have deliberately analyzed in the light of Spinoza's *conatus*.

Self-repair crosses epochs and societies, taking on specific modes of expression in every case, but in the contemporary Western world it manifests in unique forms and with unprecedented intensity. The contemporary age of psychological self-repair is rooted in "expressivist" modernity and draws sustenance from the unprecedented growth of individualism and the transformations of neoliberal capitalism. Subject to the diktats and injunctions of performance, loosened from traditional bonds of solidarity, disaffiliated from social structures of protection, the contemporary individual takes upon his or her own shoulders the difficulty of being and becoming. Even the possibility of psychological reconstruction, given the cost of treatment, is far from being available to all. The age of self-repair, unequally shared, also presupposes sufficient time and resources to have any hope of reviving one's *conatus*.

NOTES

1. D. Andler, *La silhouette de l'humain. Quelle place pour le naturalisme aujourd'hui?* Paris: Gallimard, 2016.
2. G. Ryle, *The Concept of Mind.* Chicago: University of Chicago Press, 2000 [1949].
3. D. Parfit, *Reasons and Persons.* Oxford: Oxford University Press, 1986.
4. The dialogue between Ricœur and Changeux (*What Makes Us Think?* Trans. M.B. Debevoise. Princeton, NJ: Princeton University Press, 2010) seems to me to be a useful guide for understanding the distinction between a dualism of substance (from the Cartesian tradition) and a dualism of discourse or perspective (from phenomenology). When the philosopher writes that the brain cannot be said to "think," he is not

implying that there is something else, some "additional fact" (for example an immaterial substance sich as the soul) that does the thinking. The brain remains the material, neural, basis for all thought: "Relying ... on the resources furnished by phenomenology," writes Ricœur, "I will restrict myself, modestly but firmly, to considering the semantics of two distinct discourses—one concerning the body and the brain, the other what I will call the mental. My initial thesis is that these discourses represent heterogeneous perspectives, which is to say that they cannot be reduced to each other or derived from each other. In the one case it is a question of neurons and their connection in a system; in the other one speaks of knowledge, action, feeling ... acts or states characterized by intentions, motivations, and values" (*ibid.*, p. 14). This is why thinking subjects do not relate directly to their brain or to "its" neurons (but rather to thoughts, feelings, emotions, etc.): discourse about the brain is typically third-person discourse, even when uttered by the brain's owner. However, this dualism of perspective in no way justifies an ontological dualism of substance: to affirm that there are two or more perspectives (on the brain and on "the mental") is not to imply that there might be two substances of differing nature (soul and matter). One of the aims here, which forms the subtext to the dialogue between Ricœur and Changeux, is to see whether we can establish a third category of discourse (without recourse to Spinoza's God): a mixed discourse, for example a neuropsychological discourse that integrates both discourse on the brain and discourse on the psyche.

5. P. Strawson, *Individuals: An Essay in Descriptive Metaphysics*. London: Methuen, 1959.

6. The scientific quest, following in the tradition of Broca, is to map the brain by associating mental faculties (language, emotion, etc.) with the activation of certain areas of the cortex. Technological inventions, in particular functional magnetic resonance imaging (fMRI), have helped refine the "brain mapping" program in neuroscience: measuring activity in the cortical areas thought to be responsible for particular types of mental activity. When we read a text, for example, the ventral occipito-temporal area "lights up" in the fMRI scan. This area of the brain can therefore be assumed to be the neural cause of the activity of reading. But has this brought us any closer to knowing what it *means* to read and understand a text? We can surely assume that any reading activity, and indeed any activity that involves understanding and interpretation, depends on a neural basis. But what exactly are we measuring with fMRI? Daniel Andler, without of course denying the neural basis of thought and the importance of the invention of fMRI, points to the limitations of such an inference: "what the apparatus captures is a signal called 'BOLD' (blood oxygenation level dependent (response)), linked to variation in blood flow in the area under observation. It has long been known that there is a correlation between neural activity and the BOLD signal, but this correlation is complex and far from perfectly understood; moreover, the absence of a signal cannot be interpreted *a contrario* as an absence of involvement by the area in the performance of the task. In fact, all the areas of the brain are constantly active, and it is only by observing differences that we can make suppositions about the increased role of an area in a given process" (D. Andler, *La silhouette de l'humain, op. cit.*, p. 203).

7. P. Churchland, *Neurophilosophy: Toward a Unified Science of the Mind-Brain*. Cambridge, MA: MIT Press, 1986.

8. This limitation is also supposed to have an advantage: if our neurons were constantly renewed, how could they store information in our memory?

9. F.H. Gage, "Stem cells of the central nervous system," *Current Opinion in Neurobiology* 8, pp. 671–76, 1998.

10. SF. Sorrells, MF. Paredes, A. Cebrian-Silla, et al., "Human hippocampal neurogenesis drops sharply in children to undetectable levels in adults," *Nature* 555, pp. 377–81, 2018.

11. Elena Sender, "Arrêtons-nous de produire de nouveaux neurones à l'âge adulte?," *Sciences et avenir*, https://www. sciencesetavenir.fr/sante/cerveau-et-psy/arretons-nous-de-produire-de-nouveaux-neurones-a-l-age-adulte_121888.

12. The brain is both part of the body like any other organ and also unique in that it can, thanks to specific cells (neurons), transmit (and receive) information to (and from) all the other cells. Nerve cells are unlike other cells due to their ability to act on other cells, via electrical and chemical signals, and modify their state. Neurons exist for other neurons and for all the cells in the body. Neurons literally *represent* the state of the organism and transform it. As Damasio points out, the brain, by virtue of its dense neural tissue, is able to constantly map not only its own interactions with the outside world but also the internal operating state of the body. It is thanks to the brain that the body can become an object of the mind: "Body and brain are engaged in a continuous interactive dance. Thoughts implemented in the brain can induce emotional states that are implemented in the body, while the body can change the brain's landscape and thus the substrate for thoughts" (A. Damasio, *Self Comes to Mind*, op. cit., p. 96).

13. M. Thiebaut de Schotten, M. Urbanski, H. Duffau, E. Volle, R. Levy, B. Dubois & P. Bartolomeo, "Direct evidence for a parietal-frontal pathway subserving spatial awareness in humans," *Science*, 309 (5744), pp. 2226–28, 2005.

14. A. Damasio, *Self Comes to Mind*, op. cit., p. 48.

15. In Damasio's model, the scale ranges from the protoself (elementary feelings of existence) through the core self (which is about how the organism acts upon and relates to external objects), to the autobiographical self (a reflexive form, both past- and future-oriented). Each layer of the self is interdependent on the others.

16. The brain can simulate certain bodily states in its somatosensory regions as though they were about to happen.

17. *Ibid.*, p. 53.

18. Jean-Pierre Changeux, *What Makes Us Think?*, op. cit. p. 62.

19. An action on the brain that is not directly physical or chemical, that is, which operates via the psyche, has—according to the monist hypothesis—a neural correspondence by virtue of the correlation described earlier. When we speak of the psyche, we refer not only to the conscious psyche, but also the non-conscious psyche, without reducing it to the Freudian model of the Unconscious. A large part of the psyche never comes to the consciousness of the subject, even though it handles a considerable number of operations, including in highly complex mechanisms of reasoning (what Damasio calls the cognitive unconscious, which is sometimes more

efficient than the cognitive conscious). Consciousness is merely the tip of the psychic iceberg.

20. The fact that there are no lesions in the brain to account for these mental illnesses does not imply (and this is central) there is no neural basis to these illnesses and their symptoms, even if the Freudian "topics" (such as the first topic: "conscious-preconscious-unconscious") came to be constructed independently of any neurological correspondence or foundation (as neuroscientists invariably point out). It is possible, for example, to "map" the visual and auditory hallucinations of psychotic patients by using a point-of-view camera. While many psychoanalysts are resistant to introducing any form of neurological causation into their model, a school of neuro-psychoanalysis is beginning to develop, mainly in the USA (and particularly under the impulse of Mark Solms), to foster dialogue between the two rival sciences.

21. S. Freud, *Papers on Metapsychology and Other Works*. London: Hogarth, 1957.

22. *Ibid.*, p. 245.

23. P. Ricœur, *Oneself as Another*. Chicago: University of Chicago Press, 1994.

24. S. Freud, *op. cit.*, p. 249.

25. Joël Clerget, "L'irréparable outrage," *De la réparation* (Christophe Schaeffer ed.). Paris: L'Harmattan, 2010, p. 65.

26. M. Klein (with Joan Riviere), *Love, Hate and Reparation*. London: Hogarth Press, 1953.

27. According to Klein, the depressive position is normally experienced around the middle of the first year of life and is liable to reappear during early childhood and indeed throughout life, especially when the subject is faced with the ordeal of bereavement. In an initial phase, the earliest phase in the child's psychic development, the main anxiety centers on the survival of the self. In the depressive position, the anxiety extends to the object (mainly the mother-object): the "good" and "bad" aspects of the mother are no longer seen as separate but are attached to the same object. Consequently, explains Klein, the child's anxiety is transposed to the mother-object as a whole (in an ambivalence of love and hate).

28. *Ibid.*, pp. 59–60.

29. *Ibid.*, pp. 67–68 (the italics are Klein's).

30. D.W. Winnicott, *Human Nature*. Philadelphia: Brunner/Mazel, 1988, pp. 73–74.

31. Simone Korff-Sausse describes the case of one of her patients, a victim of coercive control. Traumatized by the tragic death of her brother when she was young (she was supposed to be keeping an eye on him at the time of the accident), the patient ("Christine") experiences and relives—the analyst tell us—a structural guilt, maintained by a tyrannical, alcoholic mother, who abused her when she was a child. By pathological identification, the victim incorporates a guilt that the controller never feels, seeking to minimize her own actions, and taking the blame for failings that the controller will not admit to: the victim becomes guilty instead of the controller, while the controller becomes a victim in her place. This and other such cases raise the question of the victim's own involvement in the pathogenic structure of the relationship to the tormentor: "How can one relinquish being the object and subject of such a passion? After leaving her husband, Christine finds it hard to invest in new sexual

relationships; they seem insipid to her. If the new boyfriend doesn't persecute her on the telephone, if he doesn't make jealous scenes, doesn't open her mail, doesn't hit her, then surely, he doesn't really love her . . . something is missing. Anyway, how could he love her, when he is so nice in every way, and she is just a 'piece of filth'? That, after all, is how her mother loved her: by denigrating her, criticizing her, dragging her through the mud, making her feel ashamed every day. Is there any other way to love someone? She could not break free from this setup until the day she managed to make the connection between her mother and her husband, and became aware of her murderous hatred toward them both. 'The terrible, destructive hatred . . . is perhaps the heaviest burden of soul murder,' writes Shengold. It comes down to 'wanting to kill the parent without whom one cannot live'" (S. Korff-Sausse, "La femme du pervers narcissique," *Revue française de psychanalyse*, 2003/3 (Vol. 67), p. 938). This analytical explanation raises the general problem of the victim's complicity—even desire, albeit unconscious—in acting as easy prey for the coercive controller. It runs the risk, however, of downplaying the responsibility of the controller, who seeks to gain power over and enslave the other.

32. S. Freud, *op.cit.*, p. 256.

33. *Ibid.*, p. 256.

34. E.W. Straus, *The Primary World of Senses*. New York: Free Press of Glencoe, 1935. pp. 318–20.

35. F. Gros, *A Philosophy of Walking*, trans. John Howe. London: Verso, 2014.

36. David Le Breton, "La marche est souvent guérison," *La philosophie de la marche* (ed. N. Truong), Editions Aube/Le Monde, 2018.

37. *Ibid.*, p. 73.

38. S. Tesson, "La marche est une critique en mouvement," *La philosophie de la marche, op. cit.*, p. 17.

39. S. Tesson, *Sur les chemins noirs*. Paris: Gallimard, 2016 [*On the Wandering Paths*, trans. Drew Tesson. Minnesota University Press, 2022, forthcoming].

40. *Ibid.*, p. 41.

41. David Lucas, "La philosophie antique antique comme soin de l'âme," *Le Portique* [online], 4-2007 | Soin et éducation (II), posted June 14, 2007, accessed October 9, 2018. http://journals.openedition.org/leportique/948.

42. Plato, *Meno and Other Dialogues*, ed./trans. R. Waterfield. Oxford University Press, 2009.

43. Plato, *Timaeus and Critias*, trans. R. Waterfield. Oxford University Press, 2008.

44. Plato, *The Last Days of Socrates*, trans. H. Tredennick, H. Tarrant. London: Penguin, 1993.

45. P. Hadot, *What is Ancient Philosophy?* Trans. M. Chase. Cambridge, MA: Belknap Press, 2004, p. 67]

46. Plato, *The Last Days of Socrates, op. cit.*, p. 120.

47. Another physician-philosopher, Nietzsche, took the opposite route, treating this "ascension" as a mortal illness, a death-wish, like that of Socrates, an idol in his twilight, who wanted to die in order to distance himself from the tomb of passions and sensations (F. Nietzsche, *Twilight of the Idols*, trans. D. Large, OUP, 2008).

48. For Nietzsche and his disciples, like Deleuze, it was the other way round: ridding oneself of the soul (as a metaphysical substance) to repair the body, find new vitality in the body, restore the body to its full capacity.

49. Plato, *Alcibiades*, N. Denyer (ed.). Cambridge: Cambridge University Press, 2001.

50. See in particular Foucault's analysis of the *Alcibiades* (*L'herméneutique du sujet* (January 6, 1982). Paris: Gallimard, 2001, pp. 33 ff.): the injunction to take oneself as an object of care is linked to the exercise of power (and has nothing to do with narcissistic withdrawal, such as a cult of the self).

51. P. Hadot, *What is Ancient Philosophy?* op.cit., p. 65.

52. *Ibid.*, p. 121.

53. *Ibid*, p. 123.

54. *Ibid.*, p. 124.

55. J. Robion, *Les réparations thérapeutiques*. Paris: L'Harmattan, 2017, p. 29.

56. *Ibid.*, p. 36.

57. The analytical cure refers, of course, to the means rather than the end, and takes different forms depending on each school of psychoanalysis.

58. *Ibid.*, p. 37.

59. *Ibid.*, p. 41.

60. The notion of *trauma*—etymologically from the Greek for "wound"—was developed in the field of psychoanalysis and psychiatry in the twentieth century. One of the first fields of objectivization and application of the concept of trauma, as a violent emotional shock (abuse, rape, war, terrorist attack) causing lasting impairment or even functional incapacity in the patient, was that of North American military psychiatry, which developed the concept of post-traumatic stress disorder or PTSD to recognize psychological victims of war whose symptoms were not identified by the usual medical classifications. See Didier Fassin and Richard Rechtman, *The Empire of Trauma: An Inquiry into the Condition of Victimhood*, trans. R. Gomme. Princeton: Princeton University Press, 2007.

61. E. Werner, R. Smith, *Overcoming the Odds: High-Risk Children from Birth to Adulthood*. New York, Cornell University Press, 1992.

62. J. Bowlby, *Attachment and Loss*. New York: Basic Books, 1973, 1980.

63. Among his many successful works, see B. Cyrulnik, *Resilience: How Your Inner Strength Can Set You Free from the Past*, trans. D. Macey. New York: Tarcher, 2011.

64. Biological, and even genetic, psychiatry have incontestably influenced Cyrulnik's work, as he freely admits. Genetic factors are thought to intervene in the synthesis of an amino acid that carries serotonin (a neurotransmitter that acts directly on mood). But genetics, because it is channeled by the affective and social environment, is never the sole explanatory factor of resilience, which is seen more as a dynamic and interactive process. For Cyrulnik, resilience is not a sum of dispositions and qualities established once and for all (e.g. at birth) but a lifelong transactional process that establishes "arrangements and interactions between what we were as we developed and what the environment placed around us" (B. Cyrulnik, *Les âmes blessées. Paris:* Odile Jacob, 2014, p. 285).

65. B. Golse, "Le concept de réparation dans le champ de la pédopsychiatrie et de la psychopathologie infanto-juvénile," in *De la réparation* (Christophe Schaeffer ed.). Paris: L'Harmattan, 2010, p. 33.

66. B. Cyrulnik, *op. cit.*, p. 15.

67. *Ibid.*, p. 298.

68. P. Chamoiseau interviewed by Michel Peterson, *Potomitan*, http://www.potmitan.info/divers/imaginaire.htm.

69. See, for example, the ethnopsychiatric work of Viviane Romana: http://www.ethnopsychiatrie.net/karayib.htm.

70. Gathering elements of history and experience together into a single story with a plot.

71. The psychologically irreparable can produce even more devastating effects than destructive repair. There is no shortage of illustrations, in life and in art. Claude Chabrol's unforgettable *The Butcher* (1970) is a fine study of the irreparable, about the unlikely encounter between inconsolable lovesickness (the teacher Miss Hélène played by Stéphane Audran) and the haunting memories of war (the butcher Paul played by Jean Yanne). Paul's irrepressible compulsion to kill is never repaired; it is only interrupted by his romantic projection onto Hélène. If Paul is not simply the wild animal depicted in the cave paintings at the start of the movie, despite the blood of his victims on his hands (human and animal blood, he tells us as he dies, smells the same), it is through the suspension of love that he neutralizes, for a time, his murderous impulses. Feelings of love restore him to his humanity (despite his irreparable crimes), for which he yearns for reciprocal confirmation in a final, dying, kiss.

72. S. Tisseron, "La réparation, des chemins inattendus," in *De la réparation, op. cit.*, p. 21.

73. What we call "destructive repair" is not far removed from what Schumpeter, in the economic domain, calls "creative destruction," namely the process of economic sectors disappearing simultaneously with the creation of new economic activities.

74. There was a time when the question of "repairing the mad" did not arise: before what Foucault (*Madness and Civilization: A History of Insanity in the Age of Reason*, trans. R. Howard. New York: Vintage, 1988, p. 38) calls the "Great Confinement" (particularly the Parisian edict of 1656) and the great split between reason and madness, when the mad would wonder freely around villages, unless they were shut away in attics and cellars. The wholesale confinement of the mad, from the seventeenth century onward, motivated both by their lack of usefulness and the protection of society, did not initially lead to therapeutic care. Internment did not yet equate to treatment for those judged to be incurably ill.

75. Forman's movie came out, paradoxically, at a time when Western psychiatry, post-60s, was becoming relatively more humane, with fewer cases of administrative confinement, and greater use of psychotropic drugs to "free" patients previously condemned to a life of internment. Raymond Depardon, in his superb documentary *San Clemente* (1981), shot with a shoulder-mount camera and a handheld tape-recorder in a psychiatric hospital near Venice, subtly depicts the striking contrast between an institution that in many ways echoes the asylums of old and a transformation in the attitude of the personnel towards the patients (listening, mediation, group meetings with families who complain about a lack of organization). As he wanders the corridors of

San Clemente, destined shortly for closure, Depardon (whose camera arouses mixed reactions, from friendly curiosity to undisguised exasperation) sheds a candid light on the life of the patients, some of whom shuffle around looking haggard and at a loss, while others seem to relish their apparent liberty.

76. E. Goffman, *Asylums*. New York: Anchor, 1961.

77. B. Cyrulnik recounts an interview with a Russian psychiatrist colleague shortly after the collapse of the Berlin Wall who justified the internment of dissidents by saying: "They want what is best for us and govern in the name of the people, so you have to be mad to oppose them" (B. Cyrulnik, *Les âmes blessées, op. cit.*, p. 154).

78. G. Deleuze & F. Guattari, *A Thousand Plateaus*, trans. B. Massumi. Minneapolis: University of Minnesota Press, 1987.

79. L. Boltanski & E. Chiapello, *The New Spirit of Capitalism*, trans. G. Elliott. London: Verso, 2007.

80. A. Ehrenberg, *Le culte de la performance*. Paris: Fayard, 2011.

81. Y. Chappoz & P.Ch. Pupion, "Le New Public Management," *Gestion et management public*, vol. 1/2, no. 2, 2012, pp. 1–3.

82. A. Ehrenberg, *The Weariness of the Self: Diagnosing the History of Depression in the Contemporary Age*, trans. D. Homel *et al.*, Montreal: McGill-Queen's University Press, 2010.

83. Silicon Valley, the richest and highest-achieving region in the world, also has one of the world's highest rates of suicide and depression—and LSD usage—among executives and engineers. For the new management ideologues of Silicon Valley, depression is no longer seen simply as a sign of weakness, but as a necessary stage in the employee's questioning of their own habits and structures of thought with a view to better future performance. Get depressed, in order to come back stronger and smarter.

84. C. Taylor, *The Sources of the Self*, Cambridge, MA: Harvard University Press, 1992, p. 508.

85. A. Gefen, *Réparer le monde*. Paris: Editions Corti, 2017, p. 11.

86. G. Deleuze et F. Guattari, *Kafka: Toward a Minor Literature*, Minneapolis: University of Minnesota Press, 1986.

87. Ph. Forest, *L'enfant éternel*. Paris: Gallimard, 2013.

88. C. Laurens, *Philippe*. Paris: Gallimard, 2008.

89. L. Adler, *A ce soir*. Paris: Gallimard, 2001.

90. P. Jourde, *Winter is coming*. Paris: Gallimard, 2017.

91. A. Gefen, *Réparer le monde, op. cit.,* pp. 134–35.

92. Ch. Angot, *L'inceste*. Paris: Poche, 2001.

93. A. Ernaux, *Shame*, trans. T. Leslie, Seven Stories Press, 1998.

94. H. Duffau, *Trauma*. Paris: Gallimard, 2003.

95. E. Louis, *The End of Eddy*, trans. M. Lucey, London: Harvill Secker, 2017.

96. Y. Charmet, *Dans son regard aux lèvres rouges*. Paris: Editions le Bateau Ivre, 2017.

97. Bernard Pingaud, *Ecrire jour et nuit*. Paris: Gallimard, 2000, p. 157.

98. Gefen's observation does not cover the entire output of the contemporary "literary field," in particular the persistence of a form of literature that still sees itself as avant-garde, eschewing any therapeutic aim. This trend can be found, for example, in writers like Christian Prigent and Pierre Guyotat.

99. A. Gefen, *Réparer le monde, op. cit.*, p. 98.

100. Once again Gefen's seemingly unilateral diagnosis does not take account of all reading practices (that would call for an altogether more comprehensive sociological survey); people may read for many reasons that are not therapeutic (entertainment, education, etc.).

101. Gefen cites, for example, the Greek historian Diodorus of Sicily, who reported that the entrance to the library of Ramses II once bore the inscription "Healing-Place of the Soul."

102. *Ibid.*, p. 106.

Chapter Three

Fault and Offense

An anthropology of repair crosses a new threshold when it comes to focus on the experience of loss in its religious, moral, and social dimension. It is a new aspect of our finitude that we are about to explore: not the vulnerability of the living entity affected by a wound, an amputation or an imbalance, nor the emotional fragility of the mind mourning the disappearance of a loved one, but the fallibility of a being susceptible to doing evil and committing offenses.

What losses does religious, moral, and social repair seek to address? They take a host of forms: loss of purity, loss of innocence, loss of self-esteem . . . and with a host of implications. They relate, of course, to modes of repair, of which we will draw up a detailed typology in order to understand the analogies with the *reparatio* in the world of living matter and in the life of the mind. Purification, repentance, and apology are to the religious, moral, and social *reparatio* what scarring is to organic repair and the work of mourning to psychological repair. It is once again through analogy, as a disposition to see similarity-in-difference, that we need to approach the models of repair, but now armed with new forms of specialist knowledge: religious anthropology, moral philosophy and the sociology of interpersonal interaction.

The profound aspiration of any religious, moral, and social repair is to mitigate or even erase an impurity, a fault, an offense, and return to the *status quo ante*, in the hope of recovering purity, innocence and redemption by means of specific *reparatio* (purification rituals, confession, indulgences, prayers, apologies, offerings, etc.). But this profound aspiration is held in check by nagging guilt, by the impossibility of redemption, and by the resentment harbored in other people's hearts. These avatars of the irreparable stand in the way of the already difficult return to a state of innocence. More fundamentally, the ethical model of repair—as a normalizing format for human conduct and the persistence of troubled consciences—must be subjected to critical examination.

Beyond the religious matrix, the social world can be perceived as a vast set of reparative exchanges aimed at immanently regulating interactions when they are subject to disruption (insults, offenses, violence, etc.) before involving the state and the objective constraint of the law. There are no social facts without social control, which presides over the repair of face-to-face interactions in potentially conflictual situations.

POLLUTION AND PURIFICATION

Repair can only be conceived of for *finite* beings: beings that are vulnerable, fragile and fallible. In the moral and religious register, the anthropological category of fallibility borrowed here from Paul Ricœur[1] sheds light on how Man's constitutive weakness makes evil and wrongdoing possible. Philosophical tradition has left us a legacy of valuable reflections on the pathos of human fallibility. The Platonic dialogues of the previous chapter portray human misery as imprisoned in corporeality after the soul is "mixed in." Prone to error and easily misled, fallible Man is more fallible than ever at the moment when the soul falls into the body. The mythological language of fall, of lapse, of mixing would later feature largely in Christian theology and philosophy, and in the writings of Pascal: "And what completes our inability to understand things is that they are not so simple in themselves, and we are made up of two different kinds of opposing natures, body and soul."[2] Pascal, however, adds the notion of *disproportion* to better express human finitude, understood here as our limited ability to know anything (in our relative powerlessness), hemmed in as we are between two infinites (the infinitely great and the infinitely small): "For in the end, what is humanity in nature? A nothingness compared to the infinite, everything compared to a nothingness, a midpoint between nothing and everything, infinitely far from understanding the extremes; the end of things and their beginning are insuperably hidden for him in an impenetrable secret."[3] This disproportion,[4] which recurs in a different form in Descartes' *Fourth Meditation* (between finite understanding and infinite will) and up until the phenomenology of Ricœur (between the finite perspective of perception and the infinite scope of language), is not limited to the ability to know. It is manifest with still greater pathos in its practical (i.e., moral) dimension when humanity conspires to hide, or hide from, the meaning of its condition by losing itself in distractions and waywardness. For Pascal, the worst thing was not to do evil, but to refuse to recognize it and admit the natural unhappiness of our feeble, mortal condition. Only by steadfast conversion to the faith can we, if not change our condition, then at least give it new meaning.

Pascal's legacy, rich as it is, is of course only one of many historical testimonies to the way mankind has expressed—and still does express—its own fallible condition in myth, religion and philosophy. But we must start from here, from an anthropological reflection on fallibility, to understand how the discourse on evil and wrongdoing came into being, and how exactly the different religious worlds have sought to repair them. Many are the ways in which religious cultures portray humanity's being-at-fault.

Ritual pollution, or defilement, is an example that is near-universal, or at least widely found in most magical-religious systems. We have already seen some telling instances in our examination of witchcraft practices and magical bodily repair. Defilement presents as a mode of expression of evil and wrongdoing, as the transgression of a taboo, transmitted by physical contact and contagion. Defilement is the physical outcome of the violation of a symbolic and prescriptive order. The stain left by defilement, experienced subjectively as pain, shame and fear, is in itself a corporal punishment intended as a form of vindictive atonement. Defilement is a physical mark that betrays a moral blemish. The stain can spread to all or part of the body, but sex and sexuality are its primary modes of propagation:

> Thus one is struck by the importance and the gravity attached to the violation of interdictions of a sexual character in the economy of defilement. The prohibitions against incest, sodomy, abortion, relations at forbidden times—and sometimes places—are so fundamental that the inflation of the sexual is characteristic of the whole system of defilement; so that an indissoluble complicity between sexuality and defilement seems to have been formed from time immemorial.[5]

Defilement is, historically, one of the oldest magical-religious manifestations of the human condition of being-at-fault. We find its trace in Ancient Israel, for example, in the prophet Isaiah's vision in the Temple: "And the foundations of the thresholds shook at the voice of him who called, and the house was filled with smoke. And I said: 'Woe is me! For I am lost; for I am a man of unclean lips, and I dwell in the midst of a people of unclean lips; for my eyes have seen the King, the Lord of hosts!'" (Isaiah 6:4–5).[6] Cultural anthropology and the sociology of religion analyze defilement not as an isolated phenomenon but within the framework of a symbolic system. If we follow Mary Douglas,[7] the apprehension of defilement, of pollution, of dirt, should be seen as signaling the infringement of a given order: "This is a very suggestive approach. It implies two conditions: a set of ordered relations and a contravention of that order."[8]

This sullied condition can be remedied by means of acts of magical-religious repair. Repair in this case implies, as Douglas says, restoring order to the symbolic system: where defilement disorders, repair reorders. This might take the form of the *wedding ritual* designed to neutralize the impurity of sexuality by framing it within strict rules of alliance and reproduction, with the virginity of the future spouses being held up as the guarantee of the purity of the marriage sacrament itself. Or it might be through the intervention of an external power, divine or quasi-divine, that comes to wipe clean the initial defilement, as in Isaiah's vision when one of the seraphim (an angel with three pairs of wings) flies up to him holding a burning coal and saying: "Behold, this has touched your lips; your guilt is taken away, and your sin atoned for" (Isaiah 6:7). Once again it is through contact—in this case the pure contact of a pure being—that the impurity of defilement is cleansed. The profound aspiration is to regain a lost purity, as the psalmist pleads: "Have mercy upon me, O God, according to thy loving kindness: according unto the multitude of thy tender mercies blot out my transgressions. Wash me thoroughly from mine iniquity, and cleanse me from my sin. . . . Create in me a clean heart, O God" (Ps. 51). Repairing defilement often requires a specific ritual to be performed by the polluted person. The *purification ritual* can take multiple forms: washing, distancing, burning, expelling and spitting.

Purification rituals, such as ablutions, may have a reparative function (when the defilement is already present) or a prophylactic function, to prevent the risk of impurity. The same ritual can fulfill both functions at once, as is the case with ritual baths and ablutions in Islam: the small ablutions (wudu, وُضُوء) and the great ablutions (ghusl, غُسْل), which make use of water, and the dry ablutions (tayammum, تَيَمُّم), which use earth, stone and sand. These purification rituals confirm the importance of sexuality (small ablutions are required after pleasurable genital contact) and of contact with blood (grand ablutions are required after women's periods) as prime vectors of impurity. To have the desired effect, purification by ablution must follow a ritual, a chain of sacred acts: washing both hands up to the wrist three times after saying "bismillah"; taking water into the mouth and nose and spitting it out again (three times); and washing the face, hands and feet (three times). The precision of the gesture, the repetition and sequencing of the acts and the accuracy of the incantations are believed to guarantee the efficacy of the purifying *reparatio*; efficacy meaning the possibility of restoring the purity sullied by the initial defilement. There, where the defilement entered the body by contact or contamination, it must be washed away by the act of purification. The purifying repair seeks to restore the initial state of purity or—if the defilement goes back to our origins—to construct an ideal state of purity.

SIN AND REDEMPTION

It is not easy to distinguish defilement from sin as a manifestation of evil and wrongdoing. Historically, the two terms have been in constant circulation in the mythical-religious universe. Sin, in other words, can be expressed as defilement. The seraph who wipes away Isaiah's defilement at the same time pardons his sins. Psalm 51 reflects the same intention: "Wash me thoroughly from my iniquity and cleanse me from my sin! . . . Purify me with hyssop, and I shall be clean; wash me, and I shall be whiter than snow." While the symbolism of wrongdoing is expressed above all in defilement by physical contact or contamination, the symbolism of sin has, one might say, a broader spectrum. If we follow Ricœur on this point, one of the symbolic translations of sin, as it is expressed in Ancient Israel, is the violation of the original covenant of a people with its god. Sin always takes place "before God": "for relations of contact in space, relations of orientation are substituted; the way, the straight line, straying, like the metaphor of a journey, are analogies of the movement of existence considered as a whole. At the same time, the symbol passes over from space to time."[9] The sinner is the one who moves away from God, from his precepts, who turns away from his love, and suffers his wrath in return. It is in the form of accusations that the Prophets harangue those who have broken the Covenant, who have forgotten God, who have followed a tortuous path: injustice, in the case of Amos; adultery in that of Hosea; and with Isaiah, arrogance. Sin can reveal either an original curse—which would evolve into original sin in the Genesis myth (evil entered the world, for all mankind, by the original act of wrongdoing)—or the transgression of prescribed rules (adultery, idolatry, lust, etc.). The two orders of things are not mutually exclusive, but they involve different modalities and different scopes of reparation. It is one thing to be able to repair a broken commandment, quite another to be able to repair the original misdeed that sows the seeds of evil in the heart of every man and woman.

Acts or rituals of purification can of course, as with defilement, serve as *reparatio* for sins. But the range of reparation for sins is wider. If sin is understood as waywardness, as the "crooked path," as the broken Covenant, then its religious repair must be understood as a "return" to the Sacred Order and Relationship, as a restoration of the primitive bond: "In repentance and rest you will be saved" (Isaiah 30:15). What, then, are the *reparatio* that aspire to this return to the original Covenant? There is *redemption*, that act of divine origin, which consists in freeing someone from servitude, or from a debt, or from a moral fault. Redemption can apply to any act of any individual who has transgressed against a prohibition, an order, or a commandment. It can apply to an entire people: the paradigm case is found in the Exodus. Egypt being, in the Hebrew Bible, a symbol of captivity and more generally the sign of all that is wrong with the human condition, the escape from servitude is, by contrast, associated with redemption: "I am the Lord, and I will bring you out from under the yoke of the Egyptians. I will free you from being slaves to them, and I will redeem you with an outstretched arm and with mighty acts of judgment" (Exodus 6:6).

Redemption can even apply to the whole of humanity, breaking the original curse of sin by an extraordinary act that Christianity has elevated to the status of a liberating sacrifice in the death of Jesus Christ. Jesus is the foundational repairer of Christian monotheism. Christ being, according to Christian theology, God made Man, he redeems, by his sacrifice, the sins of humanity, and saves it from the slavery of evil. Sacrifice gives humanity back its freedom: the freedom once again, even after this founding act, to do evil and commit new sins unless mankind embraces unconditional faith in Jesus the Savior (Romans, 3:24–30).

Rituals of atonement and forgiveness, or pardon, are religious *reparatio* that also seek to liberate, to write off a debt, to wash away sins. They are found in the three great monotheistic religions, and also in Jainism in India (in a ritual called *pratikramana*, performed to ask for forgiveness of faults). In Ancient Israel, atonement was thought of as a restoration of the original Covenant, as holding off God's anger for the faults committed by his people ("Accept this atonement for your people Israel, whom you have redeemed, Lord," Deut. (21:8)). Atonement, at the same time as it frees mankind from debt, opens up a new future:

> Pardon is already fully evident in this restored capacity of knowing oneself in one's true situation in the bosom of the Covenant. Thus the penalty, felt as an affliction, is a part of punishment and of pardon at the same time. By the same token, "pardon" *is* "return"; for return, *a parte Dei*, is nothing else than the taking away of blame, the suppression of the charge of sin: "I have acknowledged my sin to thee, I have not concealed my iniquity. I said, I will confess my transgressions to the Eternal! And thou hast wiped out the penalty of my sin." (Psalm 32:5)[10]

Thus atonement puts an end to waywardness and error. Later Christian theology would propose other formulations and expressions of atonement, such as in Pierre Abelard, Paul Tillich, or René Girard: the death of Jesus on the Cross is a symbol of unconditional love which serves as the example for any Christian liable to be transformed by this founding gesture (in response, for example, to a "mimetic desire").

The act of atonement can emanate from the sinner him or herself through acts of contrition and *practices of self-flagellation*. Flagellation, or scourging—a torture inflicted on Jesus by the Romans—became a practice of expiation and penance in the Middle Ages, most strikingly through the movement of the Flagellants who went from town to town armed with whips and singing the Song of Songs, symbolically reliving the Passion in order to redeem their sins in the hope of reaching the Kingdom of Heaven. Like the rites of purification, the practices of scourging and self-flagellation are *reparatio* that are applied directly to the body (unlike prayers and hymns): the body must suffer, as the body of Jesus suffered, to extirpate and redeem sin. But evil must come out from the place where it entered. Self-flagellation is still practiced in some Catholic orders and is also practiced in some Shiite orders during the procession (Tatbir) that marks the end of Ashura (the day that commemorates the massacre of Imam Hussein and his family by the Umayyad Caliphate). Tatbir, however, does not have the same reparative function as Christian penitential self-flagellation. It is less about atoning for sins than about reliving the work of mourning the death of Muhammad's young grandson, Imam Hussein ibn Ali, who was killed at the battle of Karbala. In either case, the body must be scourged and sacrificed to stigmatize a loss (the death of Hussein ibn Ali, the death of Christ, the loss of innocence).

Sacrifice plays such a cardinal reparative function that it runs through most magical-religious worlds. Ritual sacrifice is a paradoxical form of *reparatio* in that it aims to amputate or take away something, or someone, in response to an initial loss. Sacrifice aims to give something *more* (and, correlatively, to lose something *less*) to make good the loss caused by a supposed, alleged or imagined fault (or simply to test one's faith or to signal submission to a superior). Sacrifice is thought of as a trial by ordeal, as restoring a balance (giving something extra to compensate for a loss; losing something to restore the founding relationship), or as re-establishing a symbolic order (in the sense of Douglas). Sacrificial practices vary according to the categories of offense. Among the Dinka (a farming people of South Sudan) the sacrificial beast is cut: "longitudinally through the sexual organs if the sacrifice is intended to undo an incest; in half across the middle for celebrating a truce; they suffocate it for some occasions and trample it to death for others."[11]

The least one can say is that sacrificial *reparatio* come in many forms. It might be the sacrifice of an animal, as among the Dinka; it might be the sacrifice of oneself, of one's body, even of one's life (as in the sacrifice of Jesus); it might be the sacrifice of one's possessions or of one's own flesh and blood (as in the sacrifice of a child) thus becoming a *reparatio* of *offering*, even if not every offering necessarily has a reparative function; it might be a sign of attachment, devotion and love ("Therefore, I urge you, brothers and sisters, in view of God's mercy, to offer your bodies as a living sacrifice, holy and pleasing to God—this is your true and proper worship" (Romans 12:1)). Sacrifice can therefore take place without any initial fault, unless we assume an original fault that makes everyone a sinner. Eternally indebted "before God," Man must never cease from sacrifice, making offerings in order to redeem a loss for which he is not responsible as an individual, but as a member of a sinful humanity.

If we follow René Girard,[12] sacrifice is thought of, once a scapegoat has been designated, as a regulating process that assuages, at least for a time, the rivalry of mimetic desire. The "meaning" of the sacrifice can vary greatly from one mythical and religious system to another. In most Greek myths and non-Judeo-Christian religions, the sacrificial victim, Girard tells us, is assumed to be guilty in the manner of Sophocles's Oedipus. In other words, there is always a good reason to sacrifice a victim who is guilty from the outset, and this "good reason" is, in one way or another, a response to the risk of violence engendered by mimetic desire. It is in the Hebrew Bible that we find, by contrast, the first manifestations of the innocent sacrificial victim and a critique of the mechanism of sacrifice (already in the transformation of human sacrifice into animal sacrifice in the story of Abraham and Isaac), even if sacrifice is omnipresent. This is well illustrated in the Judgment of Solomon (1 Kings 3:16–28) when, presented with two prostitutes fighting over the custody of a child, the King says: "Cut the living child in two and give half to one and half to the other." While one of the two prostitutes accepts Solomon's judgment, the other refuses and prefers to give up her child in order to save him: "Please, my lord, give her the living baby! Don't kill him" (1 Kings 3:26). In this parable, we are dealing with two irreducible categories of sacrifice: the selfish sacrifice of the "bad" prostitute who agrees to sacrifice the child, and the self-sacrifice of the "good" prostitute who agrees to give up the child so that he remains in one piece. For Girard, the first sacrifice metaphorizes the structural violence of human societies and must, as such, be denounced. The second, very different, sacrifice foreshadows the Christian profession of faith. For it is in Christianity, according to Girard, that the meaning of sacrifice takes on a radically new dimension, bringing to awareness the innocence of the sacrificial victim, through the death of Jesus himself: "Jesus saves all human beings because of his revelation of the scapegoat mechanism, which also deprives us more and more of sacrificial protection, therefore forcing us to abstain from violence if we want to survive. In order to reach the Kingdom, man has to renounce violence."[13]

The anthropological meaning of the Gospels is to lay bare the violence inherent in mimetic desire, in the logic of the scapegoat (Christ is despised by the crowd, by Pilate, by the Jews) and in the ultimate sacrifice of an innocent: "The god of Christianity isn't the violent god of archaic religion, but the non-violent god who willingly becomes a victim in order to free us from our violence."[14] The fact remains, however, that contrary to Girard's hypothesis, Christianity does not have the sole monopoly on this meaning of sacrifice. We find expressions of it in Orphism, a Greek mystical and religious current that condemned blood sacrifice,[15] as well as in Jainism in India, which rejects the sacrificial order.

The key point, for our purpose, is that the sacrificial rite and the rite of anti-sacrificial atonement represent two antithetical ideal-types of magical-religious *reparatio*, one based on the logic of violence, scapegoating, and perpetual mimetic rivalry, the other on a logic of superabundance and unconditional love, for example following the model of *imitatio christi*. There is still sacrifice—supreme, foundational sacrifice—but it is paradoxically exhibited in order to denounce its own internal logic (violence, scapegoating, rivalry, innocent victim) and propose a path of human regulation that would break away from such logic and at the same time restore the covenant between man and God: this is "the idea of personal salvation, available through the spirit of Christ and his Father as a result of the Cross, which has re-established the direct relationship between man and God, which has been interrupted by the original sin."[16]

Magical-religious *reparatio* (rites of purification, rites of atonement, acts of redemption, sacrifices, offerings, etc.) are not mutually exclusive within the same religious system. As with sin and defilement, as modes of being-at-fault, they can exist side by side without contradiction. What is remarkable about them is the repairer/repaired dyad: *Who is being repaired? Who is doing the repairing?* In most cases, it is incumbent upon the one rightly or wrongly declared to be the wrongdoer to make reparation to a symbolic order violated by his act and, in the monotheistic religions, always "before God." Transgressing a prohibition or a commandment always amounts to harming God. Under this logic, the repairer is the sinner and the repaired is God himself and, through him, everything that he upholds. This is how we are to understand ritual sacrifices (whether of animals or humans) and offerings: reparation must be initiated by the one who committed the fault (the repairer), while the repaired is the one who is its alleged victim.

The configuration is radically different when the repairer is not the actual wrongdoer, but the one who was the victim of the fault committed. This is the precise intention of the sacrifice of God in the Christian *kerygma*. The Christian God smashes the mold of the justice of equivalence and vindictive ritual (if Man has sinned from his origin, he must redeem his fault for all eternity), offering instead a logic of superabundance (the gift of a single being breaks the cycle of debt and sin). But it is not men who sacrifice themselves because they have sinned: it is God, by sacrificing his son ("My God, my God, why have you forsaken me?"), who redeems the sins of humanity. The repairer, in this rite of expiation, is God, and not sinful humanity.

The aim of all magical-religious repair is to erase, remove or mitigate the original evil or wrong: to restore the state of purity before defilement, to reinstate the Covenant before it was broken, to return to the path of faith before going astray, to regain innocence after sin. There is no guarantee, however, of the effectiveness of repair founded on belief: the sense of defilement may persist after a ritual of purification; guilt may resurface after a ritual of atonement or a sacrifice. More than any other act of faith, magical-religious repair is always confronted with the believer's uncertainty: *Am I pure again? Am I still guilty? Are my sins redeemed?* Even the removal of a bodily affliction can be ascribed to some cause other than the reparative act itself. When the repairer is the alleged wrongdoer, atonement can come up against the silence of "before God" and give way to doubt: *Am I forgiven for my sins?* These doubts and uncertainties are already the first intimation of the irreparable.

As with any reparative practice, we must remember that even if the defilement is washed away and the guilt of the believer is assuaged, some traces of the actual history of being-at-fault will always remain. Debts can be paid or written off, but not time, nor the memory of the event. Yahweh, through an act of expiation, frees the Hebrews from the yoke of the Egyptians (a servitude that symbolized the breaking of the Covenant) but God's chosen people will never return to the situation prior to that ordeal. They become *something else* after this rupture. In this sense, the time of servitude is irreparable, even if the debt is lifted. For good reason, Deuteronomy enjoins Israel to honor this founding act of remembrance: "Be careful that you do not forget the Lord, who brought you out of Egypt, out of the land of slavery" (Deut. 6:12). Injunctive memory is there to bring to mind the time of the irreparable.

The most insidious aspect of irreparability lies in the believer's sense of never being released, of never being able to redeem the fault, of being forever defiled, despite all their reparative acts. It is no longer only time that is irreparable, but the debt that places the sinner in the position of eternal repairer. This is true even for Christian theology: despite the expiatory sacrifice of Jesus, every Christian is "free" to choose between good and evil, and doubt hangs over them until the Last Judgment. It is in this sense that original sin, as an evil that emerges in humanity as a whole, is distinguished from guilt, as an act that each individual "begins" anew. Ricœur underlines the contrast:

> the confession of sins completes this movement of the internalization of sin in personal guilt: the "thou" that is summoned becomes the "I" that accuses itself. But at the same time there appears the shift of emphasis that makes the sense of sin turn toward the feeling of guilt; in place of emphasizing the "before God," the "against thee, against thee alone," the feeling of guilt emphasizes the "it is I who . . ."[17]

As the psalmist confesses: "For I know my sin, and my fault is always before me. Against thee, thee only, have I sinned; I have done that which is evil in thy sight" (Ps, 51:3–4). Guilt becomes truly alienating when the believer constructs himself as endlessly indebted, when reparation becomes interminable, when the irreparability of the fault never ceases to haunt his moral conscience. All acts of purification are in vain: the believer will still feel defiled, and for all time. All acts of repentance, contrition and atonement are in vain: the believer will still feel himself to be a sinner. The irreparability of guilt culminates in the scrupulous conscience whose religious movement Ricœur traces back to the Pharisees: the scrupulous conscience is a conscience which never feels at ease, which always adds new obligations, takes on new burdens, multiplying rites and constant casuistry.

Unremitting scrupulousness leads to the hell of guilt and points to a pathological function of magical-religious repair evident in its very excess: the bad infinite. Saint Paul was one of the first (Nietzsche and Kafka would eventually follow) to testify to the "curse of the law," whose strict observance becomes stronger than the commandment of love:

> For just as through the disobedience of the one man the many were made sinners, so also through the obedience of the one man the many will be made righteous. The law was brought in so that the trespass might increase. But where sin increased, grace increased all the more, so that, just as sin reigned in death, so also grace might reign through righteousness to bring eternal life through Jesus Christ our Lord. (Romans 5:19–21)

It is the very existence of the law that exhibits sin:

> Scrupulousness, reinterpreted by the Pauline experience of the curse of the law, appears in a new light: it too becomes the expression of an "evil infinite" that answers, from the side of conscience, to the "evil infinite" of the indefinite enumeration of commandments. At the limit, distrust, suspicion, and finally contempt for oneself and abjectness are substituted for the humble confession of the sinner.[18]

Awareness of the irreparable constantly relaunches the process of repair in a vicious circle that locks the scrupulous into what Hegel classified as the "bad infinite" (*das Schlecht-Unendliche*) and Freud as obsessional neurosis: the being-at-fault sets itself the task of obeying every religious command in order to make reparation for its faults; its failure in this task increases its sense of guilt, once again triggering the process of observance and so on and so forth (until the very endeavor of seeking to root out sin is cast into suspicion and becomes a new fault in its own right).

CONFESSING ONE'S FAULTS

It could be said that the pathological function of magical-religious repair reaches its pinnacle in the practice of confession. Is not confession the symptom of a conscience mired in remorse and guilt, chained to the past of its own actions? That is certainly one of its shortcomings, which Nietzsche in his time already diagnosed as a reactive conscience caught in the grip of resentment. But confession can also have its reparative virtues. We need only look at the wide variety of fields in which confession is encountered (religion, law, morality, politics, psychology) and the many ways it is expressed (self-confession, extracting a confession, "fessing up," etc.). Jérôme Porée has tried to extract a sort of common phenomenological core, defining confession as the: "Act of a conscience that declares itself guilty and thus proves itself capable of repenting."[19] However, this definition is not entirely "neutral" since it privileges the active (positive) form of confession:[20] the conscience "declares itself" guilty so as not to be "declared" guilty by a higher authority, for example, as it would be in the passive (negative and constrained) form of the extorted confession: *confess your fault*. Still less neutrally, this definition adds an element missing from the usual properties attributed to confession: repentance. With this added condition, confession looks not only to the past (by looking back at the fault committed), but also to the present and to the future (through repentance).

But what has confession got to do with magical-religious repair? Not all confession is religious. While not limited to religion, confession is certainly one of its historical paradigms, through the model of the confession of sins, one of the pillars of Catholicism. And yet confession, unlike rituals of purification or expiation, is not directly reparative. Confession is first of all an act of acknowledgement, in the sense of identifying facts or events in the present of discourse ("something has happened"), with a moral evaluation ("this something is wrong") and, above all, with self-attribution and self-accusation ("I am responsible for this wrong; I am guilty"). Such an acknowledgement supposes, as Porée rightly points out, a permanence of subject between the one who committed the wrongful act in the past and the one who acknowledges its wrongdoing today. Regardless of the changes that have affected the identity of the confessant, the acknowledgement of the act outlives the temporal variations of the subject.

However, confession, even of a fault, is not an act of acknowledgement like any other. Acknowledging that one has committed a reprehensible act is not necessarily a confession. For there to be confession, as Foucault tells us, there must be "a certain cost of enunciation" for the one making the confession.[21] Confession is always presented as a test for the person who makes it, and demands personal commitment—in short, *exposure*—from the subject. The statement of the confessing subject contains an assertion about a past reality and a self-identifying reference, but there is also an additional ordeal: having to say something about oneself, something that one finds hard to admit and would prefer to conceal. It is only a confession because there is a hidden meaning, a meaning that one wants to hide. To acknowledge something without difficulty, even without suffering and without shame, is not to avow or confess, especially for those who are accustomed to hearing a variety of hypocritical and insincere half-confessions. This test of truth is not only valid in the case of a confession extorted by a third party; it is also valid when the confession is made at the subject's own voluntary and spontaneous initiative.

If confession is about admitting a past fault, under testing conditions, what about reparation? Confession is not reparation, but it can tend in that direction, at least if we add the act of repentance. Of course, a fault admitted is not necessarily a fault forgiven. And one can express deep regret without seeking to make reparation for the fault committed (just as one can regret having done something without apologizing for it). However, repentance can *point the way* towards reparation. *The Confessions* of St. Augustine remain an admirable testimony to a repentance that calls for repair, even if it comes in the form of a request where the repairer is not the sinner, but God himself: "The house of my soul is too narrow for thee to come in to me; let it be enlarged by thee. It is in ruins; do thou restore it. There is much about it which must offend thy eyes; I confess and know it. But who will cleanse it?"[22] The request for reparation shifts here from the literal (repairing the ruins of the house) to the figurative (repairing the soul of a lost sinner) and is juxtaposed with prior confession (avowing the dilapidated state of the soul under the gaze of God). Whether the act of repair is initiated by the sinner or by someone else, including the victim of the fault, it can, after repentance, partake in releasing the sinner from his fault. Confession does not therefore automatically have a negative, alienating, and pathological meaning. It can ease the conscience, without necessarily leading to a "good conscience." By signaling a request for forgiveness, confession can denote what Nabert calls "a desire for regeneration."[23] And though Spinoza assimilates repentance to a "sad passion" (much as Nietzsche would later compare it to a "reactive affect"), it is fair to say that authentic confession, without being able to return to the state of innocence, does revitalize the *conatus* (Nabert's "original affirmation"), but at the price of an effort of work (Porée's "work of repentance"). It is at this price that confession, pointing toward repair, is a "release" from the weight of debt, albeit in suffering. Ricœur remains very much within this legacy:

The confession expresses, pushes to the outside, the emotion which without it would be shut up in itself, as an impression in the soul. Language is the light of the emotions. Through confession the consciousness of fault is brought into the light of speech; through confession man remains speech, even in the experience of his own absurdity, suffering, and anguish.[24]

The symbolic representation of the confession of wrongs is already, for Ricœur, a way out of blindness: coming forward to speak of wrongdoing liberates the confessing subject. The verbalization of the confessed fault is emancipating.

In order for there to be a confession, the subject must clearly remain, as we stressed above, in some way the same between the moment when the fault was committed and the moment when it is admitted and regretted. Repentance, however, accompanied by a demand for reparation, at the same time commits the penitent to transform. In the process of reparation, the confessant operates a self-transformation ("I have sinned but I shall sin no more"), perhaps even a conversion in the radical Augustinian mode ("I was a sinner, from now on I will follow the way of Christ"). Here we find the meeting point between repair and self-care that we touched on in the previous chapter: moral repair implies a process of self-transformation. Porée speaks of *creative reparation* to describe the emancipatory process of confession accompanied by forgiveness or rehabilitation:

> Rehabilitation prolongs the work of repentance for all to see. It "verifies" in its own way the implied utterance contained in the utterance of the confession. It could be described as a form of *creative reparation*. There is creative reparation just as there is creative fidelity. Both presuppose a man capable at the same time of remembering the past and of projecting toward the future, striving less to become what he once was than to become what he is not yet.[25]

This notion of creative reparation is central to understanding the fact that the reparative act never leaves the repairer unchanged. The repairer will never be the same as before committing the misdeed. Reparation directly engages a process of self-transformation.

Christian iconography has bequeathed us masterful works that testify to the "double-sided" nature of confession, looking on the one hand toward evil and the guilty conscience, and on the other toward repentance and redemption. El Greco, for instance, dedicated a series of paintings to the Penitent Magdalene. In his "Penitent Magdalene" (ca. 1580–1590), which now hangs in the Cau Ferrat Museum in Sitges, this "double-sided" aspect is expressed on the canvas by an opposite movement of the body (accompanied by Magdalene's gaze). The vermillion-robed figure, in a first movement, stretches her left arm and hand downwards, fingers pointing to a human skull. This first movement refers to vanity,[26] to death, to the vain and fleeting nature of human life, to the temptation of evil, to wrongdoing, and to representations of Magdalene as a sinner, a prostitute, possessed by "seven demons." This first movement is motivated by a guilty conscience but is counterbalanced by a movement of the right arm, carrying her hand directly to her breast, toward the heart; the hand hides the partial nudity of her body while at the same time revealing the intensity of her spiritual love, reinforced by a gaze of devotion that is focused on Jesus, on a crucifix leaning against a rock. This second movement refers both to penitence (regret for the faults borne by the lower hand) and to the path of redemption, conversion and devotion. This is the other face of Magdalene, no longer the sinner, but the woman who will be held up as a saint (hence the title *Santa María Magdalena* that El Greco gives to his painting), Jesus' most devoted female disciple, who was there at his crucifixion and who, above all, witnessed his resurrection. El Greco's genius lies in the way he composed, with his own distinctive talent, a single scene that combines fault and redemption, temptation and conversion, confession and repentance, guilt and faith in a contradictory movement of the hands and body, in which one movement (Good) is intended to surmount the second (Evil), just as the crucifix surmounts the skull of vanity.

Magical-religious repair, creative as it is when iconized by El Greco, can leave the marks of its more somber side when it turns to destruction. This form of repair is self-destructive, as we saw, when the guilty conscience succumbs to the Pauline curse of the law, and to resentment of a past constantly dwelt upon but never overcome. Destructive repair culminates in confession made under constraint; even if it is internalized, it is still vertically dependent on an institution, a confessor, or a director of conscience.

As much as Ricœur and his disciples put us on the path of creative reparation with confessional repentance, it was Foucault, following Nietzsche, who unmasked the darker side of religious reparation, after denouncing "the millennial yoke of confession."[27] The interest of his later writings and lectures[28] lies in the distinction he makes between two modes of outward display of the truth of the self in the formative early centuries of Christian monastic institutions. These modes of display can be likened to magical-religious *reparatio*. The first *reparatio*, known to the Greek Fathers as *exomologesis*, designates the admission of sins expressed through a penitential ceremony that was not so much spoken as acted out on the body of the sinner (wearing the cilice, dressing in rags, smearing the body with ashes, etc.):

> Tertullian has a word to translate the Greek word *exomologesis*: he said it was *publicatio sui*, the Christian had to publish himself. Publish oneself, that means he has two things to do. One has to show oneself as a sinner; that means, as somebody who, choosing the path of the sin, preferred filthiness to purity, earth and dust to heaven, spiritual poverty to the treasures of faith.[29]

In this respect, *exomologesis* is not directly a reparative technique. It is about exhibiting one's fault for all to see, in one's sullied flesh. *Exomologesis*, which finds its inspiration in martyrdom, becomes a reparative technique insofar as it manifests, at the same time, the sinner's desire to free himself from this world, to rid himself of his impure body, and to gain access to the spiritual life; in short, insofar as it assimilates to repentance. Self-transformation is demanded: a becoming-other which calls for self-renunciation (self-maceration, self-mortification, etc.). The work of repentance, a precondition for self-conversion, has nothing to do with a gentle letting go; it requires a form of self-sacrifice that makes it a kind of *destructive reparation*.

Quite different is the model the Greek Fathers called *exagoreusis*, which is partly a vestige of the examination of conscience developed, as we saw, in the Stoic and Epicurean schools, and which becomes instituted, with St. John Chrysostom and especially with St. John Cassian, in the form of confession. Like *exomologesis*, *exagoreusis* implies a process of renunciation and self-sacrifice, as well as repentance and self-conversion (*metanoia*). The two practices differ in their technical dimension: whereas the first focuses on the theatricalization of the penitent's body, the second boils down to an obligatory and constant verbalization of everything that goes on in the life of each Christian, through the continuous confession of his or her faults and the temptations to which he or she is exposed. It is by this speech act that the truth of the self is laid bare before another. A speech act which, as we noted, must come at a cost to the confessant, without which there would be no confession, the key to redemption and access to the divine light. And it is by adding the act of repentance and of penance to confession that religious reparation can take place, even if it requires sacrifice:

> We have to sacrifice the self in order to discover the truth about ourself, and we have to discover the truth about ourself in order to sacrifice ourself. Truth and sacrifice, the truth about ourself and the sacrifice of ourself, are deeply and closely connected. And we have to understand this sacrifice not only as a radical change in the way of life, but as the consequence of a formula like this: you will become the subject of the manifestation of truth when and only when you disappear or you destroy yourself as a real body or as a real existence.[30]

In this restrictive form, it is difficult to speak of confession and repentance as creative reparation. Admittedly, the penitent, if he or she finds the divine light, can hope to be delivered from evil through authentic conversion. But the *reparatio* in itself is destructive: destructive of the defiled body and of the sinful self. Furthermore, the obligation to constantly verbalize faults and temptations, even from the smallest and most unavowable recesses of the mind, converges on the normalizing and clearly repressive function of reparation, a negative function that we have already encountered in the course of our investigation. Rather than bringing liberation, confession and penitence lead to the alienation of the subject in the same familiar dead-end of a life under the curse of the law.

Do these *reparatio* belong to a bygone era? At the level of religious humanity as a whole, they are still very much alive. In the secularized West, however, they are clearly in free fall: less and less do we repair ourselves "before God." No longer do flagellants roam town and country atoning for their sins and imitating the Way of the Cross; the confessionals that adorn churches are more a part of our heritage than a living symbol of penitence among believers; religious orders are losing members, there is a crisis in the priesthood. Magical-religious repair in the West seems now to be reserved for a minority of the faithful. And yet . . . *exagoreusis* has constituted and continues to constitute a dynamic paradigm for institutions other than religious ones, and for other forms of obligation to tell the truth about oneself. Whether in medicine, psychiatry, or the law, confession and repentance have become structuring forms in our societies, so much so that Foucault had no hesitation in describing Western man as a "confessing animal."[31]

Though confession lives on and thrives in different forms, Foucault, in later texts, also insists on the transformations evident in its practices. Whereas *exagoreusis* substantially bound the obligation to tell the truth to self-sacrifice, modernity has retained the requirement to tell the truth, but purged it of its sacrificial component: "That was the aim of judicial institutions," writes Foucault, "that was the aim also of medical and psychiatric practices, that was the aim of political and philosophical theory—to constitute the ground of the subjectivity as the root of a positive self, what we could call the permanent anthropologism of Western thought."[32] The sacrifice of self-sacrifice among the Moderns and the positive emergence of the self do not, however, imply that the repressive component of confession and repentance has disappeared. From there flows the entire project of self-reeducation, as promised by modernity.

But even if it has been stripped of its sacrificial logic, has confession, accompanied by repentance, really deserted the contemporary world? This is the anti-Foucauldian thesis that Porée defends. From being a confessional animal, he suggests, Western man has become a dumb animal in search of innocence. The reign of the guilty has given way to the era of the innocent victim. Post-modern man has become ever more incapable of repentance because he feels fundamentally not guilty, and so ever less inclined to repair his faults, which are *de facto* denied: "The end of confession? One might equally well call it the end of guilt. Confession, after all, supposes guilt. And today we are forced to recognize . . . the profound aftershocks that the guilt-free culture has sent through our ways of acting and feeling."³³ The post-modern age of innocence brings with it the end of the reparation of sins.

This seems like a fair diagnosis, at least if we consider that the Church has largely lost its reparative mission and the faithful have deserted the confessional. Or more likely the other way round: it is partly because the Church has lost its influence and its aura that the sense of religious guilt has declined (and with it the injunction to repent) in our societies. Secularization has clearly affected the role and importance of magical-religious *reparatio*. But does this diagnosis apply beyond the religious sphere, at least for part of the Western world, as Porée argues? In part; but only in part. On one level, the phenomenon of "de-guilting" has impacted every social, political and legal sphere, as we will see in detail in the following chapters. The importance that our societies accord to the "innocent victim," the way criminals see themselves, or are themselves seen, as victims . . . these are "symptoms" of the end of guilt. The "everyone is guilty" of the Judeo-Christian testament has yielded to the age of "everyone is innocent."

This diagnosis, however, invites another, which testifies to the fact that the deguilting of which Porée speaks reflects only part of the reality. Guilt is expressed differently, by other means. The confessional animal has not gone away. We find it exposed in public, staged in the media or before "grand juries" (such as Bill Clinton's confession about his relationship with Monica Lewinsky), to say nothing of the show trials of the Soviet era.³⁴ We find it again, more discretely, privately even, in the offices of psychoanalysts and psychologists, which have largely replaced the confessionals. Confession and repentance have not disappeared, nor has the accompanying sense of guilt. The confessional animal has metamorphosed, into other voices and into other places. Just as philosophy has been largely superseded in its reparative vocation by the world of personal development, so the Church has lost out to secular institutions in its reparative mission. Sin, guilt, confession and repentance have become "psychologized" and politicized (witness the political uses of repentance) just as they were leaving behind the religious framework in which they were born.

APOLOGIZING FOR OFFENSES

Save for those societies in which religious life governs most of day-to-day existence, defilement and sin do not cover the whole spectrum of fault and guilt and so do not call for magical-religious *reparatio*, which are particular in that they are always expressed, in one way or another, "before God" or before some sacred order. The transgression of a prohibition (dietary, sexual, etc.) is always construed as an offense against a supreme being and the order of which it is the guardian (for example, the Islamic notion of "haram"). The work of reparation then seeks to restore a harmony that has been violated by the offense committed, and to bring about—before God, to regain his protection and his love—a process of rebalancing, a kind of magical-religious homeostasis.

Broadening the spectrum of fault and culpability means that the offense can affect (and be interpreted as affecting) beings that are not associated with a magical-religious universe. This is the case in everyday interactions when we voluntarily or involuntarily infringe the moral or physical integrity of others in the form of offenses, insults, or affronts, to say nothing of physical violence, crimes and misdemeanors. In our secular societies, as Goffman points out after Durkheim, rituals and sacredness have been largely displaced onto society itself and the interactions of its members: "What remains are brief rituals one individual performs for and to another, attesting to civility and good will on the performer's part and to the recipient's possession of a small patrimony of sacredness."[35]

Though long neglected by the predominantly quantitative social sciences, the secular rituals that govern face-to-face interactions were subjected to close scrutiny in the work of the American sociologist. "Remedial exchanges," as Goffman calls them, are key components of such interactions. Anyone can, of course, believe that they are wrongly accused, can plead good faith or, conversely, can refuse to make reparation even when they admit that they are the perpetrator of an offense. The fact that a wrong has been done does not imply that reparation automatically follows. Reparation may be agreed to, or simply denied and refused by the person believed to be—or who believes him or herself to be—the offender. This is why fragments of the irreparable, though often minimal, are such an integral part of our everyday (family, professional, emotional, etc.) existence, among the many aggravations that are our daily lot.

It is because non-repair, the refusal to repair, is recognized as a very human possibility that societies have instituted a whole range of instruments, rituals, and mechanisms to enforce reparation when an offense is alleged. In this sense, justice, the subject of the next chapter, is an immense reparative machine for imposing reparation, after a trial. But law and justice are not the only ways in which obligations to repair are sewn into the fabric of social relations. Any anthropology of repair must be able to account for remedial exchanges that take place in the heat of social interaction, outside the objective constraint of the law. It would be impossible for social systems to systematically resort to judicial arbitration to remedy all the offenses of daily life. Remedial exchanges are thus part of the vast mechanism of social homeostasis; a society that could not generate its own remedial exchanges would be quite impossible to live in.

The spontaneous character of remedial exchanges does not mean that they take place without social control and without internalized obligation. Individuals do not constantly reinvent the way to repair an offense. There is always social oversight in the obligation to repair a public offense. Moreover, remedial exchanges follow socially typified behaviors, behaviors likely to be reproduced in similar situations, and ideal models of reparation, which of course vary across history and across cultures. Anthropologically speaking, it is not atomized individuals who enter into a process of reparation. Reparation is, structurally, a relationship. It can be analyzed, with certain reservations, in the light of the Maussian structural model of the gift[36] as revisited by Vincent Descombes,[37] drawing on the pragmatism of Peirce.[38] In the exchange of the gift, individuals do not exist in themselves but only in relation to each other, in relationship mode. It is the relationship that gives them meaning: they exist as a dyad, that is, as giver and receiver. The gift institutes not individuals but correlated persons, like any structural system (just as the signs in a linguistic system constantly refer to each other in correlative, distinctive and oppositional pairs). Analogously, we could say that reparation institutes at least two correlated persons: the repairer and the repaired, who form the dyadic structure at the basis of all reparation. If the gift constitutes a social institution, it is because these roles are predefined by *mediation* (in the Hegelian sense adopted by Peirce), in this case obedience to a set of rules. This is why there is no purely dyadic structure, but always, from the Peircean perspective, a *triadic* structure. It is through the rule of giving (the obligation to give, and the obligation to receive and to give in return) that the giver/receiver dyad is imbued with meaning.

Although the rule is different, we find a similar triadic structure in the ritual of reparation. It is the rule (the obligation to make reparation after committing an offense) that mediates and defines the relationship between repairer and repaired. Of course, transgression of the rule is always possible, but only at the cost of further disruption to the relationship. The ideal-typical interaction model for successful reparation is as follows:

A offends B (relationship disrupted);
A gives *x* (apologies, gifts) to B by way of reparation (reparative act);
B accepts *x* from A by way of reparation (relationship restored).[39]

Unlike the Maussian gift, however, the social obligation of reparation always stems from an experience of initial loss (a diminution of another person's physical or moral integrity). The repairer must agree to give something *extra* to compensate for the loss suffered by the other, however small. The ceremonial gift (unlike the free and unconditional gift of the philosophers) is, like the potlatch rituals, conceptualized within the framework of a general system of exchange and recognition between clans—as Marcel Hénaff has shown,[40] in the footsteps of Marcel Mauss—and does not stem from an initial loss. When, on the other hand, the ritual of the ceremonial gift is disturbed,[41] and one of the groups feels offended, the ritual of exchange can become one of reparation. These two logics of interaction, because they correspond to different modalities, can exist in complementarity. If the ritual of reparation is sufficient to re-establish exchange and trust between the groups, then the ritual of giving can again resume its cycle.

While the objects exchanged in ceremonial giving are always precious objects or beings, in the case of reparations they can be purely verbal (such as apologies). Reparation does not necessarily have to be embodied in a thing, although it may also involve the giving of objects. In ceremonial giving, moreover, the obligation to give, receive and give in return does not end with the countergift; it is embedded in the politics of recognition, in games of alliance and prestige. The cycle of gift and countergift between clans is virtually endless. In some specific cases, the social obligation of reparation can also repeat this cycle, but for different reasons, when the repairer never feels that he has done enough, or when the repaired does not accept reparation, or demands more.[42] In more favorable cases, however, where B accepts x by way of reparation and feels restored to integrity, the cycle of reparation ends, without the need to start a new cycle.

Unlike remedial exchange, which generally takes place on the basis of interpersonal relationships, ceremonial gift-giving is collective from the outset (involving groups and clans) and may go beyond the framework of exchanges between two groups. A case in point is offered by the Maoris of New Zealand:

> if A gives a gift to B who then offers it to C, then when B receives a gift from C he will have to offer it to A, or C will have to give a countergift directly to A as a reply to the gift he received from B. There is a clear explanation for this: When the movement of reciprocity involves transmission through several parties, it must return to its source; this constitutes the spirit of the thing given, called *hau*.[43]

This particular logic does not easily map onto remedial exchange: the offended party expects to receive reparation from the actual author of the offense. But the intervention of a *third-party repairer* (parents, guardians, the state, etc.) may be justified when the offender (for example a very young child, or someone suffering from a mental pathology) is clearly incapable of making reparation for the offence on their own behalf.

The ritual of giving and the ritual of reparation nevertheless share a common component that enables them to be seen as a particular type of triadic structure. In Peirce's classical model, as Hénaff demonstrates, the gift relationship, defined by a law or convention, consists in the handing over of a good from A to B. But in the case of ceremonial giving—and also of reparation—a *commitment of the self* (even if it is collective) is required:

> It is the giving of oneself through the mediation of something. The third-party element carries the self of the giver; it is his *guarantee* and *substitute*. With respect to the ceremonial gift a second level of triadic relationships must therefore be considered. There is a shift from the neutral phenomenon of the transfer convention—the basic triadic structure—to the *personal gesture* of commitment to the recipient. In this case, to give is to give oneself according to a law.[44]

The same process is at work in the case of remedial exchange: the act of reparation is also a commitment of the self by the repairer to the repaired. Moreover, the reparative act and the substitute that is exchanged are preconditions for the interpersonal exchange.

Reparation in face-to-face verbal interactions is often presented as performative (a "speech act" in the sense of Austin and Searle): to say is to do. Saying "I'm sorry" is not a proposition about an observed state of affairs; it is a case of doing something (repairing) by saying it. But, like any speech act, it must meet certain "felicity conditions" if it is to have the desired effect. In what follows, I present these as distinct clauses, most often implicitly accepted by the parties, which set out the conditions for a socially effective reparation, that is, one designed to close the cycle of debt (from the offender to the offended) and of loss.

An *acknowledgment clause*. This is about acknowledging that something has happened, that it is a fault, that one is responsible for the offense, and that one recognizes the legitimacy of the other person's claim to have been offended and to obtain reparation. This acknowledgement may be entirely implicit and condensed in the remedial exchange itself. Saying "I'm sorry" or "Forgive me," after committing some act of clumsiness that has hurt someone, is at the same time to acknowledge a fault, to regret it, and to seek to repair it. Of course, the acknowledgement-of-fault clause may be hedged in by precautions or attempts to minimize it (acknowledging only part of the fault, recognizing shared liability, claiming good intentions or extenuating circumstances, etc.). The test of acknowledgement, when it is not self-evident, can give rise to all kinds of disputes, justifications, and controversies about the facts themselves, the circumstances, or the intentions (for example, whether the offence was deliberate or accidental).

A *sincerity clause*. In face-to-face interactions, the offended party, to obtain "satisfaction," is entitled to expect not only reparative action from the offender, but a correspondence between action and intention. It is of course impossible to fathom the true intentions of the offender, but there is a whole range of bodily signs (intonations, looks, mimics, etc.) that help to infer an intention (sometimes wrongly) from a sequence of actions. While the philosopher, especially one of a Kantian persuasion, will be concerned with the purity of the intention, the sociologist will focus mainly on how beliefs about the attitude of the repairer affect the offended party. Sociologically, what matters is not the actual sincerity of the repairer but the belief that it arouses (or not) in the offended. Even in very brief remedial exchanges, there is always a test of sincerity. Confessing a fault with a sarcastic smirk, or apologizing with a scowl, is unlikely to satisfy the offended party and complete the cycle of reparation. Likewise, overdoing it with a litany of apologies may seem suspicious. And there are plenty of atypical situations where the test of sincerity is overlaid by the test of guilt. This happens, for example, when two people accidentally collide with each other, without it being clear who is responsible: both may apologize at the same time (in this case, the roles of offender and offended, repairer and repaired, cut across each protagonist), or the scene can give rise to a test of guilt (*who is to blame?*), with each expecting reparation from the other.

A *proportionality* or *fairness clause*. Offenses in ordinary interactions vary on a scale from minor annoyances to altogether more serious attacks on other people's physical, moral and social integrity. Reparative rituals provide us socially with an equally wide range of *reparatio* for adjusting the reparation to the gravity of the offense. Reparation is said to be successful when the offended party feels that the offender's reparation is proportional to the injury suffered. A simple apology is unlikely to make up for repeated displays of contempt, let alone deliberate violence, toward another. Conversely, offering money or a gift to somebody one has accidentally bumped into would generally be seen by the offended party as disproportionate and might even make them feel uncomfortable. In the brief exchanges that surround minimal offenses, the proportionality clause does not usually give rise to much deliberation between the parties, so long as the reparation corresponds to what is typically expected in such situations. The test of proportionality or fairness comes into play, however, when the offended party believes that the reparation is inequitable or when the offender believes that the offended party's claim for reparation is disproportionate. The test of fairness can, at the same time, feed back (and the reverse is also true) onto the sincerity clause (if the offender doesn't give enough, then he can't be entirely sincere) and onto the acknowledgment clause (the offender doesn't fully admit the gravity of his act).

The appreciation of the offense is always relative. Relative, of course, to the "lived experience" of the offender and the offended, to their life histories, to their moods of the moment, to how they identify and are identified (with their fair share of prejudices) in terms of age, gender, race and class. Although sociology generally tries to steer clear of psychology, it is essential to take this "subjective" dimension into account in order to understand how two distinct individuals—or even the same individual in two different states of mind—can react differently to a similar offense. On the other hand, this "subjective" factor is not sufficient to interpret the appreciation of the offense. Hence the importance of "sociologizing" the reaction to public offending. Firstly, because the offence may concern, including in face-to-face interactions, individuals who are together in a group: what Goffman calls the "withs."[45] For example, when a couple out walking are verbally accosted in the street by a passer-by, the offense affects not only each individual as an individual, but also in so far as they are taken and understood to be a member of the couple. The same applies when the offence is directed at one of the groups to which we belong (be it family, class, race, profession or other category): it is a collective self that is directly targeted. Not to mention the cases where the offence is conveyed remotely, without the flesh and blood presence of those concerned (such as libelous attacks in the press or on social networks).

The social dimension of the appreciation of an offence is also a factor in the way the isolated individual relates to it. We can speak here of social and cultural patterns in the appreciation of offences, that is, structural frameworks that interpret and classify sequences of actions in terms of categories of offense (rudeness, blasphemy, insult, contempt, etc.). It goes almost without saying that these patterns are highly dependent on each society and culture: greeting a person of the other sex in the street may be interpreted as a mark of disrespect in certain traditional societies, whereas greeting only people of one's own sex from a group of people may be seen as a mark of sexism. Gallantry may be appreciated as a mark of courtesy or condemned as a form of machismo. In racist and colonial societies, for a Black person to refuse to give up their seat to a White person on a public bench or on a bus (or for them to sit in the spaces reserved for Whites) will be seen by the dominant racial class as an affront (and conversely as an injustice by the racially dominated class). At the same time, these social and cultural patterns for the appreciation of offenses are always situational and context-dependent. Having close body contact with a person (including of the opposite sex) in the subway during rush hour, despite the discomfort caused, would rarely be classed as an offense; the experience would be very different if the subway train were half empty. Being the butt of a few jokes in a friendly and relaxed context will not carry the offensive charge that it might in a more tense interaction.

The one thing that doesn't change is that the offense always presents as an attack on another person's physical, moral, or social integrity. What Goffman, putting an ethological spin on it, calls a violation of the "territories of the self": the way individuals (be they "singles" or "withs") attempt to exercise a certain right over a given space. Any unauthorized encroachment on this private preserve of the self may—depending on subjective experience, social patterns, and the situation—be seen as an offense.[46] Individuals (both singles and withs) always endeavor to protect their own patch by marking their territory (as animals do) in all sorts of permanent or temporary ways (such as leaving a personal belonging on a seat to indicate that the place is already taken).

The territories of the self are not only physical; they are always physical and moral, as are the ways of saving what Goffman calls "face," as a social form of the self-ideal, as the sacralization of the subject: "The term *face* may be defined as the positive social value a person effectively claims for himself by the line others assume he has taken during a particular contact."[47] The consideration that individuals feel they are owed varies according to their rank, class, sex, age, situation and experience. Everyone is expected to do their best to avoid making others lose "face," allowing them to maintain or save face if caught in an awkward situation. Not being greeted in return (deliberately) by someone we have greeted is not directly an attack on the physical territories of the self, but it is an affront to our "face," to our social self-esteem. If we "lose face" (stammering in public, stumbling) through our own fault, then the shame is our own; if we shift the blame onto others, that shame is accompanied by a sense of having been offended. It is easy to imagine a long inventory of offenses in the public space, from attacks on the integrity of the territory of the self to attacks on the integrity of our "face": encroachment on our own physicality, an insistent or indiscrete stare, a condescending tone, the theft of personal belongings, being cut off in traffic, cut off in a discussion, or cut in front of when standing in line, greeting someone without being greeted in return, being pushed aside in the street, and so on.

In the course of an average day spent in various public spaces, it's a fair bet that we will have been at least once in the position of offender and/or of offended, sometimes without having offered (or received) reparation, sometimes without even realizing that we have been offended (for example, by a very indiscrete glance that we failed to notice) or have given offence. What should intrigue the observer is, if anything, the opposite phenomenon: given the constant risk of potential offense as soon as we interact on the public stage, and given the constant claims to territory, it is surprising that there are not more actual offenses.[48]

Why do we not spend all our public time repairing? Why are remedial exchanges, though they do indeed structure social interactions, not permanent? Because there are other social rituals which, instead of jeopardizing other people's territory or face, aim on the contrary to respect and preserve them. These are what Goffman, after Durkheim, calls "positive" rituals, because they aim to pay homage, to offer symbolic gratification to others, to maintain their "face" and "make room" for them. Such "supportive interchanges" in Goffman's phrase, represent "the ritualization of identificatory sympathy":

> The needs, desires, conditions, experiences, in short, the situation of one individual, when seen from his own point of view, provides a second individual with directions for formulating ritual gestures of concern. Here we find the indulgences and solicitousness that hosts provide by way of food, drink, comfort, and lodging; here "grooming talk," as when inquiries are made into another's health, his experience on a recent trip, his feelings about a recent movie, the outcome of his fateful business; here the neighborly act of lending various possessions and providing minor services.[49]

All such supportive or positive rituals of everyday life mark an "attention," a "thoughtfulness" for others, and thus help to maintain, and even reinforce, their social ideal of the self. Our societies, secularized as they are, have preserved positive rituals, which sometimes even resonate directly with strictly religious rituals, to mark a particular interest (notably through offerings) in a person's temporality, like the ritual of birthdays.

The persistence of positive or supportive rituals only partially accounts for the relative weakness of actual offenses, compared to what they might otherwise be. There is a third category of rituals, which Durkheim calls "negative rituals" and Goffman "avoidance rituals." They can also be called prophylactic rituals insofar as they aim to prevent an offense (and consequently its reparation). It is not necessarily a question of acting to affirm another person, but rather of avoiding anything that might cause them to lose territory or face. Goffman coins the term "face-work" to designate everything people do to ensure that their actions do not cause anyone, including themselves, to lose face. The whole point of tactfulness is to save the face of other people without losing one's own: "Face-work serves to counteract 'incidents'—that is, events whose effective symbolic implications threaten face."[50] Avoidance rituals in social interactions play a similar function, analogically, to disease prevention actions among living organisms, or actions to guard against emotional fragility at the psychological level. Prophylactic social rituals are many and varied: keeping one's distance in public places; avoiding close contact with strangers; refraining from staring;[51] steering clear of certain topics of conversation that might make someone feel uncomfortable and "lose face"; withdrawing from a gathering (or not joining in) if one is liable to offend someone; exercising "studied inattention" when someone else is in an embarrassing situation (such as when they trip up). Some prophylactic rituals require thoughtful attention on the part of the subject (being careful about what one is going to say in a discussion so as not to offend anyone; spacing out guests at a dinner table, and so on); others, no less fundamental, are more pre-reflective. One such is what Goffman calls "scanning" (to avoid a collision), which is used particularly in the context of pedestrian traffic in urban areas:

> When a pedestrian in American society walks down the street, he seems to make an assumption that those to the front of a close circle around him are ones whose course he must check up on, and those who are a person or two away or moving behind his sight-line can be tuned out. In brief, the individual, as he moves along, tends to maintain a scanning or check-out area.[52]

It is when "supportive interchanges" prove impossible and avoidance rituals fail, when offense has been given, that remedial exchanges come into play. Remedial exchanges can therefore be seen as rituals of substitution, offsetting the absence of supportive and avoidance mechanisms, and/or the absence of a legal test and objective legal constraints. In some cases, the offender himself, acknowledging his fault, takes the initiative of reparation (without waiting to be asked by the offended party). In others, the demand for reparation may come from the offended, either because the offender has not acknowledged his fault, or because he refuses to make reparation. In certain specific cases, the demand for reparation may come from a third-party who enjoins the offender to make reparation (a bystander to a public scene who becomes an accuser, parents correcting their children, etc.).

THE IRREPARABLE AND
THE SOCIAL OBLIGATION TO REPAIR

Why do individuals tend to make amends for their offenses in the public arena when, for the most part, they do not run the risk of any judicial sanction? The sociological explanation lies in the function of social control, in the Durkheimian sense, exercised in the form of a ritual that is imposed on individuals from the outside. If he refuses to make reparation, the offender risks social condemnation; he is desecrating both the sanctity of another person (the person as endowed with rights and worthy of respect) and the sanctity of the rules of civility. This condemnation propagates a negative image that devalues the "face" of the offender, not only for having offended, but even more so for refusing to make reparation (if, of course, he feels that he is at fault). As Goffman writes, "their failure to commit themselves to this social mechanism can reflect more harshly on them than does the original offense."[53] The offender's social image, with the accompanying sense of guilt, is likely to be strongly tainted by the negative reflection emanating from the offended party, from any witnesses present at the time of the offense, and ultimately from society as a whole.

The refusal to make reparation also flies in the face of the socially structuring function of the Golden Rule, initially formulated in a religious context, but now very much a part of secular lore: "Do not do to others what you would not want done to you." If this reciprocal and reversible rule is broken, it places the offender in an internal contradiction: "If I do not repair this offense, then I must accept that I in turn will not receive reparation for any equivalent offense. In other words, if I am to be consistent, I must agree to repair an offense that I myself have committed, an offense for which I would equally want reparation if something like it were done to me." Of course, all sorts of denials and justifications can be invoked, up to a certain tolerable limit, to relieve oneself of guilt in an effort to escape this internal contradiction (minimizing one's own responsibility, finding extenuating circumstances, etc.).

We can follow Goffman in distinguishing between three forms of procedure, three reparative techniques—three *reparatio*—commonly used to compensate for or mitigate an offense in face-to-face interactions. Firstly, *accounts* come into play once the offending act has been done. The offender accounts for his actions in a way that is socially acceptable to the offended party, in order to explain the meaning of the offending act. This may relate to the actual responsibility for the act (by claiming, for example, to be wrongly accused), to the intention behind it (by claiming that its was well-meant or, in the case of an act of revenge, by justifying the malicious intent), to the context (by invoking circumstances to rationalize the act), or to the very knowledge of the offending act (by pointing out, for example, that one is a stranger in a foreign land). The offender can therefore declare himself entirely innocent, partially guilty or entirely guilty. Further sub-distinctions can be made among these types of account, as between *explanations*, *excuses* and *pretexts*:

> An explanation can be defined as an account that attempts to exonerate the offender fully by providing details concerning what it was he was actually about, this being offered after the virtual offense but before blame has been imputed openly. An excuse is an account provided in response to an overt or implied accusation but presented as only partially diminishing the blame. A pretext is an excuse provided before or during the questionable act.[54]

There is no guarantee, however, that such accounts will satisfy the offended party and bring the cycle of offense to a close. A process of reparation does not necessarily mean actual reparation when the repairer is still an offender, and the repaired is still offended. The offender's account, especially if expressed clumsily, can even aggravate the offense and have the opposite effect to reparation ("You don't mean a word of it," "You're just looking for excuses," "You always have a good reason," "It's never your fault"). For the account to have the desired effect, it must satisfy the three clauses we identified earlier (acknowledgement, sincerity, proportionality).

This is also true of the second *reparatio*, namely *apologies*. For minor offenses during brief interactions, simple apologies usually suffice; for more serious offenses, apologies usually need to be renewed and sustained ("I'm really sorry," "I feel awful about this"), or even accompanied by other acts (self-punishment, offerings, sacrifice, privation, etc.). Even more so when the same offense is repeated several times. The repetition of the same offense calls for an additional measure of reparation compared to what is generally accepted for the same offense in isolation. For example, unintentionally stepping on someone's toes once can be redressed by a simple apology. If the same offence is repeated several times, simple apologies will rarely suffice; they will have to be backed up by additional actions (for example, a commitment to change, to not repeat the same offence in the future).[55] Repeating the same offense (even if rationalized as involuntary) against the same person directly questions the sincerity clause (*Is he doing it on purpose? Is he making fun of me?*) and the proportionality clause (*This time I'll make him pay*!!).

Depending on the seriousness of the offence, apologies may imply not only a spoken act (except, of course, in written apologies) but also a particular type of body language and facial expression that must satisfy the sincerity clause (a gesture of the hand, a look of contrition, etc.). As Goffman rightly says, any form of apology presupposes a splitting of the self into two parts: a blameworthy part, which expresses embarrassment or regret, in short a self that deliberately devalues itself (by agreeing to lose some "face") and may even overdo it somewhat (in its eagerness to be forgiven); and another part that sympathizes with the blame-giving and seeks to repair the offense (while at the same time trying to regain some "face"). Reparation, as a process of rebalancing, concerns both the offended (regaining lost face or territory) and the offender (repairing one's reputation after being found to be at fault). In other words, face-to-face reparation, when it succeeds, is a mutual face-saving operation by the protagonists. To make good the initial loss (of esteem or territory), reparation offers a kind of restitutive or compensatory process. The acceptance of apologies and the gratification that punctuate remedial exchange act as operators that sacralize the social ideal of the self and ensure correlative conformity with the sanctity of the social norm. Conversely, in the absence of reparation after an offense (or if the reparation is judged to be insufficient), it is the "face" of the offended party that is devalued, in fact doubly devalued: both by the initial offense and by the refusal to make reparation.

Unlike accounts and apologies, *requests*, as Goffman calls them, generally occur prior to a potentially offensive event. They differ, however, from avoidance rituals in that requests anticipate that a potential offence will occur (and therefore do not seek to avoid it): "A request consists of asking license of a potentially offended person to engage in what could be considered a violation of his rights. The actor shows that he is fully alive to the possible offensiveness of his proposed act and begs sufferance."[56] This is, at the same time, a paradoxical form of reparation, since the event has not yet happened and the potential offender may encounter a refusal on the part of the potential offended. Requests seek to mitigate the offensiveness of the act by alerting the potential offended of a possible threat to their territory or face. But because requests can be legitimately refused, they also leave a degree of initiative to the offended, should they decide to reject the intrusion. Requests are marked socially by a whole range of highly ritualized and typified formulations: "Might I bother you?" "I hate to trouble you, but . . ." "Do you mind if I cut in front?," "May I take your arm?," etc. The fact that these registers of request are so highly ritualized increases, in principle, their acceptability, although without guaranteeing that the request will ultimately be granted. This ritualized character is such that, in some circumstances, for minor virtual offenses, refusing such a request may be publicly interpreted as a sign of bad faith, even as an affront. This is the case when the potential offender has in fact little choice but to commit a minor offense (such as having to squeeze past someone to retrieve something or to get out of a subway train). The offense could paradoxically turn back on the potential offended: if he ignores the request, the offended could well become the offender, and have to make amends in turn! Caught at his own game, the offensive offended party may then be criticized for being either over-sensitive or standoffish.

In what sense, however, can we assert that an offense is repaired? In the ideal-type model of remedial exchange, the ritual is supposed to end in gratification. But there are plenty of cases in everyday life where the ritual is impeded. These are among the many—often small and inconsequential—instances of the irreparable that individuals are heir to in the course of day-to-day life, either because the offender was unaware of his offense (and there was no way to make him aware of it), or because he refuses to acknowledge his fault and make due reparation, or because he downplays his responsibility and offers only grudging reparation. Just as there are degrees of reparability, so there are degrees of irreparability. There is that which has not been repaired, that which cannot be repaired (as when the offender cannot be called to account), and that which is deemed forever irreparable.

The irreparability of the offence is not only due to a failing on the offender's part (such as a denial of guilt); it may also result from the offended party's refusal to accept reparation when, for example, they feel that the apologies are insincere, or that the offer of reparation is not proportionate to the offense, or indeed that the offense is such that no reparation can ever hope to compensate for it. Despite the best efforts of the repairer, reparation is seen by the offended party as a waste of time when the act is deemed to be so wicked (a gratuitous insult, an inappropriate gesture, etc.) that it makes any form of forgiveness difficult or impossible. The irreparable takes on a radical form when the offense is judged to be out of all proportion to any existing regime of reparation. The irreparable here clearly raises the issue of the principle of equivalence or magnitude, by which the harm (the offense) is weighed against the compensation (the reparation); this relates directly to our proportionality clause. The restitutive logic of reparation for the offence does not here correspond to the equivalence that operates when x is paid out in compensation for the loss of y. In other words, the offended party B's loss of x (face, esteem, territory, etc.) should correspond to a compensatory equivalence y, z, i, j (apologies, gifts, justifications, etc.) in what A (the offender/repairer) is offering or in what B is demanding. The difficulty of assessment lies in the fact that what is lost and what is repaired belong to two different orders of things (unlike, for example, a modality of exchange in which A lends x to B who then gives x back to A). The challenge is to find a way of comparing the incomparable.

Even if the offended party deems the offer of reparation to be "proportionate" to the offense suffered, there always remains a gap between the nature of the loss and the nature of the compensation, a gap that marks any restitutive logic with the stamp of the irreparable. This problem, so central to the field of legal reparations, as we will see, is already evident in the social repair of ordinary interactions. The problem deepens when the offended party considers that no offer of reparation can compensate for the harm suffered. By definition, in that case, the proportionality clause cannot be fulfilled, because no equivalence can be established between the offense and the reparation. No form of apology will succeed in restoring the "face" either of the offended or of the offender. Each will have lost face as a result of the interaction, with no hope of regaining it. The offended remains offended (and the repairer is still an offender) without the sense of having been repaired. The irreparable generally arises either because the ritual of reparation has not been initiated—or has remained partial or incomplete and has failed to lead to acceptance (of apologies) or to some form of gratification—or because no reparation can compensate for the offense suffered (the "radical irreparable").

To this radical irreparable, we must add a relative irreparable. Apologies, however sincere, and the acceptance by the offended party of the proposed reparation, do not wipe clean the history of the offense. At different scales of gravity, the offense can leave traces, even when it has been excused, much like—to use a living analogy—scarring after a burn.[57] When the offense occurs without gravity during very brief exchanges with anonymous people in public places, a relative form of amnesty is generally *de rigueur*. The offence will leave little or no trace; everyone will easily regain face and will go on their way with no hard feelings. When, on the other hand, the offense is on a more serious level, the offended party may, despite accepting reparation, continue to feel that their face has not been entirely restored, and may harbor lingering resentment. More seriously still, when the interaction took place with someone close, the emotional charge may be more painful, especially if the offense is renewed. Though excused, the past offence, far from being forgotten, may be brought to mind in other circumstances, accentuating the seriousness of the present offence and changing the whole set of interactions. Insofar as reparation never enables a return to the situation prior to the harm, insofar as the offense is inscribed in time and in memory, it can rise up at any moment and disrupt future interactions. In this sense, an offense, even if it is excused when reparation is offered, is never certain of being definitively repaired, as long as it persists in the memory of the offended. Forgiving is not forgetting.

Religious societies have historically dictated the standard model of reparation for faults, and for a substantial part of humanity still do, whether the fault is the transgression of a prohibition or a commandment, or an original misdeed that weighs on the destiny of all mankind. In every case, reparation is demanded because a sacred order has been violated. Whether expressed in the symbol of defilement, as a stain, or in the language of sin, as a deviance, the fault demands specific (magical-religious) *reparatio* from anyone who hopes to be reintegrated into divine protection and the sanctity of the community: acts of purification, confession and repentance, acts of atonement and redemption, offerings and sacrifices. The secularization of Western societies has undoubtedly transformed the nature of being-at-fault at the same time as we have witnessed a significant decline in magical-religious repair, which clings on in the practices of a minority of the faithful. In the West, mankind no longer carries the mantle of the "confessional animal" that Foucault denounced in the 1960s, as the influence of the Church was fading. Less guilty, at least in religious terms, Westerners are *de facto* less quick to make amends for their faults.

But the beast of confession, atonement and redemption still has life in it. It has metamorphosed: it has migrated into psychologists' practices and is sometimes exhibited at staged political events. The obligation to repair faults has nevertheless retained its ordinary character in face-to-face interactions. The decline of the religious sacred has not affected the social sacred (and the sanctity of its members): any infringement imposes an obligation to repair. Though—at least for part of humanity—we may make reparation less often "before God" or before a confessor, we are still obliged to make reparation before society and those who stand before us. Of course, social agents don't spend all their time making reparation, despite the constant risk of offense. Supportive rituals and avoidance rituals exist for a reason: in order not to have to undertake reparative rituals, in order to prevent any potential offense. The reparative rituals so necessary to social interaction, in the shape of typified practices, come into play when avoidance rituals have failed. As a form of social control, reparative rituals ensure social homeostasis, in the absence of the constraints of the law. But this ever-fragile homeostasis is itself threatened when the cycle of offense remains unresolved because the offense is considered irreparable, because the offender refuses to make reparation, or because the offended refuses to accept it. Neither supportive rituals, nor avoidance rituals, nor reparative rituals will ever resolve all the offenses, not even the minor ones, that haunt our daily lives. When reparative social exchanges fail, it is the vocation of positive law to fill the void, assuming that the offense can be translated into a lawsuit.

NOTES

1. P. Ricœur, *Freedom and Nature: The Voluntary and the Involuntary*, trans. E.V. Kohák. Evanston: Northwestern University Press, 1966.
2. Pascal, *Pensées and Other Writings*, trans. H. Levi. Oxford: Oxford University Press, 1999, p. 71.
3. *Ibid.*, p. 67.
4. A disproportion that in no way prevents Pascal from encouraging the exercise of reflection: "All mankind's dignity consists in thought" (Fragment 626).
5. P. Ricœur, *The Symbolism of Evil*, trans. E. Buchanan, New York: Harper & Row, 1967.
6. For context, in the reign of King Uzziah (791–740 BCE), accused of impiety and religious insincerity, a divine punishment was visited upon Isaiah and on the "people of unclean lips" ("Ah, sinful nation, a people laden with iniquity," Isaiah 1:4).
7. M. Douglas, *Purity and Danger: An analysis of the concepts of pollution and taboo*. London: Routledge, 2001.
8. *Ibid.*, p. 36.
9. P. Ricœur, *The Symbolism of Evil, op. cit.*, p. 74.
10. *Ibid.*, p. 237.
11. M. Douglas, *Purity and Danger, op. cit.*, p. 115.
12. R. Girard, *Violence and the Sacred*, trans. P. Gregory. London: Bloomsbury Academic, 2013.

13. R. Girard, *Evolution and Conversion: Dialogues on the Origins of Culture*. London: Bloomsbury Academic, 2007, p. 148.
14. *Ibid.*, p. 152.
15. Giuseppe Fornari, "Labyrinthine Strategies of Sacrifice: The *Cretans* by Euripides." *Contagion: Journal of Violence, Mimesis, and Culture*, vol. 4, 1997, pp. 163–88.
16. R. Girard, *Evolution and Conversion, op. cit.*, p. 148.
17. P. Ricœur, *The Symbolism of Evil, op. cit.*, pp. 103–4.
18. *Ibid.*, p. 145.
19. J. Porée, *Phénoménologie de l'aveu*, Paris, Hermann, 2018, p. 12.
20. This is the essence of what Porée is advocating in his essay, presented as an attempt to rehabilitate confession.
21. M. Foucault, *Mal faire, dire vrai*, edition compiled by Fabienne Brion and Bernard E. Harcourt. Louvain: Presses universitaires de Louvain, 2012.
22. *Augustine: Confessions and Enchiridion*, ed., trans. A.C. Outler, Louisville: Westminster John Knox Press, 2006, p. 34.
23. J. Nabert, *Eléments pour une éthique*, Paris, Aubier, 1971.
24. P. Ricœur, *The Symbolism of Evil, op. cit.*, p. 7.
25. J. Porée, *Phénoménologie de l'aveu, op. cit.*, p. 73.
26. The Vanitas genre in art was inspired by *Ecclesiastes* 1:2 ("Vanity of vanities! All is vanity").
27. M. Foucault, *The History of Sexuality, Vol. 1*, trans. R. Hurley. New York: Pantheon, 1978.
28. See in particular "Christianity and Confession," a lecture given at Dartmouth in 1980 (republished in M. Foucault, *About the Beginning of the Hermeneutics of the Self*, trans. G. Burchell. University of Chicago Press, 2016, pp. 53–92).
29. *Ibid.*, p. 60.
30. *Ibid.*, pp. 73–74.
31. M. Foucault, *The History of Sexuality, op. cit.*, 59.
32. M. Foucault, *About the Beginning of the Hermeneutics of the Self, op. cit.*, p. 75.
33. J. Porée, *Phénoménologie de l'aveu, op. cit.*, p. 60.
34. Which Costa-Gavras depicted in all its crookedness and cruelty in *L'Aveu* [The Confession] (1970).
35. E. Goffman, *Relations in Public: Microstudies of the Public Order.* New York: Basic Books, 1971, p. 63.
36. M. Mauss, *Sociologie et anthropologie*, Paris, Presses universitaires de France, 1950.
37. V. Descombes, *Les institutions du sens*, Paris, Editions de Minuit, 1996.
38. C.S. Peirce, *Reasoning and the Logic of Things*. Harvard University Press, 1992.
39. The ideal-type model of the ritual of reparation of an offense may sometimes end with the expression of thanks (gratitude) by the offender toward the offended party for accepting the reparation in accordance with the following process: offense, offer of reparation, acceptance, gratification.

A offends B;
A gives *x* to B by way of reparation;
B accepts *x* from A as reparation;
A thanks B for accepting reparation.
For example, in an ordinary reparative conversation:
A: "Excuse me" (reparation);
B: "Think nothing of it" (acceptance);
A: "Thank you" (gratification).

During very brief exchanges in public spaces, however, it is common for the repairer, often in a hurry, not to wait for the moment of gratification after a minor offense (a quick "Sorry!" and then he is gone). At the same time, the gratification may not be verbal; it may be limited to a simple gesture (a nod of the head, a smile, etc.). And then there are some atypical cases that need to be considered: A may have felt that he offended B, without B feeling hurt. A may feel obliged to make reparation to B, without B feeling any need for it, in which case A's reparation may paradoxically trouble B. Conversely, B may feel offended by A without A having intended to give offence or even seeing his act as offensive (in some interactions, simply looking at somebody too insistently can be interpreted as an aggressive act that calls for reparation).

40. M. Hénaff, *The Philosophers' Gift*, trans. J-L. Morhange, New York: Fordham University Press, 2020. It is, in Hénaff's words, a set of "public procedures of reciprocal recognition among groups." In the case of the potlatch rituals of the indigenous populations of the northwest coast of America, the exchange obeys an agonistic logic between clans: "A chief gives a celebration in the name of his group to honor another chief who is dealt with at the same time as a party to be treated and a rival to be challenged. The high value of the gifts offered (emblazoned copper, woven blankets, furs, food) is meant to make a reply difficult. The chief most capable of giving excessive gifts gains honor and prestige, but no additional power" (*Ibid.*, p. 32).

41. For example when one clan refuses to give or to receive, when a group gives too much or too little, or gives back a good exactly as it had been received.

42. In this case the model would be:

A offends B;
A gives *x* to B by way of reparation;
B does not accept *x* as reparation (or A continues to feel indebted to B);
A gives *y* to B by way of reparation;
B does not accept *y* as reparation;
And so on.

43. M. Hénaff, *The Philosophers' Gift*, *op. cit.*, p. 33.
44. *Ibid.*, p. 44.
45. E. Goffman, *Relations in Public, op. cit.*, p. 19.
46. This is the case, to use part of Goffman's classification, for the *body* proper (the carnal envelope of any individual, and its ability to move); for *personal space*,

which delimits a relatively stable spatial framework within which any encroachment is interpreted as an intrusion; for the *stall*, a temporarily occupied portion of a public space (public benches, the beach, seats on a bus, etc.); for the *use space* (the territory situated around an individual to which he or she can lay claim in order to obtain a good or perform a task); for the *turn* (the position one is entitled to occupy in a public setting, for example in a line of people, or when waiting one's turn to speak in a discussion, etc.); and for *possessional territory* (goods and personal effects arrayed around the body as a sign of belonging). Portions of public space ("stalls") can sometimes be tested and disputed, for example when two people arrive at the same place ostensibly at the same time (the tacit rule of first-come-first-served no longer applies, except when one person feels that he or she arrived before the other), or when compelled to share zones such as the armrests between train or plane seats (common territory, perhaps, but only able to accommodate one elbow at a time).

47. E. Goffman, *Interaction Ritual*. New York: Pantheon, 1961, p. 5.

48. And yet Goffman curiously observes that "territorial claims . . . constantly introduce the need for corrective remedial work" (*Relations in Public, op.cit.*, p. 121). If this is not the case—if we don't spend all our time repairing or "remedying"—it is precisely thanks to the existence of avoidance rituals and prophylactic acts.

49. E. Goffman, *Relations in Public, op. cit.*, p. 66.

50. E. Goffman, *Interaction Ritual, op. cit.*, p. 12.

51. Goffman cites the example of public urinals where men have to be very careful and discrete about where they direct their gaze, so as no to intrude on other men's intimacy.

52. E. Goffman, *Relations in Public, op. cit.*, p. 11.

53. *Ibid.*, p. 100. Goffman insists on making a clear distinction between the two processes: one ritualistic, in that the offender has violated rules of civility that he should have followed; the other restitutive, in that it aims to compensate for the loss suffered by the offended party. The reason advanced for this distinction is that the two processes will not always carry the same weight in the offended person's demand for reparation. A person who has been robbed is looking less for remorse (for the broken rule and for her loss of face) than for the restitution of her property or for financial compensation. In other cases, the profanation of the rule and the ritual will take precedence. The offender must then "show that whatever happened before, he now has a right relationship—a pious attitude—to the rule in question; *and this is a matter of indicating a relationship, not compensating a loss*" (*Ibid.*, p. 118). This conceptual distinction does not carry over into practice: offending another person is indeed both transgressing a rule and impinging on their physical, moral and social integrity. Contrary to Goffman's assertion, even when there is no material restitution to be made to another person, repair, and in this case specifically reparation, is always a response to a *loss* (of self-esteem, social self-image, etc.) or a way of seeking to compensate for it. In other words, there can be no reparation, of whatever kind, without a correlative logic of restitution.

54. *Ibid.*, pp. 112–13.

55. I find myself at odds again with Goffman when he states that ritual activity remains much the same regardless of the severity of the act (whether a toe has been

accidentally stepped on or a destroyer accidentally sunk, to borrow his example). It is true that reparative rituals are not infinitely scalable. To take up this example, the person at fault could, in both cases, take on a contrite air and repeat the ritual formula: "Sorry!" But while a rueful expression may be enough in the case of a clumsy person who has involuntarily crushed his neighbor's foot, it is unlikely to do the trick for the captain who has sunk a ship due to a bad maneuver. Apologies and pleas for forgiveness will need to be repeated many times over with very little hope of "satisfying" the victims. It is not the rules of civility that the captain has transgressed, but respect for human life. In this case, we have left the regime of the offense behind for the regime of military law. A simple "Sorry!" will carry little weight before the tribunal, if it goes to trial. Forms of reparation (in particular, compensation) will be expected, following an assessment of guilt, couched in legal as well as moral terms.

56. E. Goffman, *Relations in Public, op. cit.,* p. 114.

57. More happily, but more rarely—without being altogether exceptional—remedial exchange may give rise, after gratification, to other forms of social ritual if the protagonists end up on good terms. The reparative ritual can then evolve into a supportive ritual.

Chapter Four

The Measurement of Harm

Social repair is not limited to the model of face-to-face interaction. Firstly, because there are regimes of offence that operate remotely, without the flesh and blood presence of the individuals concerned. New communication technologies (e-mail, social networks, etc.) have considerably increased the number of virtual offenses, which directly challenge the sincerity clause of any apology, it being impossible to rely on bodily expressions to test the authenticity of any reparation. Written offenses are that much more pervasive in that they can remain as a trace (and a latent source of resentment) stored in memory, potentially forever.

Nor is social repair limited to the strategic model of giving and taking offense that served as our guide with Goffman. Social repair is not only about responding to infringements of other people's territory or "face," but about responding more generally to multiple forms of social vulnerability, dependence and suffering. When we take on these protean social "pathologies," we displace and at the same time redeploy the dyadic structure of repairer and repaired, beyond interpersonal relationships and towards "positive" institutions (non-profits, communities, states). The offender/offended schema cannot here function as a matrix for social repair, at least when the fault is not necessarily attributable to any individual. Suffering from a loss of social autonomy, from social injustice, from social disaffiliation forces us to consider reparatory measures that mobilize institutions whose obligation to repair is not predicated on prior guilt.

Social injustice is but one of the many ways injustice can make itself felt. It invites us to think more broadly about the relationship between injustice and how to repair it. Repair refers here to a set of processes and mechanisms that aim to respond to a situation seen as unjust. Injustice can arise when one party feels aggrieved as a result of a harm that negatively affects their situation. There is injustice when a logic of equality is flouted, when equals are treated as unequal. The objective of repair is then to convert inequality into equality, to restore everyone's rights, to give everyone their fair share. But repair comes up against a whole series of difficulties that we need to examine. On what principles are we to establish an equivalence between the alleged harm and the proposed remedy? In the end, the question that arises is one of measurement: what is measurable, and what is incommensurable between the harm and the remedy? Through the incommensurable—the impossibility of establishing a just equivalence—it is the irreparable that resurfaces, to haunt any ideal of justice. It is also the nature of the thing or the person that is at stake. What should we repair? People or goods? Just how far should we repair them? It all depends on our frameworks of perception and evaluation of justice and injustice, which vary from individual to individual, from group to group, from society to society. Ever since Aristotle, two contrasting ideals of justice have existed side by side, with different conceptions of the principle of reparation (repairing harm is not the same as repairing social injustice). On the one hand we have *corrective justice*, which treats everyone in the same way according to a principle of "numerical" equality (for example, repairing a theft will consist in the thief returning what he has stolen). On the other, we have *(re)distributive justice*, which treats everyone on the basis of merit, position, competence, income, etc., according to a principle of "proportional" equality (for example, asking the rich to contribute more in taxes than the poor). Heated public debates center on which social goods should be governed by which approach (corrective or distributive), and on just how far reparability can be extended.

DEPENDENCE, CARE AND SOCIAL REPAIR

Unlike legal repair (usually by way of reparation for harm), which is clearly delimited in positive law as a form of corrective justice, the notion of social repair is not widely used in the social sciences, let alone rigorously defined. We will therefore be exploring new ground here as we seek to outline its contours. In what sense can we speak of *social repair*? We can start by distinguishing between three different orientations. The first—*social repair as a public response to offenses*—is something we dwelt on at some length with Goffman, looking at remedial exchanges in face-to-face situations between offender and offended. From here on, however, I want to examine institutional modes of social repair. The second orientation that emerges is a very broad one, in which what needs to be repaired is not an individual, or even a target group, but society as a whole (*social repair as a transformative response to social pathologies*). It applies when, as a result of major upheavals (economic crisis, war, modernization, etc.), a society is felt to have lost some of the substantive (economic, cultural, etc.) elements that previously guaranteed its cohesion, equilibrium and well-being. Social repair then describes the effort to restore, as far as possible, the order that reigned prior to the upheaval. The diagnosis is generally couched in medical metaphors ("a diseased society"). Similarly, Axel Honneth speaks of "social pathologies" (as opposed to "social injustices") when describing "the entire population" as suffering "relative to the idea of what constitutes a good life."[1] It is not some category or other of the population that is in need of repair (through positive social discrimination, for example) but society as a whole.

The third orientation of social repair (*social repair as social assistance*) is no longer aimed at the overall transformation of society in its entirety but at finding a targeted response to vulnerable populations in the name of an ideal of social justice. Here it is social injustice, as a structural or perhaps situational form of inequality, which calls for reparative intervention. It may seek to restore an earlier state (e.g., remedying the loss of position or income of a particular population group following an economic or health crisis) or to project an ideal state (e.g., establishing university quotas for minorities that suffer from structural relegation and discrimination). When target groups have always been in an unequal position relative to the wider society, there is no sense in trying to repair the situation by restoring it to some supposedly golden age before things went wrong. Repair, even if it aims at reform, can only make sense in terms of a standard that serves as a forward-looking regulatory horizon for remedying a structural state of inequality.

The definition and delimitation of what is (or is not) socially reparable is rarely self-evident. It involves frameworks of perception, evaluation and categorization of what is just and what is unjust that vary profoundly from one social group to another, and which inevitably engender disagreements, conflicts and even struggles for reparation between groups that consider themselves legitimate beneficiaries of social repair and other dominant groups that are asked (via taxation) to remedy social inequalities. Struggles for reparation can be as much about the target populations themselves, about how to categorize those entitled to reparation (underprivileged social classes, racial minorities, gendered minorities, etc.) as about the social goods to be redistributed (social position, responsibilities, civil rights, income, health, etc.). Struggles for social repair set socially dominated groups, who have an interest in extending the register of the reparable and in preserving the gains they have already made, against groups occupying a dominant position, who have an interest in restricting the scope of legitimacy of the socially reparable.

Before social repair was taken in hand by government (state or local authorities) in the form of social policy, it was administered by part of society itself (families, charities, religious institutions, mutual societies, etc.). It would therefore be poor history to equate social repair with social policy. If social repair has mainly become social policy, it is due to the gradual disappearance of traditional social solidarity and the erosion of the insurance-based social protection system, especially, in the French case, since the governments from the 1980s onward abandoned the objective, originally set by the National Resistance Council, of progressively reducing economic and social inequalities.[2] Social policies for managing poverty have replaced the objective of leveling out economic and social conditions and achieving full employment. Social repair is not a major issue in a society of full employment that effectively guarantees social protection for all. But when the social insurance system no longer fulfills its protective function, or not sufficiently, and when social insecurity and dependence are on the rise, then social repair becomes a burning concern.

If social repair, in the guise of social assistance, is not aimed at the social equalization of people's living conditions, then what is its purpose? It seeks, fundamentally, to remedy a state of dependence: a dependence so deep that it threatens the physical and moral integrity of a vulnerable population group (with each society defining and setting its own threshold, such as the poverty line). The aim of social assistance is not, for example, to reduce the income gap between the highest and lowest paid, nor is it to restore the poorest in society to their full social capacity, even if social repair policies may be accompanied by social reintegration measures (training, back-to-work schemes, and the like). The goal of social repair is not equality (numerical or proportional) or the progressive reduction of inequalities, but *assistance*. The corresponding *reparatio* are multiple: minimum old age pensions, single mother benefits, minimum wage, adult disability allowance, etc.

This mode of social repair is radically different from the remedial exchange model of everyday life. In the case of a social offense, the repairer is—with some exceptions—the offender, upon whom rest the fault, the guilt, the responsibility and the injunction to repair. In the case of a social injustice (except in the case of a private individual such as an employer guilty of unfair dismissal) the repairer—when this role is filled by a public authority—may not be responsible for the loss of autonomy of any particular individual (unless the administration has committed an error with respect to its employees or citizens).[3] In this respect, the public authorities play the role of *third-party repairer*, standing in for a naturally deficient or absent repairer, not to restore or ensure the full autonomy of the dependent (the repaired), but to ensure a minimal threshold of autonomy or social survival.

One of the main difficulties faced by requests for social repair is that they come from populations that are already fragile, precarious and poorly organized. This is not the case with the insurance system, which relies on social organizations such as unions and employers' groups that are already structured and recognized as legitimate interlocutors by the public authorities. Struggles for social repair, as a form of social assistance, are all the more precarious because they center on people who, as well as being dependent and vulnerable, are largely "unseen" and "unheard." Organizing, protesting and demonstrating presuppose a whole set of capacities, mediations and institutions generally lacking among those who live in extreme dependence.

There is therefore a strong temptation, for many of us, to want to assist the most vulnerable groups in their struggles for social repair. It is always possible (and indeed necessary) to criticize what amount to spokespersons when they "speak for," or perhaps instrumentalize, the "disqualified," the "dependent" or the "vulnerable" without really knowing their situation. However, social philosophy and social action can be justified in order to "somehow articulate and make explicit the everyday suffering and vulnerability experienced by individuals and groups whose situation as minorities and subalterns usually prevents them from expressing themselves in a way that is considered legitimate in the public sphere."[4] Nobody is denying the possibility and the legitimacy of "subalterns" to speak for themselves, when they can, to obtain forms of social repair. But in cases of extreme vulnerability, there is no other choice for spokespersons than to at least act as a "sounding board," as Franck Fischbach calls it, in order to amplify, make more visible and audible, the words of those who are often voiceless. Guillaume Le Blanc raises the same problem: "When the denial of recognition is such that it mutes the voice of the despised, how can the struggle for recognition be initiated? When the denial of recognition is made invisible to those who are despised even by themselves, how can we secure so much as the possibility of a struggle for recognition?"[5] However, rather than the traditional function of the spokesperson for the oppressed, in the Sartrean mold, what is needed is what Le Blanc calls "loudhailers" (*porte-voix*), in the sense of both lending one's own voice and giving voice to others.

This operation supposes a *translation* of the original language of precarious groups into a language that is not their own; a role Le Blanc assigns to social philosophy by way of a critique and a social clinic (in the sense of taking care). Fischbach contests the legitimacy of such a translation, which risks betraying the original utterance: "If social philosophy has a job of translation to do, it is not that of translating the ordinary language of struggle into the language of philosophy, but rather translating the expert language of the social sciences into ordinary language, so as to make the conceptual tools forged by the social sciences useful to the struggle."[6] In fact the problem, as I see it, is not the mode of translation (from the language of the precarious into the language of social philosophy, or from the language of the social sciences into the language of the precarious) but the very existence of an original language. Translating presupposes not only a source language, but also the possibility of expressing it publicly. The problem for populations in situations of extreme vulnerability is that they are dispossessed of their voice. How do we translate something that struggles even to be said? This is the central challenge facing a struggle for social repair aimed at remedying social injustice. A challenge not only in terms of recognition (respect, social esteem, etc.) in the sense of Honneth and Le Blanc, but in terms of the absence or loss of social autonomy in any form. The problem of recognition is primarily expressed as social contempt; the problem of social repair is expressed more generally as social (and economic) dependence.

Social repair, in the form of social assistance to the vulnerable, extends beyond the population groups positioned at the bottom of the social and economic ladder. Dependence,[7] though undoubtedly reinforced by increasing precariousness in social conditions, is likely to affect any person who is the victim of an absence or loss of autonomy. Even those at the top of the social ladder experience critical periods or thresholds of extreme dependence (the early years, illness, end of life). In a very broad sense, all human beings are dependent in as much as they rely on others to provide the conditions for their existence. Interdependence is an ontological fact, consubstantial with the human condition. This very broad sense does not call for any form of repair. It is the disabling or incapacitating form of dependence that directly sets us thinking about repair, especially when a person accumulates multiple forms of dependence (physical, psychological, social, economic). In this context, repairing dependence can be compared to a form of care targeted at vulnerable populations.[8] Joan Tronto refers explicitly to repair in her definition of care: "*a species activity that includes everything that we do to maintain, continue, and repair our 'world' so that we can live in it as well as possible.* That world includes our bodies, our selves, and our environment, all of which we seek to interweave in a complex, life-sustaining web" (the italics are hers).[9]

The interesting thing about Tronto's approach, apart from her stance against a "maternalist" vision of care, is its distinction between different phases of care, which resonate with this particular modality of repair for vulnerable groups: "caring about" (recognizing and paying attention to a person's specific needs); "taking care of" (responding to a need); "care-giving" (all the efforts and practices designed to relieve, treat, comfort, reassure and administer to the dependent person); and "care-receiving" (the set of procedures for verifying that the care given matches the initial need). The scope of the aims (maintain, continue, repair) and activities (curative and preventive work, educational work, social work, housework, etc.) that fall under the heading of care is very wide, though it doesn't include all social activities. It would be wrong, however, to equate all care practices with a reparative aim or activity; repair is just one aspect of the aims and activities that relate to taking care. On the one hand, when the aim assigned to a care task is to maintain and continue "our world," there is nothing strictly reparative about it. When a parent feeds their child, when a teacher presents a lesson to their students, it would make no sense to say that they are "repairing" these people, even if they are taking care of them. When, on the other hand, the care activity is preventive, it still cannot be assimilated to an act of repair. When a nurse or caregiver moves an elderly person to protect them from the sun, they are not meeting a need for repair. Care, in other words, can be classed as a reparative practice if it responds to a loss of autonomy in a person who is becoming dependent (or who is already chronically dependent). Feeding a child is not a reparative activity, but treating their grazed knee most certainly is. Vaccinating an elderly person against the flu is not a reparative activity, but helping them with the housework, because they can no longer physically manage it, is. The same activity can, however, have different aims (for example to repair, to prevent or to maintain), as we saw in our reflections on living things, with the example of the bear applying a paste made from saliva and roots to its fur both to repel insects (prevent) and treat wounds (repair). Providing food and shelter for a homeless person can be an act of repair (if they are ill), of prevention (to protect them from insecurity), or of maintenance (ensuring their subsistence). It is therefore very much the *meaning* that the care staff and the vulnerable person give to an activity that defines and delimits the repairer-repaired relationship.

Feminist theories of care also shed light on the status and gender of those who tend to occupy care-related social functions, whether reparative, preventive or maintenance-related. Care work (helping, assisting, feeding, keeping clean, keeping safe, and so on) is mostly performed by women, and notably by women of "subaltern" status (domestic childcare providers, nurses and care assistants, teachers, nannies, etc.). This social fact attests that women are more concerned than men about relationships of dependence and vulnerability. But this attentiveness is not, if we follow Carol Gilligan's thesis,[10] a natural disposition peculiar to the female gender; it is the product of differentiated socialization. While boys tend to be brought up with an ideal of independence, girls are trained into a more relational subjectivation, more attentive to attachment and to dependence. These social predispositions explain why repairers, in the care professions, tend to be women. The ethics promoted by care by no means suggest that this social tendency should remain the norm: it is purely *de facto* rather than *de jure*. It is consequently possible and indeed desirable to recruit a more gender-diverse care workforce.

Social repair, in its three forms (the global repair of society; social repair as social assistance for the disadvantaged; social repair as *taking care* of the vulnerable), inevitably comes up against limits that take the form of the irreparable. On the one hand, the dominant trend towards greater social and economic injustice far exceeds the means implemented by contemporary governments to deliver social assistance policies, to say nothing of countries where social repair policies are virtually absent. Neo-liberal states have not only abandoned the project of social equalization once championed by the political ambitions of the post-war period, but they have also abandoned the attempt to underwrite a substantial share of social misery; as a result, a structural social irreparability persists and is, if anything, growing, through lack of political will. The dominant "realist" argument plants and nourishes the idea that not everything can be repaired socially, that there is a kind of inevitability about not being able to remedy social injustice, that the growth of social precarity is in some way irreversible. It is as if our governments had abandoned the project of "paying off" part of the social debt towards the poor and were now prepared to tolerate a structural component of social irreparability.

Moreover, as we noted earlier, social repair as social assistance does not really aim to restore full social capacity when it is addressed to structurally deprived or dependent groups who, in some cases, do not even take the step of applying for social assistance. Going back to the previous situation would make no sense here. The reparative norm is less about regaining full social autonomy than about enabling a state of social survival. Social repair as social assistance is, in practice, partial and incomplete.

The limits of social repair must also be probed from the point of view of the a-reparable. The questions that we touched upon with Canguilhem, on the repair of living matter, and subsequently on psychological repair, arise again at the social scale. The application to the social field of medical metaphors around the normal and the pathological, for example "social pathologies," are a clear pointer. What we need to examine is the particular norms that serve to justify policies of social repair. In what sense can social precarization be seen as the sign of a "sick body," as opposed to whatever we might mean by good social health? What norms do we presuppose when we define a type of social normality? By dressing the wounds of the social through a "social clinic" might we not diminish our ability to criticize the social norms that govern the neo-liberal mode of regulation in our societies? The difficulty lies in being able to justify a social clinic for the most deprived without losing sight of a critique of the neo-liberal norms that contribute structurally to social disqualification and precarization.

This difficulty only increases when the social clinic project is challenged by a fraction, even if it is only a small fraction, of those it is designed to help. It is at this level that the question of the a-reparable emerges most keenly, when individuals refuse to see themselves as socially "a-normal" and in need of treatment or repair. Take the case of "work" as a structuring norm that delimits the normal (those who work) from the a-normal (those who do not work and are consequently dependent). Guillaume Le Blanc formulates the problem well:

> the question arises as to how to explain the normative presuppositions of social care without unduly binding care itself to a philosophy of care that would at best encompass it as a form of therapeutics, and at worst would open the door to a burdensome philosophy of social normality, whose main effect would be to do violence to lives socially viewed as abnormal by considering them from the outset as needing to be corrected, put back on the normative track. If so, care would be more like stripping the flesh off ordinary lives than providing compassionate support for their creative potential, a potential scorned by social norms.[11]

What is socially objectified as a stigma (precarity, welfare dependency, etc.) may be lived from the inside as an alternative lifestyle and an implicit criticism of the norms of social life (having to work, having to live like other people, etc.). In these specific cases, it is a way of laying claim to the socially a-reparable, of refusing to be considered "ill" or "abnormal," and of refusing to have to be repaired. This is the problem some social and healthcare workers are occasionally confronted with when individuals (such as the homeless) refuse to be taken into care. The survey by Patrick Cingolani, cited by Le Blanc, reflects the choice of a precarious lifestyle as a correlative critique of a normalized social life. He quotes a certain Ghislaine: "Well, you either make your own little life for yourself, by yourself, like, on the inside . . . or you stay right out of it, which ain't easy either. But no, I don't see myself living like most folks: nice and quiet, you get a job, you do your eight hours, you come home, you go to bed . . ."[12]

This critique of repair as normalization should not be allowed to reflect discredit on the idea of social repair itself. A philosophy of social repair must be able to articulate, albeit not without tension, a justification of the social clinic when it stems from a demand expressed—at least implicitly—by vulnerable populations, *as well as* a justification of the social critique both of the neo-liberal norms that underlie social precarization and, indeed, of the reparative norms themselves, when they impose a form of social normality that overrides any positive affirmation of social marginality.

JUSTICE, CRIME AND REPARATION

Social injustice does not cover the whole spectrum of injustices that are likely to require repair and reparation. Rather, it invites a more general reflection on the significance of justice and injustice, through which reparation can take on meaning. It is of course in the field of law that repair—under the guise of redress, remedy and reparation(s)—comes into its own as a particular response to a particular form of injustice: that is, damages for damage (or loss, injury or other harm). The transformation from subjectively experienced offence to judicially assessed complaint presupposes a whole series of conditions, ensuring that not every failure of remedial exchange is going to culminate in a legal process; far from it. On the one hand, there must be institutions, legitimized as such, whose mission is to deliver justice, to arbitrate between contending parties, to give each party its due following an adversarial debate. Without the existence of a third party, based on a corpus of objectified laws and an impartial judge, the legal remedy—if there is one—cannot be described as "just." On the other hand, the person who feels they have been offended has to initiate a process to file a complaint with the competent institutions. The obstacles (psychological, social, etc.) are so numerous that many presumed victims do not cross this threshold, particularly in sex-related cases (rape, harassment), for fear of being exposed, of being unable to cope, and for fear of the consequences: retaliatory measures in their personal and professional lives.

There is nothing automatic (except in serious cases such as blood crimes, where the justice system can kick into action without a complaint being filed) about converting a subjectively experienced offense into a judicially assessed process. The unrepaired, though not in itself irreparable, is an omnipresent fact of social life. This is why social movements such as *#MeToo* today seek to denounce a "culture of impunity," particularly in certain forms of violence against women. The problem is not only one of law (and justice) in the treatment of a case (notably the statute of limitations); there are social and psychological issues around the act of filing a complaint and making an offense public. There is, however, a category shift between denouncing an offense publicly on social networks and having a case mediated by a court of law.

Finally, it must be possible to qualify the experienced offence (a condition for bringing a case before a judge) with reference to the prevailing positive law, which by definition varies from one society to another. Refusing to greet someone may quite reasonably be experienced as an offence by the person insulted in this way, but it is difficult to convert it into a complaint that can be dealt with by a judge. Not every lived offense translates into a codified law. Even when it does, controversies can persist over how it should be categorized in law (moral or sexual harassment; sexual assault or rape; insult or defamation), not to mention the absence of substantive evidence or the existence of time limits, so much so that many cases are simply shelved. It is only after a trial, after deliberation, that a complainant can be legally qualified as a victim and demand reparation for the harm suffered. A subjectively experienced complaint does not necessarily entail a legally determined victim. Repairing an offense through the payment of damages is a path with an uncertain outcome. Unlike remedial exchanges in the heat of day-to-day interactions, the legal repair of harm, if it happens at all, is by definition a process that takes time, involving mediation, arbiters, witnesses, a specific codification of the adversarial debate, a body of law, etc. And there is no guarantee that the complaint will result in an order for reparation.[13] The obstacles that arise in filing a complaint are further compounded by uncertainty about the award, to say nothing of the actual modalities of reparation. But this is also the condition for the subjectively experienced offense to be legally recognized as a harm, without which there can be no "just" reparation.

Unlike remedial exchanges, based on social or moral obligation ("social force"), the legal remedy imposed by a judge does have a coercive character ("legal force"). Though one can flout social constraints and refuse to apologize for an offence at the request of an offended party, one cannot, in principle, once all means of redress have been exhausted, oppose an obligation of reparation issued by a judge at the end of a trial.

In what sense, however, can we speak of the purpose of justice as being reparative? It is by no means certain that all systems of justice have a reparative mission. This takes us back to the canonical distinction between justice as a regulating principle of what is *just*, and justice as defining what is *lawful*, that is, which conforms to positive law and encompasses all of the positive institutions responsible for laying down the law and delivering justice. It is in this sense that Aristotle, in chapter 5 of the *Nicomachean Ethics*, affirms that "Both the lawless man and the grasping and unfair man are thought to be unjust (1129 a 38)."[14] Thus a man, according to a certain idea of what is "just," can be described as unjust when he displays greed, even without this leading to harm and a corresponding demand for reparation. At first sight, then, the question of reparation should only arise in the case of "corrective justice," that is, where the law has been broken and the physical or moral integrity of a (natural or legal) person has been violated.

So should we exclude "distributive justice" from the scope of repair? Aristotle reminds us that distributive justice is "that which is manifested in distributions of honor or money or the other things that fall to be divided among those who have a share in the constitution (for in these it is possible for one man to have a share either unequal or equal to that of another."[15] Distributive justice is not in principle reparative if it merely involves dividing up honors or riches, unless there is a prior situation that could be described as unfair. If I distribute slices of a cake equally to "equal" persons, I am indeed respecting the principle of "distributive justice," without it being in any way reparative (the situation was initially equitable, unless, for example, on a previous occasion, I gave a larger share of a cake to one person at the expense of another). In other words, distributive justice becomes reparative when it becomes *re*-distributive (i.e., when it seeks to re-allocate "shares" that are thought to have been unfairly distributed in the past). This is how we can justify a redistribution policy that derogates from the principle of numerical equality in order to "give more to those who have less" (granting social benefits to the most disadvantaged without allocating them to everyone). The distribution here is not based on an equitable situation but on an inequitable one, which is why, in this case, (re)-distributive justice does indeed seek to repair a situation that is considered unequal: justifying a *de jure* inequality (only some people have the right to receive a benefit or a larger share than others) in order to repair *de facto* inequalities.

Depending on the political regime, the types of goods that can be shared—and the criteria for sharing them—may, as we saw, be subject to controversy, debate and sometimes struggle. In an aristocratic regime, it will be considered "fair" to give larger shares, or more aptly "privileges," to those of noble lineage. Distributive justice, though fair by its own criteria, could therefore be described as unfair under a different regulating principle (such as a democratic regime). Re-distributive justice is only fair in itself if it satisfies a proportional equality which, Aristotle tells us, requires at least four terms: "The just, too, involves at least four terms [A, B, C, D] and the ratio [A/B and C/D] . . . is the same . . . for there is a similar distinction between the persons [A and B] and between the things [C and D]. As the term A, then, is to B, so will C be to D."[16] But this proportional justice can only become reparative if it seeks to address a situation that is initially seen as disproportionate. Thus, in a meritocratic regime, if A is considered more deserving than B, but obtained fewer rewards than B in an earlier distribution (B was over-rewarded and A under-rewarded; B is in surplus and A in defecit), then repair via redistribution will consist in restoring proportional equality, attributing more rewards and honors to A than to B because the former is considered more deserving.

While distributive justice is only reparative under certain conditions, corrective justice is reparative by definition in that it seeks to respond to a wrong or harm that one person has done to another, and in that it seeks to remedy an initially unfair situation. Unlike distributive justice, corrective justice—Aristotle insists—does not concern itself with the quality of people (for example, their merits) but only with their actions. If it seeks equality, it does so not according to the principle of proportional equality, but according to the principle of numerical equality:

> For it makes no difference whether a good man has defrauded a bad man or a bad man a good one, nor whether it is a good or a bad man that has committed adultery; the law looks only to the distinctive character of the injury, and treats the parties as equal, if one is in the wrong and the other is being wronged, and if one inflicted injury and the other has received it. (1132 a 1–9)[17]

Aristotle further distinguishes between two "kinds" of corrective justice: one that aims to remedy relationships that were initially established by mutual consent (e.g., in the form of a contract) but which have subsequently harmed one party through the fault of the other (e.g., by breach of contract), and one that aims to remedy relationships where there was no prior mutual consent (cases of theft, imprisonment, assault, murder, etc.).

Where does repair come in here? In reestablishing an equality that has been flouted by the fault of one party to the detriment of another. The harm is manifested in the fact that one is "in defecit" and the other "in surplus." Repair, in this case, means subtracting the surplus that has benefited one (the guilty party) and restituting it to the other (the victim). Repair equalizes and restores an "intermediate" between too much and too little. It is not about awarding the victim more than he or she lost as a result of the harm (that would only generate a new inequality), nor indeed less (in which case equality would not be restored). Corrective justice is only "fair" if it is strictly numerical, that is, mathematically speaking, if the judge determines that the same quantity (C) is to be subtracted from (B), who is in surplus due to the harm, and added to (A), who is in defecit due to the harm, making them equal again.

This eminently mathematical solution for repairing harm nevertheless raises formidable problems in practice. When the harm concerns a quantifiable material asset (such as the theft of a personal object), equalization may be relatively straightforward, under certain conditions. An objective measure (restitution of the object or compensation) may make it possible to restore equality, even if the reparation or correction may also include a *supplement* for loss of enjoyment (the fact that the victim was unable to use the stolen object for a time), not to mention the psychological or social consequences of having been robbed, especially if physical assault was involved, or a private place broken into. Even in this relatively uncomplicated case, the process of equalization is more complex than Aristotle suggests: the "defecit" for the victim cannot be measured simply in terms of a material loss that need only be restored in order for equality to be reestablished. Even if the victim feels that their rights have been restored, there will still remain something irreparable, which resides in the very fact of having been robbed.

It is easy to imagine how the problem becomes even more serious, as we shall see in positive law, when the harm suffered concerns a physical or moral injury that entails potentially irremediable and irreversible loss. How can the process of equalization be assured in this case? Here, we are at the heart of the irreparable, where the justice system struggles to evaluate the reparations that are supposed to compensate for the loss suffered. The difficulty lies in the incommensurability between the nature of the loss and the nature of the reparation. They are incommensurable to the extent that no reparation can ever compensate for the harm. When the damage and the damages, the harm and the reparation, are of substantially the same nature (for example, material goods), the principle of equalization applies, under certain conditions, because there is a relatively objective measure, a common yardstick for loss and compensation that makes them comparable. We are faced with the incommensurable when the loss suffered, being irreversible, will always exceed any form of compensation. When, in March 2019, a San Francisco jury ordered the firm Monsanto to pay 80 million dollars in damages to a retiree suffering from cancer, alleged to have been caused in part by his use of glyphosate (contained in the weedkiller Roundup), they knew that even such a sizable indemnity would never give him back his health.

The nature and gravity of the harm (a deadly disease) are incommensurable with its repair (financial compensation). The difficulty of corrective justice lies in the fact that it has to repair a harm while dealing with incommensurable quantities. The process of equalization is itself put to the test of justice. Aristotle sees the difficulty, without really offering any solution: when "one has received and the other has inflicted a wound, or one has slain and the other been slain, the suffering and the action have been unequally distributed; but the judge tries to equalize things by means of the penalty, taking away from the gain of the assailant" (1132 a 10).[18] Aristotle is aware of the difficulty, hence the verb "tries" which testifies to the fact that equalization is by no means self-evident (for the judge) when it comes to remedying the harm caused by murder. How could equality be restored in favor of the victim by the punishment of the perpetrator? Taking the life of the criminal will not bring the victim back to life. It is an illusory form of equalization that defers equalization to the punishment or penalty. While Aristotle is certainly sensitive to the right of victims to obtain reparation, this example displaces the meaning of reparation, a reparation from which the victim has nothing to gain, except, perhaps, posthumous revenge.

We need to clarify the relationship between reparation and punishment. In the case of commensurable quantities, where the offender is obliged to return what he has stolen to the victim, or restore what he has damaged, the sentence pronounced by the judge tends to be a form of reparation. But when the guilty has not only harmed others, but has also transgressed the law (property rights, for example), the judge may add an additional penalty that does not directly benefit the victim. This additional penalty (e.g. imprisonment) only makes sense in relation to the law (though it may also be designed to protect the victim or others from a repeat offence). When we are dealing with incommensurables, with serious assaults on a person's physical and moral integrity, the punishment tends to take on an even greater dimension, partly disconnected from any attempt at reparation for the victim. This is what Aristotle is implying in the above example: the measure that is taken is primarily to the detriment of the offender; there is no meaningful process of retribution for the victim.

The issue we have just raised, as we trace the contours of a philosophy of justice, has direct implications for positive law. If we turn to French law, the principle of "full reparation of harm" is set out in Article 1240 of the Civil Code (formerly Article 1382): "*Any human action whatsoever which causes harm to another creates an obligation in the person by whose fault it occurred to make reparation for it.*" When the author of the action has civil liability insurance, their insurer will compensate the victim. In its principle and in its interpretations (notably in the rulings of France's supreme court, the Court of Cassation), "full reparation of harm" means that the person responsible for the harm must compensate all the harm and only the harm; the victim must be left neither poorer nor richer. If richer, we would be dealing with what might be called over-reparation (as opposed to under-reparation, which would be reparation below what is provided for by law and/or expected by the victims). Over-reparation can be legally determined when the court considers the amount paid to the victim to be disproportionate to the harm suffered, particularly in the case of cumulative reparations.[19] Over-reparation may also—at least potentially, but actually quite rarely—be experienced subjectively by the victim when the reparation awarded exceeds any expectations they may have had at the outset of the procedure.

French positive law, by rejecting both the impoverishment (too little) and the enrichment (too much) of the victim, clearly corresponds here to Aristotle's logic of equalization in corrective justice. It is, in other words, a principle of strict equivalence between damage and reparation, as the following Court of Cassation ruling confirms: "the nature of civil liability is to reestablish as exactly as possible the equilibrium that the damage destroyed, and to put the aggrieved party in the same situation as if the damaging event had not occurred" (Cass. civ. 2e, 28 October 1954, J.C.P. 1955, II, 8765). The whole subtlety here—but also the whole difficulty, as we will see—

lies in the possibility of reestablishing "as exactly as possible the equilibrium that the damage destroyed," that is, restoring victims to a situation identical to what they would have known if the harm had never happened (while ensuring that it does not make them richer).

However, this position comes up against innumerable difficulties both in principle and, above all, in practice, to do with the very possibility of delivering "full reparation of harm." In a closely argued piece submitted to the Court of Cassation,[20] law professor Vincent Heuzé offers a systematic critique of this position, clearly echoing the problem of incommensurables that we evoked with Aristotle. Heuzé is careful to distinguish the target of *full* reparation, which is by no means self-evident, from that of simple compensation. The general principle of *full* reparation is unattainable if we take it to mean a pure and simple return to the situation prior to the harm. At best, it can only be a form of compensation, which is itself problematic. The problem is most acute in the case of physical and moral injury:

> It is universally accepted that the function of the compensation awarded in such cases is not to make good the damage, i.e. to restore the state prior to the damage, but to provide financial compensation for the damage that has been irremediably caused. Consequently, the only difficulty concerns the level at which the compensation should be set in order to be recognized as satisfactory.[21]

The disparity concerns the commensurability of physical injury, especially if it is irreversible, having to translate into monetary terms a loss of a different nature. In the French legal system, the amount of compensation is set by the courts. How do they determine the amount of compensation? By a simple matter of convention:

> For example, a magistrate with no experience in this area might certainly consider that, for a mother who has just lost her five-year-old child, compensation of 100 euros would be derisory, while an indemnity of 10 million would be excessive. But, left to his own devices, he cannot say with certainty that neither of these two amounts, nor any intermediary amount, would represent fair compensation for the suffering experienced. In order to arrive at a decision, he will inevitably feel the need to find out what compensation is usually awarded in similar cases.[22]

With regard to physical injury, French legislation has undergone significant changes, particularly since the publication of the Dintilhac report in October 2005 and the "Dintilhac nomenclature" which lists the different types of injury.[23] But this list (which does not have the "force of law" and is therefore purely indicative)[24] does not set compensation scales for each category of injury, any more than does the Court of Cassation, which, while reiterating the principle of full reparation, leaves it entirely up to the judge to set the amounts. In practice, as well as referring to case law, the judge can base his decision on scales set by the Association française des assurances and by the *Gazette du Palais*.[25] The problem is that these scales are not necessarily the same from one institution to another, not to mention the evolving nature of extrapatrimonial damages, which may require the amounts to be revised if the physical injury worsens.[26]

These difficulties are reinforced by what Jérôme Porée has called "the therapeutic age of reparation" which consists of asking the justice system to respond to the suffering of victims. However, at least for certain crimes, the pain of the victims is truly inconsolable and incommensurable with any monetary expression. Moreover, there may be something immoral about wanting to establish some sort of pre-determined scale (this much for the father of a child killed in a road accident through the fault of a third party, that much for the brothers and sisters). The aporia consists in having to repair something that is, by its very nature, irreparable; in having to translate infinite pain into monetary values. The legal and moral problem of reparation for physical and moral injury lies in having to compare the value of a person, assumed to be an end in itself, with an amount of compensation that represents a value assigned to things; in other words, if we adhere to a Kantian deontology, in having to consider persons as things.

The legal principle of full reparation of harm has a more reasonable chance of satisfying a logic of equivalence when the harm is not physical or moral, but material and pecuniary. This, at least, is the case when the principle of "reparation in kind" (of which we have already glimpsed some of the difficulties in the ecological domain) can legitimately be invoked: when, for example, the offender can return the same object or another object of the same kind to the aggrieved party. In this case, it can be said, in the words of the Court of Cassation, that the reparation has "put the aggrieved party in the same situation as if the damaging event had not occurred," with the proviso that the victim was unable to enjoy the use of the property for a time following its theft or destruction, and leaving aside the psychological, social or economic impact (the theft of a car, for example, might have prevented someone from getting to work). To take account of relative impoverishment, the judge may require additional compensation, as well as restitution of the property in kind.

Even reparation in kind, in such cases, requires something other from the judge than a purely determinative judgment, in the Kantian sense of the term. It requires a form of equity, of *phronesis*, of mindfulness about the particular situation of the victim. *Phronesis* is all the more necessary when the principle of reparation in kind is manifestly not possible, and only "reparation by equivalent" is feasible. This is where the nuance becomes especially crucial between, on the one hand, putting the victim back into the same situation as if the harm had not occurred, and on the other, putting him or her back "as exactly as possible" into the pre-damage situation. This "as exactly as possible" can give rise to multiple and contradictory interpretations and many heated discussions between the aggrieved party, the guilty party, the lawyers and the judge. In the case, for example, of a demand for reparation for a work of art that has been completely destroyed (and so can neither be repaired nor restored), the principle of reparation in kind no longer makes sense. How can one even speak in this case of restoring the victim "as exactly as possible" to the prior situation? Only reparation by equivalent can be envisaged here, which raises problems of its own.

Admittedly, the problem is less dramatic than that of physical injury, since a work of art can—at least if it is quoted on the art market or has been valuated by an art expert—be subjected to a certain logic of commensurability in monetary terms, without triggering moral indignation (we are comparing the value of things with the value of other things, not with the value of a person). But in as far as the victim will not be able to recover their original property in kind, but only a monetary equivalent, it is wrong to say that they will be restored to the original situation "as exactly as possible." This is why Professor Heuzé prefers to speak strictly of "compensation" and not of reparation, at least in the narrow sense given to the term by the Court of Cassation's ruling. In other words, we could say—sticking closely to the terms of positive law—that reparation is, in practice, the exception, while compensation is the rule.

RESTORATION AND RETRIBUTION

In the legal context, reparation should be seen as a dual process: reparation of the victim (through equitable retribution for the harm suffered),[27] and reparation of the law and ultimately of the political community (through the restoration of "right"—the term traditionally used to render Kant and Hegel's *Recht*; for our purposes, the modern translation as *law* will suffice, that is, the law, which consists of many laws). It is Hegel[28] who went furthest in his determination to explore the concepts of law and justice, while minimizing the recognition of the victim. Reparation tends to coincide with the punishment of the criminal: insofar as the criminal's lawbreaking has negated the law, the punishment administered by the court consists in restoring the law. It is primarily the law, rather than the victim, that the court must repair. Punishment is thus presented as the "work of the negative," as the negation of the negation (the crime), which ensures the process of equalization and a return to the foundation of the law.

How is it conceivable that the victim, at least in the case of personal injury, is not taken into account for reparation? The reason lies partly in the question of incommensurability between the harm suffered by the victim (notably in the case of murder) and any attempt at compensation. It is because any compensatory justice for the victim is aporetic that Hegel shifts reparation onto the restoration of the law, thus justifying, where applicable, the death penalty: if the criminal has killed a person by transgressing the law, the (just) punishment (as negation of negation) must consist in taking his life. Because persons cannot be repaired like things, because any compensation for the victim of a crime is faced with the irreparable, as Hegel affirms in § 98 of the *Elements*, the only thing that can be repaired is the law that has been infringed.

It is therefore very much the criminal (rather than the victim) who monopolizes Hegel's attention in the paragraphs of his *Elements of the Philosophy of Right* devoted to crime. This is because punishment is not only an instrument for restoring the law, but also correlatively an instrument for restoring the criminal as a subject of the law (even when the justice system sentences him to death):

> Furthermore, the *action* of the criminal involves not only the *concept* of crime, its rationality *in and of itself* which the state must enforce *with* or *without* the consent of individuals, but also the formal rationality of the *individual's volition*. In so far as the punishment which this entails is seen as embodying *the criminal's own right*, the criminal is *honoured* as a rational being.[29]

Failure to punish the criminal would be to leave him outside the law, to consider him a "harmful animal." By contrast, punishing him for his misdeed—in the name of the law in order to restore the law—is to recognize him as a "rational being." In this sense, it is not the victim who must be repaired when the damage is irreparable, but the criminal himself, through punishment. A reparation, however, that can take the form of the destruction of the criminal's life when the sentence is one of capital punishment.

Hegel's philosophy of right may arouse legitimate indignation today, both in terms of the penalty (justifying capital punishment) and in terms of reparation (ignoring the victim). Solving the problem of incommensurables by shifting the meaning of reparation onto the restoration of the law sidelines the victim in a way that runs counter to the very idea of what is just. If justice is about giving the aggrieved party its due, then reparation cannot simply be limited to punishing the criminal—in the name of restoring the law—for having transgressed the law. In short, the victim must have his or her *share*. The problem of incommensurability does not imply that we should renounce all reparation, even if, at least for certain crimes, and especially mortal crimes, it will always fall short in terms of potential compensation. The impossibility of equalizing reparation for certain types of harm should not lead to a rejection in principle of compensation in any form; otherwise we risk contradicting the very idea of justice (giving people their due).

If the Hegelian solution strikes us as scandalous today, it is because the place and the representation of the victim in the contemporary era are unprecedented, due to a genuine historical revolution astutely analyzed by Didier Fassin and Richard Rechtman: "the ideological revolution produced by the concept of trauma changed the status of the wounded soldier, the accident survivor and, more broadly, the individual hit by misfortune, from that of suspect (as it had been from the end of the nineteenth century) to that of entirely legitimate victim."[30] Of course, the invention of post-traumatic stress disorder as a category by American psychiatry, and the slow institutionalization of the work inspired by Charcot, Freud or Janet in the fields of psychiatry, psychology and victimology—along with their social, political and media applications—have not been the only cognitive frameworks behind the emergence of a new figure of victimized subjectivity. The older legal invention of the crime against humanity has, as we will see in the next chapter, an equally decisive role in the recognition of victims of genocide and slavery, for example. Surely all but the most hard-bitten Hegelians would concur that listening to the voice of the victims, especially when they come from minority or vulnerable populations, marks a considerable progress in the history of justice in particular, and human societies in general.[31] Justice has, on occasion, been done, despite the long road that still remains to be traveled toward the recognition of victim status for many individuals long ignored by the judicial authorities.

At the same time, at least for certain crimes and offenses, this progress only reinforces the problem of incommensurability. The greater the place of victims in the law, the greater the problem of determining just reparation for the harm suffered. If we follow Porée, the problem is taking a particularly dramatic turn now that we have entered a new age of reparation:

> This is not the age of myth; nor is it the age of law. It is the age of the individual reduced to himself, abandoned alternatively to his own power, and lack of power. It is the age of the body in good or in bad health. For us, repairing no longer means *restoring* an order or *returning* a good, but reliving and being reborn. In place of restoration-reparation and retribution-reparation, we have substituted a lay version of the Christian resurrection: *regeneration*-reparation."[32]

This new age of reparation can be thought of, he suggests, in terms of the therapeutic: the purpose of justice is no longer simply to "give victims their due" (or to punish the guilty), but to treat and heal victims, giving them new life, so that they are born again out of their suffering.

Historically, the therapeutic purpose of justice was first problematized and developed, as Janine Barbot and Nicolas Dodier have shown, by legal professionals beginning in the 1970s and 80s, in the context of a reflection about the place of victims in criminal trials. One "pro-victim" current, linked to conservative movements in the United States, wanted at the same time to bring in stiffer penalties for criminals. A second, more liberal, current sought to improve conditions for the recognition of victims (compensation, psychological support), without leading in return to harsher sentencing. These scholarly debates were accompanied by significant legislative changes:

> In France during the 1980s, with the help of justice minister Robert Badinter, they sought an alternative to the "Security and Freedom" law and established a new victim assistance policy,[33] by creating a support network piloted by the state, the National Institute for Assistance to Victims and Mediation (Institut national d'aide aux victimes et de médiation, or INAVEM). At the beginning of the twenty-first century, jurists who identify with this liberal current have contributed to increasing victims' presence within the criminal trial itself, notably via the provisions of the so-called Guigou law on the presumption of innocence and aid to victims (named after the Socialist justice minister who championed it). In more general terms, this approach thus provides a way of grasping how the spaces of actors anchored in specialized arenas become connected to the political domain.[34]

Barbot and Dodier's field observation, in support of an ethnographic survey of the so-called "growth hormone" trial,[35] adds an extra layer of complexity to Porée's hypothesis of a therapeutic age of reparation. On the one hand, the new collective representation associated with the suffering victim, and the new legislation on victims' rights, undeniably modified the trial process. This was particularly evident in the pleadings of the civil parties' lawyers:

> The lawyers wished to explain how they had been affected by the suffering of the victims' families and stressed the necessarily divided character of their feelings. The frequent shift from "I" to "we" ("we all" or "all of us") demonstrated this desire for unanimity. Most of the closing arguments thus praised the creation, during the sequence of testimonies, of a *compassionate community* surrounding the victims—a community which encompassed the lawyers, magistrates, families and all spectators of the suffering, whatever their role within the criminal justice system.[36]

The objective, at least for the civil parties' lawyers, was to try to translate into law "the exceptional magnitude of suffering" expressed by the parents of the children who fell victim to the contamination. On the other hand, some of the actors in the trial, notably the defense lawyers, clearly distanced themselves from, and even denounced, any form of "compassion-aid" (the feeling which makes a jurist faced with a victim's suffering want to do something to help them) and any appropriation of the legal system solely to alleviate the victims' suffering: "Anxious to keep their distance from *compassion-aid*, all of the lawyers nevertheless considered that appeasement of suffering could be legitimate if it was *in addition*. In other words, a criminal trial can appease certain forms of suffering, but it can only do this effectively if it is not organised to this end."[37]

Is this an instance of the therapeutic purpose of reparation in the sense of Porée? Not entirely, or perhaps in a more subtle way. To say that a legal ruling, through penal sanction and compensation, can alleviate the suffering of the victims is not the same thing as saying that this is its purpose. In other words, the therapeutic dimension, while it may be real, is not an end in itself but an *effect* (a *surplus*, in the sociological jargon) of a decision that must be taken first and foremost in the name of the law and in accordance with the "traditional" aims of justice (punishing crime and repairing harm). Of course, the sociographic analysis of the growth hormone trial is only a case study; there is no presumption that it can be generalized to every judicial scene. But this study has the great merit of nuancing the hypothesis of a "therapeutic age of reparation," while at the same time attesting to legal professionals' reticence about making it the purpose of justice to relieve suffering. The very expression *therapeutic age of reparation* could be misleading, if we are left with the impression that the desire to alleviate the victims' pain overshadows the other aims of justice. Instead, we are forced to acknowledge the coexistence of if not contradictory, then at least heterogeneous purposes of justice within the same "age." In other words, the contemporary invention of therapeutic reparation has not eliminated the attachment of legal professionals to "restoration-reparation" and "retribution-reparation."

Porée is operating on another scale, a philosophical—and, one might say, normative—scale (in contrast to the descriptive approach of Dodier and Barbot's pragmatic sociology). For it is in terms of "pathology" that the philosopher warns of an age of reparation that is turning into "resurrection mania." It is, of course, a form of *hubris* he is denouncing, not the *hubris* of sacrifice as it might have been in the "mythical age" of repair, but the *hubris* of regeneration at the heart of the therapeutic age. The excess is inherent in the victim's own demand: to have a remedy for their suffering, to be born anew. Despite the strengthening of victims' rights, such a demand reinforces the problem of incommensurability: what reparation could ever compensate for the suffering caused by the loss of a loved one due to the action of a third party? The crisis of the therapeutic age of reparation, as

Porée calls it, also affects the justice system, which finds itself increasingly helpless to cope with victims' requests, despite the changes in legislation in their favor. In other words, while the courts tend to consider that victims ask for too much with regard to what the law can do, victims tend to consider that the system does not give them enough for the suffering they have endured: "This is where the madness lies: it is to believe that reparation can, by itself, eliminate our pain, raise us from the dead, and make us exist again. It is to ignore the irreparable."[38]

We must differentiate here between at least three reparative purposes that can be assigned to justice: restoring the law, compensating victims, and relieving their suffering. To these we must add a fourth, which directly concerns the perpetrator. The reparation of the criminal may seem paradoxical in that he is, after all, responsible for the harm, and still more paradoxical if we believe, with Hegel, that is by means of punishment that the criminal regains consideration as a rational subject, even if the judge decides to sentence him to death.

Historically, it was not always so. Not until the late eighteenth and early nineteenth centuries, in parts of Europe and in the United States, if we follow Foucault's analyses—the time of the great penal reform projects that advocated for less severe penalties—does the question of repairing the criminal begin to be problematized, publicized and institutionalized. The question does not arise before, or rather, the reverse: it is not about repairing the criminal, but destroying him or her, and moreover, making them suffer methodically and publicly in the "spectacle of torment." However, this excessive suffering inflicted on the criminal is not really seen as an equivalent to the suffering endured by the victim. Even in the absence of harm or injury to others, the mere fact of having violated the law merited punishment because any such transgression was perceived as an assault on the very person of the sovereign: "Punishment, therefore, cannot be identified with or even measured by the redress of the injury; in punishment, there must always be a portion that belongs to the prince, and, even when it is combined with the redress laid down, it constitutes the most important element in the penal liquidation of the crime."[39]

This is why punishment is presented as a political ritual, staged in the public square, by which the affront of lèse-majesté must be washed clean by the torture of the criminal (every crime, Foucault suggests, contains the seed of regicide). Reparation is thought of above all as the reconstitution and restoration of sovereign power (and never as the rehabilitation of the criminal). In the course of this morbid ritual, the logic of equivalence plays out on a certain level, when the staging of the torture echoes certain elements of the crime (such as setting up the scaffold at the very scene of the crime, piercing the tongue of blasphemers, and so on). But at the same time it is overwhelmed by a logic of excess, in the administration of suffering to the criminal out of all proportion to the suffering endured by the victim:

> Although redress of the private injury occasioned by the offence must be proportionate, although the sentence must be equitable, the punishment is carried out in such a way as to give a spectacle not of measure, but of imbalance and excess; in this liturgy of punishment, there must be an emphatic affirmation of power and of its intrinsic superiority.[40]

This additional suffering, of which torture is the dreadful expression, does of course have a reparative purpose: as well as the harm done to the victim, it is necessary to add to the convicted person's lot of suffering both the additional cost of restoring the law, and the vengeance of the sovereign (this increment of pain is an integral part of the political economy of punishment). In addition to this reparative function, the punishment has a genuinely prophylactic purpose. The public staging of the torture must have a terrorizing effect on the onlookers who have gathered to watch the spectacle: the example of suffering exhibited in the punishment of the criminal must instill into the heart of every subject the desire never to undergo the same fate, to forsake all criminal acts, and thus avoid the implacable force of royal justice.

Historicizing the reparative purpose of justice is a way of showing that until the end of the eighteenth century, repairing the victim took second place,[41] repairing the guilty was irrelevant, and the only thing that mattered was to restore the rule of law and the omnipotence of the sovereign. The gradual transformation of the system of punishment correlatively modified the aim of reparation. The disappearance of torture as a *reparatio*, increasingly considered inhuman as well as ineffective (due to the prestige that surrounded the sacrifice of certain criminals, held up as true heroes, to the intense annoyance of the legal authorities) and the gradual generalization of imprisonment gave the convict a new status: worthy of being repaired, in the sense of correcting their vices and reeducating their souls. Whereas repairing the victim can now be thought of both as restoring what they are owed and as relieving their suffering, repairing the guilty can be seen as the moral rectification of an evil inclination and as their rehabilitation as a subject of law.

A distinction is henceforth made between the criminal act and the person who committed the crime. The criminal may, under certain conditions, have a destiny beyond his guilty act. It is not only the criminal act that must be repaired (by compensating the victim and restoring the rule of law), but also the criminal himself as a rational being, the main vector of this transformation being the prison system. Prison is certainly viewed as the institution that protects society by isolating criminals. But it is also conceived of as a place for the moral regeneration of criminals, following a model that draws part of its inspiration from the monastic institutions. Punishment is meted out in a house of "correction," redolent of a journey to conversion, under the constant watch of correctional officers. Isolation in cells has both a preventive function (to avoid the bad influence of other inmates and the risk of escape) and a reparative mission: the criminal, through the psychological shock of solitude, must look back on his crimes, ponder them, and embark on the straight and narrow path of redemption. The cell-bound *reparatio* of the criminal may at the same time be accompanied by religious *reparatio* within the prison walls (chaplain visits, morning prayer rituals, atonement for sins, confession).

The moral rehabilitation of the criminal also involves the obligation to work. The length of the sentence is set according to the time needed to correct the vice. Daily toil must instill new habits into the convict, drumming virtuous new routines into the body and the spirit, to enable economic reintegration, for some, after release:

> The reason given was that idleness was the general cause of most crimes. An investigation—no doubt one of the first—carried out among those sentenced under the jurisdiction of Alost, in 1749, showed that malefactors were not "artisans or labourers," but "idlers given up to begging." Hence the idea of a house that would in a sense provide a universal pedagogy of work for those who had proved to be resistant to it.[42]

The correction of the prisoner was subsequently overseen by new technicians (in addition to chaplains, guards and judges): doctors, psychologists, social educators, teachers . . . all tasked as much with alleviating the sentence as with leading the criminal onto the path of virtue and social reintegration. The prison system condenses within itself a substantial share of the ideal-type models of repair: bio-medical *reparatio*, psychological *reparatio*, moral *reparatio*, social *reparatio*. Even if sentenced to life or, worse, death, the prisoner must still be able to benefit from the attention of the psycho-medical-legal complex (including recourse to psychopharmacology before mounting the scaffold).

This attention becomes altogether more acute when it has a prophylactic objective, to prevent reoffending by "releasable" prisoners. The same techniques (work, prayer, solitary confinement) can have both a reparative function (to expunge the sinfulness from the criminal) and a prophylactic function (to prevent the crime from happening again): "The 'reformatories' were mechanisms directed towards the future; they too were intended not to efface a crime, but to prevent its repetition."[43] These "reformatories," however, came up against harsh statistical realities: far from being a school for reform, prison has become, for some prisoners, a top-flight school for crime and a fast track to radicalization.[44] Elevated, contrary to the wishes of many of the great penal reformers, into a generalized model of punishment, prison now largely signals the complete failure to repair the criminals themselves (in the sense of moral and social correction).

The question of the suffering inflicted on the criminal must also be considered. The abolition of torture clearly marks a fundamental break (and an undeniable step forward)[45] in the history of penal policy: the tortured body is no longer the medium on which the violence of the sovereign must be exercised. But have softer sentences necessarily eradicated all the forms of suffering that afflict the criminal's body? Far from it. Though the stated objective is to take away a good or a right (freedom) rather than to chastise the flesh, the modern punitive system has never renounced the idea that the criminal should suffer more than others. Prison can also mean hard labor, rationing, overcrowding, sexual deprivation, beatings, bullying and "the hole." Symptoms such as these inspired Foucault to write that there remains a "trace of torture" in the modern mechanisms of criminal justice: "a trace that has not been entirely overcome, but which is enveloped, increasingly, by the non-corporal nature of the penal system."[46] Since the publication of *Discipline and Punish*, faced with prison over-population and rocketing rates of recidivism, substitution measures have of course been encouraged and supervised.[47] But prison remains the norm for our penal systems.

What lies behind the persistence of this "trace of torture" in the convict's sentence that is added to the victim's retribution? There is, within the sentence, an *additional* suffering allotted to the criminal, quite distinct from what is due for the harm done to the victim: the criminal must not only settle his debt to the victim, it must also cost him *something more*. In practice, the equalization of justice aims not only to subtract from the criminal the share that he unduly took from the victim, but also to subtract a positive share (freedom, for example, or civil rights) or add a negative share (the suffering of isolation, overcrowding, etc.). One way or another, the criminal must pay more and enjoy less. It is this logic of punishment, going beyond the logic of compensation due to the victim, which perhaps finds its source in the "trace of torture" that France's modern penal policy has retained from the Ancien Régime, despite its project of humanizing sentences.

The distinction in French positive law between criminal liability and civil liability overlaps neatly with both the philosophical and historical debates around the reparation of harm. Strictly, reparation does not arise in the case of criminal liability, which is based on the obligation to answer for infringements of the law (from simple fixed-penalty offences to misdemeanors to serious crimes). In this facet of liability, we find again Hegel's justification for ignoring the victim: what has been violated is the law, the fundamental values of a society, of the state. Criminal liability is concerned only with sanctioning behavior considered to represent a violation of public order; it does not set out to repair the harm done to a victim. Even when victims are directly affected by a crime or misdemeanor, no compensation can be claimed for the victim from the perpetrator in the name of criminal liability. Only in the case of particularly heinous crimes, such as crimes against humanity, may the accused be tried in the presence of a limited number of individual victims, as was the case, for example, during the Nuremberg trials[48] or during the first *épuration* (purge) in newly-liberated France in 1944–1945. It is the Public Prosecutor (*Procureur de la République*), representing the state, who directly prosecutes criminals for breaking the law. The response is repressive, and also non-reparative, in the narrow sense of compensating the victim. In a broader sense, criminal liability does, however, imply a form of reparation, precisely in the Hegelian sense of restoring the law. In this sense, the punishment, in the name of criminal liability, takes the form of "a negation of negation." While this penal response wards off the risk of the victim taking hidden revenge on the guilty (by obviating the need to do so), the question remains open as to whether it does not simply displace vindictive justice, by making it the business of the state, or of society at large.

Civil liability, by contrast, directly involves reparation to the victim and is not in principle intended to be "punitive," at least in French law. We now have, on one side, the dyad criminal liability/restoration of the law, and on the other, the dyad civil liability/retribution of the victim. Liability, as we saw earlier, is framed by Article 1240 of the new Civil Code: "Any human action whatsoever which causes harm to another creates an obligation in the person by whose fault it occurred to make reparation for it."[49] The civil liability of a malefactor can be invoked only after a "civil party" plaintiff has filed a claim. For the same case, for example a crime, the accused can potentially be held doubly liable: criminally liable by the prosecution, and civilly liable by the victims and their lawyers. In other words, the accused can be both prosecuted by the state (to restore the law through punishment) and sued by the civil parties (to win retribution for the victim through compensation).[50] Civil liability can only be invoked if three criteria are met: one, the harm must be categorized as material (loss or damage of property), bodily (e.g., a wound), and/or moral (e.g. reputational damage);[51] two, there must exist established facts (*le fait personnel* [personal liability], *le fait d'autrui* [vicarious liability] or *le fait de la chose* [liability for the actions of things]); and three, it must be possible to establish a line of causality between the originating event and the harm. Absent any one of these conditions, no claim for compensation is admissible. In other words, the plaintiff can only become a victim, and demand reparation, if a causal link can be established between the act and the injury.[52]

It is easier to grasp these difficulties if we draw upon the notion of reparative configuration or "*dispositif*" theorized by Janine Barbot and Nicolas Dodier, initially derived from a Foucauldian framework of analysis. The sociologists define a *dispositif* "as a prepared concatenation of sequences, intended to qualify or transform a state of affairs through the medium of an assemblage of material or language elements."[53] A *dispositif* arranges heterogeneous elements that might be material (the courtroom, indemnities) linguistic (legal texts, narrations, indictments, pleadings), interacting agents (magistrates, defense lawyers, civil parties' lawyers, state representatives, victims, witnesses, experts), and sequential actions (trial, appeal, compensation, etc.). The sociological value of the notion of reparative *dispositif*, as a specific *reparatio* applied to the law, takes multiple forms. It resides first of all in the importance given to operations of qualification, in their many manifestations: the elaboration of a doctrinal corpus by legal professionals on the purposes of the law; the estimation of the harm by the victim; the legal categorization of the case by judges; the narrations of witnesses. The problem is that these qualifications can give rise to different interpretations, different frameworks of evaluation ("normative repertoires") of the facts, of the legal texts, of the degree of liability of the defendants, and at least as many controversies. For example, individuals may consider themselves the victim of a harm without being able to translate it into the categories of the law, or without the case being taken up by the courts, or indeed without their demand leading to effective reparation.

The second benefit offered by the notion of reparative *dispositif* lies in its dynamic or processual character, which at the same time entails the possibility of transforming a state of affairs (for example, transforming a subjectively experienced harm into legally mandated reparation through the mediation of a trial):

> The existence of arrangements, and thus of flexible or intangible dependences between various elements, means that a concatenation of sequences already exists as a potentiality—that it is "prepared." Individuals can experience this chain as a constraint or draw on it as a resource. The dependences between the elements within an arrangement are the result of a prior history.[54]

The reparative *dispositif* does not begin with the act of compensating the victims, but in a chain of actions that begins with the filing of a complaint and the constitution of civil parties, a set of actions *in light of which* the process of reparation is carried through with teleological intent by a series of actors. While there are formal procedures to be complied with (for example, filing a complaint, for the civil parties), the process is not linear and can be broken off (if the plaintiff withdraws his or her complaint, or if the courts do not take up the case). At this stage, the aforementioned difficulties that arise in finalizing the reparation process become clearer; a process that is always uncertain even before the trial takes place, to say nothing of the delays in the payment of reparations.

VENGEANCE AS AN INSTITUTION

The problems posed by civil liability are of a different nature to those posed by criminal liability, even if the greater consideration given to the suffering of victims has been accompanied, in some legal systems, by an increase in the punitive aspect of sentencing, most notably in the Anglo-American legal practice of "punitive damages." The main problem is to know whether, even in contemporary judicial systems, the penal sanctions still contain vindictive residues that hark back to Foucault's "trace of torture."

This "making the convict suffer" is something that a philosopher like Ricœur is quick to denounce as an "intellectual scandal, in terms of criminal justice, this suffering inflicted on the guilty by the penalty, a suffering that seems to be added from the outside, by the judicial institution itself, to the suffering initially felt by the victim of a harm or injury."[55] An "intellectual scandal" because nothing, outside of what ought to be the strict rationality of justice (giving the victim their due for the harm suffered), justifies this additional suffering visited upon the criminal. An "intellectual scandal" because this excess suffering is to be understood more in a logic of revenge than of justice. An "intellectual scandal" because the rationale for justice is to substitute the figure of *Dikē*, representing debate, distance and conciliation, for the cycle of violence, whereas the suffering applied to the guilty perpetuates both the violence and the repetition of vengeance. Admittedly, it is no longer the personal vengeance of the royal sovereign being exacted throughout the country on the tortured bodies of the condemned, but it is perhaps a substitute, albeit a less severe one, in the name of more abstract and impersonal figures such as society or the state. In the punishment of the criminal, does not society also claim its due, taking collective revenge, beyond its legitimate self-protection? Is this not the "trace of torture," which has metamorphosed with the political transfer of sovereignty?

In the end, whenever reparation is sought for a harm suffered, the relationship between justice and vengeance hangs in the balance. And this relationship is more complex than it seems. More complex, first of all, because vengeance is indeed a way of repairing damage, a reparative technique, a *reparatio*. Though one might hesitate to qualify it as philosophically or legally "just," vengeance can in itself correspond to a logic of equalization (as payment in return) if the "counterblow" is substantially equivalent to the initial "blow received." *A contrario*, vengeance would be "unjust" if the reprisal violence were disproportionate to the initial violence (for example, taking revenge for an insult by delivering a mortal blow). Accordingly, major institutions of vindictive justice such as *vendetta* in the Mediterranean regions (mainly the Balkan region, southern Italy and Corsica) operate a strictly codified form of equalization. One such institution is the *Kanun*, stemming from medieval customary law, which still resurfaces today, after the fall of communism, in some parts of northern Albania. The *Kanun* is not solely concerned with vendetta, known as *gjakmarrje* ("blood-taking"), but one of its "books" deals with the rules of honor. Faced with the impossibility of suppressing inter-clan warfare, the *Kanun* was designed as a framework to contain its excesses. The *Kanun* is therefore anything but blind and unrestrained revenge: it seeks to establish a degree of "measure" and a certain equalization: it is forbidden to eliminate a man in the presence of his wife; the killer is obliged to attend the burial of his victim; one must not murder children under 15, women, or the elderly . . .

The resurgence of blood feuds in Albania since the 1990s can be explained by several factors that converge on the idea that state justice is less effective than that practiced in the name of the *Kanun* in suppressing blood crimes:

> The abrogation of the death penalty by the state due to international pressure in 1999, the new European Standards for prisons, and the flexible nature of imprisonment, combined with the corruption of the judicial system have provided everyday people with normative and practical arguments that state law lacks the intention to punish proportionally according to the crime. Notions of balance, fairness, and proportionality are at the core of locally-defined justice and are organically integral to the ideals of customary law and practices.[56]

It is remarkable, in Nebi Bardhoshi's ethnographic investigation, that one of the regulating ideals of "the just," in the Aristotelian sense of fairness and equity, should be assimilated locally to vindictive justice, rather than state-instituted justice. However, vindictive justice, unlike blind revenge, is justified for these practitioners not only because it is rooted in a traditional legitimacy (in the Weberian sense) that goes back to the Middle Ages, but also because it is strictly framed by a logic of equalization.

Although they could not claim to be so rigidly codified, ordinary social interactions—far away from the societies where vendettas rage—are peppered with small daily acts of revenge, which are not usually punishable by law (or, at least, no complaints are filed), in professional, family, friendly or amorous relationships. Ricœur pieces together the ideal-type:

1. It begins with a harm that goes beyond material damage or physical injury: it is a moral harm, an affront to honor, in terms of esteem, measured against the norms shared by the familial (in the broad sense) reference group. Let's call it an "attack on one's reputation";
2. An instant reaction: anger, which is a passion, a feeling directed against the attacker;
3. The desire for retribution contained within the anger, whereby the passion of anger is transformed into active intention;
4. The actual revenge, at some point in the future, understood as "payback."[57]

What Ricœur breaks down analytically into a series of steps in the process of revenge can be enacted instantaneously (rendering blow for blow, on the spot) or it may take more time to mature (making the revenge sometimes more formidable). In other words, vindictive reparation can be immediate or delayed. As we saw with offenses, revenge can be expressed collectively if the harm concerns a collective person (such as a family or a clan): an attack on the reputation of one member is *de facto* an attack on the collective itself, which can in return exercise vindictive justice not necessarily on the person directly responsible for the offence, but on any member of the offending collective:

> The transition from the psychological level of the vindictive to the social level of the vindicatory takes place when it is not a question of individual revenge, of taking justice into one's own hands, but of doing justice, of avenging the *life capital* of the group to which one belongs, and which has been unjustly belittled, disregarded and disrespected. It is not a question of punishing a guilty person, nor of annihilating an enemy, but of *redressing the balance of power* between adversaries by a face-to-face exchange, before adversity turns into hostility.[58]

Anthropologically speaking, vindictive reparation is assimilated to a system of exchange, much like traditional exchanges of gift and countergift but, as it were, in a negative way: the blow given must be answered by a blow in return, which may generate a new counterblow, and so on. In this sense, vengeance sets out to equalize losses and misdeeds.

If the institution of vengeance is a social and historical fact that must be analyzed as such—described and explained in its logic and its manifestations—we cannot but be challenged by it philosophically. Is only excessive vengeance to be condemned, or is all vengeance by nature unjust? The great founding texts are full of stories of violence that fully justify vengeance in the name of the damage suffered, and especially in the name of the one who exacts vengeance. The theme of the "avenging God" runs through the entire Hebrew Bible, from Exodus,[59] to Deuteronomy[60] to the Psalms.[61]

Vindictive justice is sometimes exhibited in all its implacable logic as violence and excess in the Greek tragedies, from Sophocles' *Electra* to Euripides' *Medea*, the better to denounce it. The genius of Euripides' play is that it arouses, in the reader and the spectator, a feeling of ambivalence, "a suspension of the soul," as Spinoza would say. On the one hand, the spectator can only sympathize with the unjust fate suffered by Medea, betrayed and repudiated by her ex-husband Jason (who marries another woman, the daughter of King Creon), a husband for whom she has sacrificed everything out of passion. On top of this betrayal comes forced exile and separation from her two sons. The terrible misfortune that befalls Medea makes her the victim of a twofold injustice and of twofold male domination: both marital (that of her ex-husband) and political (that of Creon, who seeks to exile her). A sense of injustice wells up in the spectator; an injustice that demands reparation.

On the other hand, the mode of reparation chosen by Medea to exact her own justice generates a sense of dread. The crime of passion is not directed against Jason, but against what is most dear to him (his new wife and two sons). This is no immediate revenge taken on the spur of the moment; it is planned and calculated revenge (making Jason believe that Medea's anger is appeased, in order to trick him and make it possible to poison his new wife). The terrifying logic of revenge reaches the height of unease when Medea prefers to sacrifice her two children rather than see them live far from her, for the sole reason of making Jason suffer. The moral scandal lies in placing the thirst for revenge above maternal love in the economy of virtues and motives for action. Infanticide is the dreadful instrument of her dark design. Medea's righteous indignation, as a wife and mother, cannot justify her decision to sacrifice her own children in order to repair her injured honor.

Beyond Euripides' tragedy, is there really no place for revenge? If it does not correspond to any logic of equivalence, if it is all about excess, revenge will not find an advocate to defend it among philosophers. The scandal of Medea lies not only in the use of revenge as reparation, but also in the excess (and cruelty) with which it is acted out: the excess of retaliation (murder by poisoning and double infanticide) to compensate for disgrace and exile. When, by contrast, it seeks to equalize the original crime in its content, revenge—as Hegel asserts at the end of the paragraphs of the *Elements* devoted to coercion and crime—does indeed correspond to a logic of "retribution": "In this sphere of the immediacy of right, the cancellation [*Aufheben*] of crime is primarily *revenge*, and its *content* is just so far as it constitutes retribution."[62]

Surprisingly, and in another register, Aristotle also comes up with some justifications for revenge, though less in the *Nicomachean Ethics* than in the *Rhetoric* (1386 b 13),[63] as a response to the anger aroused by an affront or an offense. This unabated anger which is, once again, that of Medea toward Jason: "I will bring misfortune upon your house." Revenge is certainly a matter of passion, like anger, which is its primary impulse, and cannot be elevated to the rational conduct of justice. But it is not a wild, irrational passion: it proceeds from a sense of injustice, from indignation, from humiliation. There is therefore, in the desire for revenge, a desire to obtain justice, even if it must be by one's own hand. "Just vengeance" cannot then be dismissed as an oxymoron. Nevertheless, the fact remains that only justice, in the full sense of the word—because it puts a distance between the parties by means of a third party, and because it is governed by reason, which measures, compares, and equalizes—has full legitimacy to regulate our institutions. But when justice is lacking, when justice is absent or corrupted, what remedy is left for subjects to respond to a harm? There may of course always be the radical posture of non-violence, refusing to respond to an affront with revenge, or to meet vengeance with vengeance, exemplified in the Christ-like gesture of loving one's enemy. But can we condemn—in a state that can only be qualified as natural, or pre-legal—a degree of vengeance as a measured response to the injustice suffered? In the absence of a justice system instituted and recognized as such, might not vindictive reparation have good cause to exist?

In taking a more complex view of the relationship between justice and vengeance in terms of reparation, we are not only asking whether "just vengeance" can be justified. As if in a mirror, we are also probing the persistence, as we saw earlier, of a vindictive logic in instituted justice, which culminates in the penalty inflicted on the criminal. The share of "justice" in revenge is the inverted reflection of the share of revenge in justice. The question is whether we can defend ourselves against the "intellectual scandal" of the suffering of the convict, symptomatic of the vindictive underlay of instituted justice. The need to eliminate the remnants of vindictive reparation from penal rationality concerns not only the additional suffering of the criminal, but also the risk of an infinite regression of vengeance itself. The feeling that there are traces of vengeance in the penal sanction could lead to vengeance in return, and so on, a contradiction that Hegel is alert to: "Thus revenge, as the positive action of a *particular* will, becomes a new *infringement*; because of this contradiction, it becomes part of an infinite progression and is inherited indefinitely from generation to generation."[64] If so, crimes would not be prosecuted and punished as "*crimina publica*" but as "*crimina privata*" (§ 102).

In as much as Hegel fully justifies the exercise of punishment (including the death penalty) in the rationality of the law, he offers no escape from the contradiction he denounces. In its determination to punish by inflicting suffering, justice—while clearly distinct from vengeance in "form"—remains dependent on it in "content." The problem therefore remains unchanged: how can one conceive of a judicial reparation of harm that is free of all vindictive logic, a system of justice that limits itself to giving victims their due? The solution would be to decorrelate the sanction from the punishment, that is, to break away from a "punitive" justice that seeks to make the guilty suffer as part of a vindictive process. Such a solution clashes head-on with the criminal justice system and with part of our common sense, especially for certain criminals (child-killers, pedophiles, rapists, war criminals). The gravity of certain crimes generates an immediate emotional response: the criminals must pay for what they have done. There is, in these knee-jerk reactions, something of the anger of which Aristotle speaks: a passion perhaps, or rather an emotion, but one that proceeds from "just" indignation about particularly heinous crimes.

And yet, if instituted justice is indeed governed by an ideal of reason, the judge has no other choice than to keep indignation at arm's length when it flirts with the anger of vengeance, at least in the name of a regulating ideal, even at the risk of being misunderstood and pilloried by public opinion. Eradicating any form of "hardship" from the sentence would undoubtedly be an objective as undesirable as it would be impracticable, at least when the real or presumed threat that the criminal represents makes it necessary, for everyone's right to security, to isolate him at least for a time from his fellow human beings. But isolation necessarily means deprivation for the prisoner. This share of hardship in the sentence is not *a priori* correlated with a vindictive logic or with the will to make the convict suffer, beyond the retribution of the victim. It is less an act of punishment for the deed committed than an act of prevention aimed at future crimes. It is what justice, and more generally the state, owes to its citizens to ensure their protection. The essential thing is that this element of hardship, of which prison isolation is only one technique among others (and not always the most effective), serves an objective of prevention and not of vindictive reparation, on pain of falling back into a mortifying contradiction. The essential thing is that the sanction should adhere as strictly as possible to the compensation of the victim for the harm suffered. The essential thing is that the judicial decision puts an end to the dispute, by separating "mine" from "yours," drawing a line under the uncertainty that hangs over the case and rendering what is due to each. It is this "definitive judgment," at least until all avenues of recourse have been exhausted, that ideally makes it possible to demarcate instituted justice from vengeance, which is potentially without end. The more the judicial decision eliminates the vindictive supplement of suffering for the criminal, the more it will be recognized as just by the convict him or herself.

THE PROMISES OF RESTORATIVE JUSTICE

This diminution in the vindictive component of the penalty may open the way to a justice that is less punitive than "reconstructive," to use the term that Antoine Garapon takes from the ethics of Jean-Marc Ferry.[65] The goal is not directly to punish, but above all to *acknowledge*: to acknowledge the complaint and the account of the victim (if their loss is proven) and their request for reparation, but also to acknowledge the justifications and reasons for action of the guilty party (if their guilt is proven), to mutually acknowledge the fairness of the decision of justice (if it is purged of vengeful anger), and to acknowledge—where applicable—the sincerity of the convicted person's request for forgiveness or their repentance for the harm done. This reconstructive justice has a "long-term end," as Ricœur would say. It does not have, like the "short-term end" of corrective justice, the aim of separating and sharing out, but rather of "sharing in" something, of re-weaving, re-mediating, re-integrating: "The end-point is neither the law, nor the victim, nor the accused; what ideas of restoration and reconstruction ultimately refer to is the organic bond that holds a human community together."[66] This long-term end of justice can still be called reparative, no longer in the sense of just retribution, but in the sense of being reincorporated into the same body after having been "separated." This remediation, at least as a regulating ideal, seeks to rebuild the social fabric and some degree of inter-understanding after the phase of conflict: "This justice of listening and dialogue aims less at repairing the past than at making people responsible for the future."[67] The utopia of reconstruction seeks, at the same time, to erase the traces of resentment after a sharing-out that fails to bring satisfaction to everyone.

In this "sharing-in," in this restoration of the bond, the convicted person, as well as the victim, must have a place. This is another, more positive, consequence of the recognition of the offender's rationality, which culminates in rehabilitation programs. If only a rational person can be punished, then *a fortiori* there is all the more chance they can be rehabilitated. Rehabilitation does not aim to forget the crime (or the victims), but to give former criminals a destiny that does not eternally chain them to their misdeeds, that is, the right to be able to start something new, an *initiative*, Hannah Arendt would argue, on the strict condition that their release, even on probation, does not represent a proven danger to others (often the subject of lengthy arguments before the sentence enforcement judge): "It is good for the potential victim that we are, as the bearer of the right to security, and perhaps also as a potential aggressor, that detainees retain the prospect of reintegration into the community of citizens and of full restitution of the rights pertaining to citizenship."[68]

Rehabilitation is not directly included in the sanction; instead, it is offered as a potential next step toward a different future for the offender, and as additional assurance that punishment is not indexed to vindictive reparation. Without even having to assume that the criminal is a product of society—in the sense that society, at least for certain crimes, has some kind of debt towards them—rehabilitation aims, at a more fundamental level, to bridge another kind of distance:[69] from exclusion and privation to the prospect of a new inclusion, to bring the prisoner back into the social body, provided that they no longer represent a potential threat to others. It is in this spirit that the French Penal Code defines rehabilitation as the act of restoring to the convicted person all the rights that he or she has lost: restoring the convicted person's honor and probity by erasing the conviction and any disqualifications and incapacities that result from it. French law further distinguishes between two types of rehabilitation: either "as of right" after the main sentence has been served (Article 133–12 et seq. of the Penal Code), or pursuant to a court decision (Articles 782 and 783 of the Penal Procedure Code). In this sense, rehabilitation allows for a form of forgetting which is well expressed in the phrase "erasing the conviction and any disqualifications and incapacities," enabling the former offender to rebuild a set of capabilities (freedom to speak, to act, to exercise their civic rights, etc.).[70] But this forgetting is only relative: the trace of the criminal's act is preserved on a judicial file and can be used against them in the event, for example, of a repeat offence. Rehabilitation, while it erases the conviction, does not erase the memory.

What Garapon calls "reconstructive justice" and Ricœur "the long-term end of justice" bear strong similarities to the notion of "restorative justice" which has gained considerable momentum in recent decades as a way of moving on from a solely punitive or retributive logic of justice.[71] Rehabilitation, even included in the Penal Code, is a step in this direction in that it provides for a follow-up to the sentence, a possibility of reconstructing the convicted person, beyond the sanction, and reintegrating them into society.

The principles of restorative justice offer conceptual frameworks and procedures for conflict resolution that are far more comprehensive and complex. First theorized and institutionalized in the English-speaking world in the 1970s and 1980s, restorative justice rose to prominence in France in a particular context that Professor Robert Cario, one of its leading advocates in the country, ascribes to three factors: "the crisis of modern criminal law, confiscated by a devastating penal populism; the consideration of the victim's right to a fair trial; and the (re)-discovery of traditional practices of conflict resolution."[72] Whereas traditional criminal justice sees the offence as an attack on the state and its values, looks essentially toward the past of the offence (except when looking to the future in order to prevent re-offending), and prioritizes sanction and punishment, restorative justice sees the offence as an attack on interpersonal relationships (and above all on the integrity of the victim), looks essentially to the future, to the reconstruction of human relations (resocializing the offender, repairing the victim, restoring social peace), and prioritizes mediation, dialogue and recognition. It is this search for social peace or social harmony that clearly brings it closer to the "long-term end of justice," where it is no longer a question of deciding between the parties in conflict, but of mending the tears in the social fabric.

The first paradox of restorative justice is that, while it differs from the criminal justice system in its principles and procedures, and clearly presents itself as an alternative, it is generally integrated into the criminal justice systems of the jurisdictions that have sought to experiment with it. In other words, restorative justice constitutes an alternative or parallel path within a wider criminal justice system. This first paradox is reinforced by the fact that the same jurisdictions may demand, for the same case, a traditional penal outcome (sanction and punishment of the offender) while at the same time calling for a restorative outcome (meetings between victims and offenders, acknowledgement of guilt, resocialization of the offender). The second paradox of restorative justice is that, though the term is a new one and reflects new approaches, it is at the same time rooted in traditional and sometimes very ancient conflict resolution practices (particularly in New Zealand and Northern Canada), some of which have subsequently been incorporated into positive law.

What makes restorative justice of particular relevance to us is, of course, its close connection to the logic of repair (so much so that it is sometimes called "reparative justice," as a semantic equivalent). While restorative justice is clearly distinct from criminal justice, it does share certain attributes with corrective justice. The main such attribute—which gives full meaning to the adjective "restorative"—consists in re-establishing a balance, in redressing a situation in the wake of an offense, and is clearly distinguished, despite the potential semantic confusion, from the principle of the "restoration" of the law inherent in penal logic. We are not very far here from the principle of equalization dear to Aristotle. In the same vein, Howard Zehr does not hesitate to make "righting the balance" or "putting right" one of the main objectives of "restoration." This objective creates an obligation for the offender towards the victim: "this implies a responsibility on the part of the offender to, as much as possible, take active steps to repair the harm to the victim (and perhaps the impacted community)."[73] However, unlike corrective justice and the principle of civil liability, which seek above all to reestablish a situation by restituting or by imposing monetary compensation, restorative justice also sets itself psychological, moral and social goals.

In Zehr's model, the victim is indeed at the center of the restorative process, but at the same time—and necessarily—at the intersection of a relationship that involves the offender and what he calls the "community." There is no restorative justice when the victim is the only stakeholder. Moreover, the needs or expectations of the victims, as identified by Zehr, are not limited to material compensation for the harm suffered. They also expect sincere and voluntary acknowledgement of the harm committed by the offender and, in certain cases, acknowledgement of the responsibility of the wider community. These conditions are not *a priori* requirements of the principle of civil liability or of corrective justice in general, for which the obligation to make reparation can be met without any formal act of acknowledgement by the offender. This acknowledgement implies particular procedures (dialogue circles, post-sentence meetings), and, with few exceptions, the voluntary presence of the victim, offender and community representatives (including members of the families concerned). Victims may also expect a form of "healing," according to the theorist, in a register that clearly borrows from psychology: "It is possible that a victim can be helped toward healing when an offender works toward making things right—whether actually or symbolically. Many victims, however, are ambivalent about the term 'healing,' because of the sense of finality or termination that it connotes."[74]

The second originality of the restorative justice system consists in the place given to the offender. Unlike in criminal or civil justice, the offender cannot be summoned or obliged to participate in restorative justice, but only, in contrast to the status of a defendant, "invited to engage" with the reparative process. Restorative justice cannot function with the logic of coercion alone. Especially so for the victim, who can legitimately accept or refuse to take part in the process. In the model imagined and, in part, practiced by Zehr, offenders are certainly encouraged to acknowledge their faults, but also to be recognized as victims themselves, at least if one considers that "many offenders have indeed been victimized or traumatized in significant ways. Many other offenders perceive themselves to have been victimized."[75] Zehr is insistent, however, that recognition of the offenders' life history must not serve as an alibi for an "excuse culture" nor detract from the offender's responsibility (acknowledgement of the offence is a precondition for the success of restorative justice). This practice must, however, take account of the offender's own "needs," to understand the reasons or explain the causes that led to their act, both for the offender and for the victim, and indeed for the "community." The system claims not to be accusatory, but instead reflective and "reconstructive." It also aims, by refusing to reduce the offender to the offence, to create the conditions for better reintegration into society, even if this is preceded, according to the penal logic, by a period of incarceration.

The third originality of the model lies in the role devolved to "communities," or at least to some of their representatives, both to recognize, where applicable, their share in the responsibility for the offending act and to support the process of "restoration" and mediation. The role of the third party, who cannot be a judge in the traditional sense, is not to pronounce a new sentence nor, should they be so minded, to contest the sentence originally handed down. Theirs is above all a pacifying mission: to promote dialogue and mutual understanding. In order for their offer of mediation and conciliation to be acceptable to the protagonists, the third party must be impartial and must employ collaborative and inclusive processes.

From the affirmation of these grand principles to the concrete practices that draw inspiration from them, there are sometimes significant gaps or at least highly specific modalities of implementation. Two examples will serve as illustration. First, the "peacemaking circles," instituted in the Aboriginal communities of Canada. These ancient practices of conflict resolution in First Nations communities have been integrated into the Canadian criminal justice system, notably to curb juvenile delinquency. In addition to "sentencing circles" to determine penalties in criminal cases, there are "healing circles" that are designed to be restorative rather than punitive:

> In a circle process, participants arrange themselves in a circle. They pass a "talking piece" around the circle to assure that each person speaks, one at a time, in the order in which each is seated in the circle. A set of values, or even a philosophy, is often articulated as part of the process—values that emphasize respect, the value of each participant, integrity, the importance of speaking from the heart, and so on.[76]

Victims, offenders, family members and community representatives are included in the encounter, with "circle keepers" (often Elders, due to their legitimacy capital) acting as "facilitators" of the discussion, and of the process of acknowledgement and reparation.

Another restorative justice mechanism, "penal mediation," inspired by Anglo-American models, was introduced into France by a law passed on January 4, 1999 (supplemented by further legislation in 1999, 2004, 2010 and 2014) in a context of penal inflation, prison overcrowding and high reoffending rates (especially in cases of petty delinquency). For the legislator, it was a matter of finding alternative modes of judicial action. The decision to initiate penal mediation belongs to the Public Prosecutor who can, depending on the case, make the opposing parties themselves act as protagonists in the conflict resolution process, under the aegis of a "penal mediator," a third party held to be impartial. In principle, penal mediation, the solution of choice in the French model, requires the agreement of both parties (victim and offender), which conditions the process of restoring the social bond.

According to Paul Mbanzoulou,[77] a specialist in the field, the principle of penal mediation has been diverted from its original objectives by the law of July 9, 2010, which modified the conditions of mediation. The process now depends solely on the "agreement of the victim" (in place of the "agreement of the parties," which included the offenders). By focusing only on the "needs of the victim," the 2010 law circumscribes one of the key principles of restorative justice, which is intended to be collaborative and "inclusive" of all parties (offender included). The penal mediation provided for by the 2010 law is, he claims, "restorative" in appearance only. In fact, if that is indeed the case, it also reveals the limits of some of the principles of restorative justice when applied to certain cases. The 2010 law focuses more specifically on "violence against women within couples, and the impact of such violence on children." If spousal violence puts mothers or partners in direct danger of death, it is hard to imagine, in these extreme cases, how the presence of offenders could be justified. Zehr does not hesitate to acknowledge these cases, which may prevent a "direct" encounter between victim and aggressor.[78]

The fact remains that the restorative justice model, for all its powerful philosophical and legal promises, has at least three limitations when it comes to its applications. The first lies in the often justified but sometimes (depending on the case) excessive importance given to the victim relative to the other protagonists, and thus to the detriment of the "needs" of the offender, in Zehr's terminology. The second, diametrically opposed, lies in the sometimes excessive importance given to the offender, whose "needs," or even the recognition of his or her own victimhood, may distort and deny the "needs" of the actual victim. The third limitation comes from Zehr's own model, in of the importance it gives to "communities." Though very well suited to certain traditional societies (New Zealand Maoris, indigenous

Amerindian villages, etc.) the model is less relevant to individualistic societies where the sense of belonging to a community does not run so deep.

Legal reparation becomes necessary when social control fails. Though each evolves in its own specific domain (biological, psychological, moral, social), each register of repair is always liable to affect the others. And though repair is a global phenomenon, a "total fact" that never presents in a unified manner, but rather in diversified and analogical ways—as repair, reparation and reparations, to say nothing of remedy, remediation and restoration—every order of repair is primed to interact correlatively with the others.

Law-based mediation, however, and the judicial process of reparation, present singular characteristics. On the one hand, the intervention of a *third party* (judge, state, mediator) with sole authority to arbitrate the dispute and to justify, or not, the award of reparations. On the other, the existence of a sophisticated codification, specific procedures, and complex mechanisms, without equivalent in the other modes of *reparatio*. There is, however, a common substrate between legal reparation and other modes of social repair. Reparation is a response to two types of loss that must be clearly distinguished: on one side, the violation of the sacredness of an order, the transgression of a law or command; on the other, the violation of another person's physical or moral integrity. At the level of justice, this dual response corresponds, in the first case, to reparation as the *restoration* of law (by punishing the guilty), and in the second, to reparation as the *retribution* of the victim (for the harm suffered). This conceptual clarification is essential for understanding the issues that arise consubstantially with legal reparation: the persistence of a vindictive logic in the restoration of the law (making the criminal pay for transgressing the order of the law); and the persistence of incommensurability between the nature of the harm suffered and the nature of the reparation determined by law. And it is here that the irreparable emerges to disrupt any attempt at legal reparation.

The fact that these issues run through the history of human societies, in their own specific ways, is sufficient justification to sketch out their anthropological implications and discuss their philosophical propositions, as we did with Aristotle. The philosophical scale is not sufficient, however, either to account for the social and cultural diversity of legal mechanisms of reparation in positive law (including forms of alternative justice such as vendetta), or to evaluate their historical transformations. Historicizing legal reparation makes it possible to understand why, today, it gives rise to questions about the unprecedented place of the victim in Western societies, at the turning point of a "therapeutic age of reparation." The end purpose of justice is now not only to restore law, to compensate the victim, to rehabilitate the guilty and to protect society, but also to relieve the victim's suffering. This "therapeutic" orientation of legal reparation resonates with what we called, at the psychological level, the "age of self-repair," peculiar to the "expressivist" culture of modern Western societies. Never before have our societies been bombarded with so many calls to repair ourselves, leading to an age of all-out "psychologization" of repair and reparation, with very real effects on legislative changes, court hearings, and the way justice is dispensed. This recent structural transformation of justice does not mean, however, that its other purposes have become obsolete. A pragmatic sociology of reparation mechanisms—reparative *dispositifs*—reveals just how attached legal professionals are to ensuring that the alleviation of victims' pain does not become the primary aim of judicial decision-making.

Faced with certain dead-ends, engendered by our criminal and civil justice systems alike, restorative justice—some of whose principles are directly drawn from traditional conflict resolution methods—has risen to prominence over recent decades. While repairing the wrongs and harms done to the victim remains at the heart of the system, its originality, when it is not circumvented in practice, consists in the place given to the offender, with the objective of restoring interpersonal relations. Looking beyond the sole logic of retribution, reparation can then be thought of and experienced as a "long-term end" of justice.

NOTES

1. A. Honneth, *Ce que social veut dire. II Les pathologies de la raison*. Paris: Gallimard, 2015 (the citation is specific to the introduction to the French edition of his *Pathologien der Vernunft*).

2. M. Foucault (*Naissance de la biopolitique* [The Birth of Biopolitics]. Paris: Gallimard, 2004) clearly demonstrates how France's new ruling elite progressively came round to this neo-liberal position.

3. The government may, however, be held indirectly responsible toward the most socially vulnerable groups due to the neo-liberal policies implemented over the last thirty years.

4. F. Fischbach, *Manifeste pour une philosophie sociale*. Paris: La découverte, 2009.

5. G. Le Blanc, *Vies ordinaires, vies précaires*. Paris: Seuil, 2007, p. 217.

6. F. Fischbach, *Manifeste pour une philosophie sociale, op. cit.*, p. 91.

7. Dependence can be defined both in terms of what cannot be done without another's help and by what lies under another's authority: "What these definitions share is that dependence is thought of as an asymmetric relationship; but whereas in the first case the asymmetry results from a constitutive limitation, in the second, it is seen

from the angle of constraint, as a barrier that can and must be lifted" (M. Garrau & A. Le Goff, *Care, justice et dépendance*. Paris: PUF, 2010, p. 12).

8. J. Tronto, *Moral Boundaries: A Political Argument for an Ethic of Care*. London: Routledge, 1993.

9. *Ibid*., p. 103.

10. C. Gilligan, *In a Different Voice: Psychological Theory and Women's Development*. Cambridge MA: Harvard University Press, 2016.

11. G. Le Blanc, *L'invisibilité sociale*. Paris: PUF, 2009, p. 167.

12. Quoted in P. Cingolani, *L'exil du précaire*. Paris: Klincksiek, 1986, p. 99.

13. In the context of her fieldwork investigation into the publicizing of the use of torture under the Chilean dictatorship, Paola Diaz highlights the translation and configuration operations involved in converting the victims' lived experience into demands for reparations according to the terms codified by transitional justice (Paola Diaz, "Les chemins de la publicisation de la torture au Chili," *SociologieS* [online], Dossiers, L'expérience latino-américaine de la sociologie pragmatique francophone, posted May 23, 2017, accessed March 28, 2019. http:// journals.openedition.org/sociologies/6281).

14. Aristotle, *The Nicomachean Ethics*, trans. D. Ross. Oxford: Oxford Univ. Press, 2009, p. 81.

15. *Ibid*., p. 84.

16. *Ibid*., p. 85.

17. *Ibid*., p. 86. In the actual practice of corrective justice, however, the judge may in some cases take into consideration the "persons," either by way of mitigation (for example by taking account of the social background of the accused) or aggravation (for example if the accused is also deemed to be dishonest).

18. *Ibid*., p. 86.

19. It is in this sense that, in two rulings given on July 11, 2017 (no. 16–83.581 and no. 16–85.580), the Criminal Chamber of the Court of Cassation reiterated that the victim may not accumulate multiple compensation payments from different persons as reparation for the same harm.

20. V. Heuzé, "Une reconsidération du principe de la réparation intégrale," https://www.courdecassation.fr/colloques_activites_formation_4/2005_2033/reparation_integrale_8065.html#_ftn1.

21. *Ibid*.

22. *Ibid*.

23. https://solidarites-sante.gouv.fr/ministere/actors/partenaires/article/nomenclature-des-postes-de-prejudices-rapport-de-m-dintilhac. The list distinguishes between "patrimonial" damage (a pecuniary loss that is temporary or permanent, such as education-related losses) and "extrapatrimonial" damage (a non-pecuniary loss that may be temporary, permanent or evolving, as in the case of pathologies like cancer).

24. In practice, however, the use of the Dintilhac nomenclature has become common practice in the courts, and an accepted reference both for judges and for experts and insurers. It is also very useful for victims, to help them list and categorize their injuries. My thanks to Marie Delbard for kindly enlightening me on these points.

25. The *Gazette du Palais*, founded in 1881, is a French review specializing in legal analysis and forward-looking legal research, considered authoritative by legal professionals in France.

26. In the case of collective (e.g., air transport) accidents, insurers set their own scales, but they are also bound by national legislation and international conventions (in particular the Montreal Convention, of which France has been a signatory since 2004) that oblige carriers to specify an amount of compensation per passenger, to pay advances without delay to natural persons, so that they can meet their immediate economic needs, and to maintain sufficient insurance to cover all liabilities. To assist the victims of such accidents, France has set up the Conseil National d'Aide aux Victimes (CNAV) created by decree in 1999: http://www.justice.gouv.fr/aide-aux-victimes-10044/la-justice-et-les-associations-10278/le-conseil-national-de-laide-aux-victimes-23095.html.

27. To avoid confusion, I do not intend to use the notion of retribution in one of its philosophical and legal senses ("retributivsm") according to which the purpose of the penalty is to "take retribution" on the offender or criminal (the Latin *"retributio"* also means "render like for like"). I prefer to see the penalty as "restoration of the law" (rather than as retribution). In other words, I associate "retribution" not with what is inflicted on the criminal but with what is due to the victim.

28. Hegel, *Elements of the Philosophy of Right*, trans. H.B. Nisbet. Cambridge: Cambridge Univ. Press, 2003.

29. *Ibid.*, § 100, p. 126.

30. D. Fassin & R. Rechtman, *The Empire of Trauma. An Inquiry into the Condition of Victimhood*, trans. R. Gomme. Princeton: Princeton Univ. Press, 2007, p. 278.

31. See in particular Act no. 2000–516 of 15 June 2000 reinforcing the protection of the presumption of innocence and of the rights of victims (notably Title II: https://www.legifrance.gouv.fr/affichTexte.do?cidTexte=JORFTEXT000000765204).

32. J. Porée, "Justice et réparation," in *Corpo, saúde e espaço público*, volume 1. Coimbra: Ariadne, 2006, p. 23.

33. See in particular the "Loi Badinter" (Loi 85–677 of 5 July 1985) aimed at improving the situation of victims of traffic accidents and accelerating compensation procedures.

34. N. Dodier & J. Barbot, "The Force of *Dispositifs*," trans. M.C. Behrent, *Annales. Histoire, Sciences Sociales,* Vol. 71, Issue 2, 2016, p. 422 of the French original.

35. These trials resulted from the damage caused to patients who, during childhood, were administered a hormone to treat growth disorders. The unintended side effects, which led to the deaths of 120 people, were caused by the contamination of an infectious agent (a prion) responsible for a fatal neurodegenerative disease (Creutzfeldt-Jakob). The authors followed the hearings of the first criminal trial, from February to May 2008.

36. J. Barbot & N. Dodier, "Dealing with compassion at work. Strategic reflexivity among court lawyers," trans. C. Hinton, *Sociologie du travail,* 57 (2015) e51.

37. *Ibid.*, e58.

38. J. Porée, "Justice et réparation," *op.cit.*, p. 23.

39. M. Foucault, *Discipline and Punish*, trans. A. Sheridan. New York: Vintage Books, 1991, p. 58.

40. *Ibid.*, p. 49.

41. To say that victims took second place does not mean that they had no place. In the criminal law of the Ancien Régime, the actual word *victime* is admittedly little used until the very end of the eighteenth century; criminal lawyers preferred to use the term *plaignant* (plaintiff). It is also true, as Eric Wenzel underlines, that the *victime* is seen mainly as the agent who enables the instigation of legal proceedings following a crime or offense. But the injured parties can, in some circumstances, obtain damages for the harm suffered: "It is worth pointing out that these ways of taking the victim into account originate in the medieval 'pecuniary composition,' largely superseded by the inquisitional procedure during the later Middle Ages, the main difference being that the pecuniary composition was a matter of private law, whereas civil reparation, by integrating the penalty system, is more a matter of public law (E. Wenzel, "Quelle place pour la victime dans l'ancien droit pénal ?" In: *Les victimes, des oubliées de l'histoire?* [online]. Rennes: Presses universitaires de Rennes, 2000 (generated March 20, 2020). Available online: http://books.openedition.org/pur/18568. ISBN: 9782753523326. DOI: https://doi.org/10.4000/books.pur.1856). Going still further back in time, to Greco-Roman Antiquity, the notion of "victim" does not have the same signification as for the Moderns, and *a fortiori* for our contemporaries: the *victima* is "the individual or the animal who is willingly or unwillingly sacrificed for the good of the City" (*ibid.*). Which is not to say that the person who suffers a loss or injury has no place in legal proceedings, though "victim" is often assimilated to the person who seeks revenge (for a detailed study of law and pre-law in Greek Antiquity, see L. Gernet, *Droit et institutions en Grèce antique*. Paris: Flammarion, 1982).

42. *Ibid.*, 121.

43. *Ibid.*, p. 126.

44. Figures on current rates of reoffending need to be handled with care, however, as they vary from one country to another (being much lower, for example, in the Nordic countries, which increasingly opt for non-custodial penal policies). In its 2013 social survey (*France, portrait social*), France's national statistical office INSEE reveals that 4 out of 10 people sentenced in France are reoffenders. The rates differ depending on the category of offence: low for serious crimes, high for cases of minor delinquency.

45. Modern penal reform initiatives undoubtedly invented a new model of social control, which has spread to other institutions (schools, factories, etc.) beyond the prison walls. What Foucault does not emphasize, however, is that this has made possible a form of inclusion—even within a process of exclusion (confinement)—by including criminals among the ranks of rational beings, capable of being repaired, and even of being restored to their rights (on this point, see Hans Joas, *The Sacredness of the Person*. Washington, DC: Georgetown Univ. Press, 2013, pp. 47–48.

46. M. Foucault, *Discipline and Punish*, *op. cit.*, p. 16.

47. Alternative sentencing measures include conditional release, suspension of sentence on medical grounds, day parole, non-custodial placement, and placement

under electronic surveillance (tagging). Prisoners may also be released on parole under certain conditions.

48. As Guillaume Mouralis shows, the victims at the Nuremberg trials were thought of as collective and national rather than as "suffering individually." Though some individual victims were called as witnesses by the prosecution, they were not accorded the same place and recognition as at the Eichmann trial, or during the second *épuration* in France, which began in the 1980s (G. Mouralis, "Retrouver les victimes. Naufragés et rescapés au procès de Nuremberg," *Droit et société*, 2019/2 (no. 102), pp. 243–60). See also A. Wieviorka, *The Era of the Witness*, trans. J. Stark. Ithaca: Cornell Univ. Press, 2006.

49. https://www.legifrance.gouv.fr/affichCodeArticle.do?cidTexte=LEGITEXT000006070721&idArticle=LEGIARTI000006437044.

50. It is important to distinguish between a fine (or fixed penalty), which is an amount owed to the state in the name of criminal liability—and thus in the name of a punitive logic—and damages, which are an indemnity owed to the victim for the harm suffered in the name of civil liability. Strictly speaking, while a fine is not a "reparation" (in favor of the victim), it can be so in a broad sense, in the name of a restoration of the law. However, some legal systems accept *punitive* damages (USA) or *exemplary* damages (UK) far in excess of the damages actually suffered, in order to penalize a particular behavior. In this case, civil and criminal liability merge into one.

51. The same offense can lead to multiple harms (burglary, for example, causes material and moral harm).

52. Procedures vary from one legislation to another. In France, the plaintiff must file a complaint and evaluate both the harm suffered and the estimated compensation required (if the case is referred to a judge, the award cannot be higher than the amount initially demanded by the victim). It is up to the victim to prove in his or her complaint that the harm was caused by an offence, that the harm is real (caused by indisputable damage), that the harm concerns him or her directly, that the person from whom he or she is demanding reparation is indeed responsible for the harm, and that the harm can be evaluated. The amounts at stake in the dispute will determine which court is competent to hear the case.

53. J. Barbot & N. Dodier, "The Force of *Dispositifs*," *op. cit.*, p. 431 of the French original.

54. *Ibid.*, p. 432.

55. P. Ricœur, "Le juste, la justice et son échec," *Cahiers de l'Herne* (spécial Ricœur). Paris: 2004, p. 293.

56. Nebi Bardhoshi, On the Anthropology of Blood-Feuds During a Time of 'Total Crisis,'" *Ethnologie française*, 2017/2 (no. 166), pp. 331–40. DOI: 10.3917/ethn.172.0331. URL: https://www.cairn.info/revue-ethnologie-francaise-2017-2-page-331.htm.

57. P. Ricœur, "Le juste, la justice et son échec," *op. cit.*, p. 296.

58. R. Verdier, *Vengeance. Le face-à-face victime/agresseur*. Paris: Ed. Autrement, 2004, p. 3.

59. "You shall not bow down to them or worship them; for I, the Lord your God, am a jealous God, punishing the children for the sin of the parents to the third and fourth generation of those who hate me," Ex. 20:5.

60. "It is mine to avenge; I will repay. In due time their foot will slip; their day of disaster is near and their doom rushes upon them," Deut. 32:35.

61. "The Lord is a God who avenges. O God who avenges, shine forth!," Ps. 94:1.

62. Hegel, *Elements of the Philosophy of Right, op. cit.*, § 102, p. 130.

63. Aristotle, *On Rhetoric*, trans. G.A. Kennedy. New York: Oxford University Press, 2007.

64. Hegel, *Elements of the Philosophy of Right, op. cit.*, § 102, p. 130.

65. Antoine Garapon, Thierry Puech, Frédéric Gros, *Et ce sera Justice. Punir en démocratie*. Paris: Odile Jacob, 2001.

66. P. Ricœur, "Le juste, la justice et son échec," *op. cit.*, p. 301.

67. *Ibid.*, p. 303.

68. *Ibid.*, p. 305.

69. P. Ricœur, "Sanction, réhabilitation, pardon," *Le juste*. Paris: Ed. Esprit, 1995, p. 202.

70. The question of the length of the sentence is of crucial importance here: beyond a certain duration, the convict is so desocialized that the prisoner's ability to readjust to life on the outside is undermined. At the same time, the judge must take account of the sentence handed down at the time of judgment (perhaps with "minimum terms"), the inmate's conduct during incarceration, the socialization environment into which the person is to be released, and the potential danger they represent. The rehabilitation requirement, as a way out of the cycle of revenge, constantly comes up against the requirement to prevent harm and protect society.

71. See, at the international level, the resolution adopted in 2002 by the United Nations Economic and Social Council on the basic principles of restorative justice and the EU Council framework decision of 15 March 2001: https://eur-lex.europa.eu/LexUriServ/LexUriServ.do?uri=OJ:L:2001:082:0001:0004:EN:PDF.

72. R. Cario (ed.), *La justice restaurative. Une utopie qui marche?* Paris: L'Harmattan, 2010, p. 9.

73. H. Zehr, *The Little Book of Restorative justice*. New York: Good Books, 2014, p. 28. If we follow Zehr's wheel metaphor, repairing wrongs and harms constitutes the center, the hub.

74. *Ibid.*, p. 29.

75. *Ibid.*, p. 30.

76. *Ibid.*, p. 45.

77. P. Mbanzoulou, "La médiation pénale en France à l'aune de la loi du 9 juillet 2010," *La justice restaurative. Une utopie qui marche?, op. cit.*, pp. 16–32.

78. The new provisions in the law of August 15, 2014, set out to rectify this bias by doing more to include the offender in the restorative mechanism. Article 10–1, for example, seeks to fulfill the basic prerequisites of restorative justice (inclusion of the victim and the offender, voluntary adherence, impartial third party, etc.): "A measure of restorative justice is one which allows a victim as well as an offender to be actively involved in the resolution of the difficulties resulting from the offense and more particularly in the reparation of any caused harm. This measure can only be implemented

once the victim and the offender have been fully informed about it and have expressly agreed to participate. It is implemented by a purposefully trained, independent third party, under the supervision of the judicial authority or the prison administration upon request. The process is confidential, unless otherwise stated by the parties or when a superior interest, linked to the necessity of prevention or repression of offenses, justifies the fact that the information relating to the implementation of the measure should be brought to the attention of the public prosecutor" (trans. Robert Cario, Benjamin Sayous) (https://www.legifrance.gouv.fr/affichTexte.do?cidTexte=JORFTEXT000029362502&categorieLien=cid).

Chapter Five

History in Debt

Tuesday, May 20, 2014, Bellefontaine, Martinique. 6:30 pm. Local women are selling fresh drinks and fruit at the windows of their little shacks. It is still very hot. Down in the harbor, everyone's attention is focused on the fishing of small mackerel: a large net is slowly being dragged ashore by a dozen fishermen. Nearby, some people are heading towards the square in front of the town hall. The brass band can already be heard. I have arranged to meet Garcin Malsa here, an emblematic figure in the political life of Martinique,[1] known locally for organizing the "Convoy for Reparations" ("Konvwa pou reparasyon" in Creole) since 2001.

In the early years, the event brought together a handful of activists, mostly from the pro-independence movement, but over the years it has attracted a growing number of supporters. On May 20, 2014, between 500 and 1,000 people came to swell the ranks. The "convoy" begins its march after the national commemorations of slavery on May 10 and ends on May 22 (a holiday in Martinique, since 1983, marking the abolition of slavery). Between the two commemorations—one national, observed throughout the French Republic, the other local to Martinique—the itinerary is much the same from one year to the next, starting at Saint-Anne in the south of the island and finishing at Le Prêcheur in the north (a municipality headed by another figurehead of local independence, Marcelin Nadeau), passing each evening through a new settlement along the Martinique coast.

The organization of this event is orchestrated mainly by the Mouvement International pour les Réparations (International Movement for Reparations) or MIR, founded by Malsa in 2001. MIR is above all active in Martinique, but also has relays in other Caribbean islands such as Guadeloupe. It presents itself as an anti-imperialist and environmentalist movement, and has made itself known in metropolitan France by filing a complaint against the French state for the harm caused by slavery, jointly with the Conseil Représentatif des Associations Noires (Representative Council of Black Associations) or CRAN, under the *presidency of Louis-George Tin. MIR is pressing for the creation of a committee of experts to list and characterize the traumas suffered. At the financial level, the organization is asking for the payment of 240 billion euros to the "Martinican people."* In addition to this pecuniary compensation, it demands that a duty of remembrance be honored by way of moral reparation. On April 17, 2019, after several years of legal proceedings (dating back to 2005), the Court of Cassation rejected the complaint filed by MIR on the grounds that the articles of the Penal Code punishing crimes against humanity "came into force on March 1, 1994, and cannot be applied to events prior to that date." The activists now hope to take their fight to the European level by bringing their case before the European Court of Human Rights.*

On May 20, 2014, in Bellefontaine, the activists' numbers continue to swell before the departure of the procession at 7 pm. I join Garcin Malsa, who, microphone in hand, quickly introduces me and asks me to explain in a few words the reason for my presence at the event. I say I am here for an investigation into the memory of slavery and the question of reparations. The mic is then passed to Louis-George Tin, who explains, at length, the need for reparations for the damage caused by slavery. At 7:00 pm, as the sun sets on the horizon, Garcin Malsa takes a torch in hand and signals the official start of the procession, while several Creole bands get into marching order. The tropical heat is almost stifling. Activists wear red scarves, a sign of revolt, and sing old slave songs in Creole. The symbolism on display is not about victimhood (minute of silence, laying of wreaths, etc.); rather, it reflects the sense of struggle, typical of what I call the anti-colonialist commemorative regime, by opposition to the victim-centered abolitionist commemorative regime (which focuses on celebrating the abolitionist Republic and on paying homage to the victims of slavery).[2] *The meaning imbued in the struggle is twofold: against metropolitan colonialism, for reparations.*

After an hour and a half of marching at a fair pace, with torches lighting the convoy's long procession through the darkness under the inquisitive gaze of onlookers lining the coastal road, there is a carefully organized break. A team of activists has already set up small stands halfway along the route where everyone can refresh themselves with free water or iced tea and recuperate with dried bananas. The break is short-lived, however, and the pace quickens still faster afterwards, until it is almost a military march. The Convoy for Reparations reverses the symbols of history: the procession, reminiscent of the old lines of chained slaves, now stands tall in the name of the struggle to repair history. At its head, Garcin Malsa, still holding a torch, exerts a real fascination over the other marchers.

After three hours of walking we arrive, exhausted, in St. Pierre, first through the narrow streets of old colonial houses, greeted by residents on the sidewalks or leaning out of the windows of their homes, before reaching the town hall square, literally packed with people. A tape recording of excerpts from Aimé Césaire's speeches on colonialism plays on repeat, until Malsa gives a speech in Creole on the demands for financial reparations addressed to the French state.

The bands then join together for a final concert before the marchers disperse at the end of the night. Tomorrow evening, we will once again take to the road with the Convoy for Reparations, this time from Saint-Pierre to Le Prêcheur, in an even larger procession.

This long descriptive passage, taken from my fieldwork journal (2014) on memory and reparations for slavery in the French Antilles, introduces a number of the issues that will arise in this, the final chapter of our inquiry into repair. The Convoys for Reparations reflect a singular form of collective mobilization, in contrast to demands for reparations in the context of standard common law procedures. Even beyond the particular case of slavery, these struggles for reparations—and (where they exist) the exceptional procedures that seek to address them—are characterized by several distinctive issues.

Unlike the models of repair that we analyzed previously—biological (scarring), psychological (the work of mourning), religious (atonement, purification), social (apology), legal (retribution and restitution)—the historical model of repair introduces exceptional mechanisms designed to take account of the loss, the amputation, and the trauma suffered. The share of the irreparable will consequently be even greater. If the expression "the age of reparation" has any meaning, it is surely to qualify our contemporary historicity, with its unique perspective on the tragedies that have disfigured previous centuries. This is not the age of mourning, but rather that of the impossibility of mourning, as though, metaphorically or analogically, the scars are unable to heal over. Nor is this the age of redemption or emancipation, which continued to leave its mark on the historicity of the Moderns,[3] for whom the sacrifice of the victims could still be justified, Hegelian-style, in the name of a more powerful Reason embedded in history and purposefully oriented toward an enlightened future. Ours is, moreover, not so much the age of reparation as that of an incessant demand for reparation that is never really fulfilled or satisfied, against the backdrop of an unprecedented rationale of victimhood. The therapeutic age of reparation directly affects the way we conceive of history. It even blurs the dividing lines between the paradigms of repair: we observe the psychologization of the law when we expect trials to relieve the suffering of victims: the moralization of politics, perhaps with religious undertones, when we expect today's governments to make gestures of repentance or forgiveness, or even atonement, for crimes committed in the past; and the judicialization of history, when we ask the law to bridge a historical gap that was once deemed insurmountable.

The age of demands for reparation, in which we live, means the possibility of constantly reopening the historical wounds of the past, even the distant past, in order to bring somebody or something to account in the present day. The age of reparation crystallizes a past that incessantly haunts the present, not just as a specter, but even more so as a debt. History has always been written by the victors, but now it demands to be judged by yesterday's vanquished and by today's presumed victims. This is very much an inversion of the "direction" of history, one that we have been witnessing for several decades, despite the obstinate resistance of the partisans of the "old" history, who seek to erase the debt by silencing it. But this inversion of the direction of history generates in return a whole series of effects and challenges.

The first issue with historical reparation, which is a keen challenge for the law, lies in our temporal distance from some of the crimes for which reparation is demanded. Even when crimes are declared to have no statute of limitations, the distant past of events makes it difficult to identify victims and perpetrators who, in today's world, would be clearly identified. How can reparation proceedings be initiated for crimes that go back a long way in time, and perhaps span several centuries (the slave trade, slavery, colonization, etc.)? The second issue, correlative to the first, is the nature of the crimes. Quantitatively, they were perpetrated in a context of violence or mass extermination. While each crime, taken individually, carries its own burden of suffering and gravity, massification multiplies its effects. Qualitatively, these crimes—such as genocide, enslavement, deportation or ethnic cleansing—have the particularity of having been committed against the very idea of a shared humanity.

It is not hard to imagine how the problem of incommensurability, already posed at the scale of ordinary law, takes a particularly problematic and dramatic turn when it comes to repairing crimes against humanity. For the presumed victims, what logic of equivalence could possibly compensate for the human disproportion of the harm and trauma suffered? Is financial compensation morally acceptable for repairing crimes against humanity? More generally, what type of reparation, material or moral, is best suited to respond to the scale of these crimes? Should a historical irreparable not give rise to a debt that is by nature unpayable? The third issue concerns the status of the actors incriminated or prosecuted for what are, most often, mass crimes. Most crimes against humanity (the Holocaust, the slave trade, slavery, etc.) were perpetrated by states, and were not considered crimes at the time they were committed. Most of the time, they were actively encouraged and legalized, such as by the *Code Noir* or the anti-Jewish laws. The status of historical actors primarily raises the problem of the continuity of the state, especially when the crimes committed date back to very remote times, under non-democratic regimes. To what extent can today's governments (and the societies that may have to contribute to reparations) be held accountable for acts committed by the state several centuries ago? The second problem, even when the crime is more recent, lies in the fact that the state risks being judge and jury. How can the state, as the guarantor of the law, ensure fair arbitration of a case in which it is directly implicated?

REPARATION AND RESTITUTION

The expression "repairing history" may sound surprising. Is history not, by definition, something that is already done and dusted? Surely whatever harm was done, was done exclusively to natural or legal persons. So how can "repairing history" make any sense? In a metaphorical sense, of course, which is the subject of a meticulous investigation by magistrate Antoine Garapon that will serve as a guide for part of this inquiry.[4] Garapon is quick to point out the ambiguity of such expressions:

> Is this not about judging the wounds of the past that can still be felt in the present? People are only ever interested in the past for reasons that have to do with the present. Unlike history, justice is not concerned with the past in order to restore it as faithfully as possible, but to bring closure to an event that has offended a political community by challenging its values.[5]

In short, wanting to "repair history" consists in seeking justice for crimes of extreme gravity that took place at a time when they went unpunished, or were even encouraged. Wanting to repair history involves mobilizing the law where it cannot usually be exercised, by bringing history, however ancient, within the reach of the law.

The project of "repairing history" is a relatively recent phenomenon, dating from the 1990s, and originating in a particular culture (the United States), in relation to a particular event (the Holocaust), with the support of a specific body of *reparatio* (civil law). In the aftermath of the Second World War, the victors sought, by organizing large-scale trials, not to "repair" history but to punish those responsible, and primarily the Nazi criminals. If there is an element of legal invention, it resides in international criminal law, which takes the Nuremberg trials as its model. The institutionalization of "crimes against humanity" in 1945, under Article 6(c) of the London Agreement, was not intended to restore looted property or to compensate victims, but only to punish criminals.

Demands for reparations, following war or conflict, are of course an ancient practice, but they arise in another international or bilateral context, and outside civil law. They are generally initiated by the victors, being in a position to impose their will on those they have defeated. The definitive instrument for war reparations is not international criminal law, still less civil law, but international treaties, such as the Treaty of Versailles (1919), which provided for the payment of compensation and the transfer of property and equipment from Germany and the Central Empires (Austria-Hungary, Bulgaria, the Ottoman Empire) to the Allies. The term "reparation" retains its full meaning under Article 231 of the Treaty of

Versailles, known as the "War Guilt Clause" which declared Germany and the Central Empires responsible for "all the loss and damage" suffered by the Allies during the war. It is remarkable, on the one hand, that the terms "loss and damage," relating to civil lawsuits for reparations, were transferred to relations between states, some of which were placed in the position of victims and the others in the position of culprits: the actors, in this process of equalization, are not individuals but states. The paradox of war reparations is that the victims (to whom reparations are owed) are at the same time the victors of the conflict, while the perpetrators (from whom reparations are demanded) are the vanquished. It is remarkable, on the other hand, that the guilt clause and the amount of reparations were not established at the end of a trial, as is customary in civil law, but on the basis of a treaty drawn up unilaterally by the victors. Finally, it is also remarkable that claims for war reparations can be made long after the fact, as is the case today with Poland, which on September 1, 2019—marking the eightieth anniversary of the invasion of the country by German troops—set up parliamentary committees to calculate the amount of loss suffered. Some Polish representatives, such as Arkadiusz Mularczyk, have ventured to quantify the damages, using a civil law model: "You take the average life expectancy of the time, you estimate how much a person could earn, pay taxes, and contribute to the gross domestic product."[6] Such extrapolations and evaluations naturally raise formidable problems, which we will need to explore at length.

There are also historical exceptions by which the vanquished, at least at the end of a particular conflict, have subsequently found themselves in a strong position to demand reparations from the victor. This was the case with the conflict between France and its former colony of Saint-Domingue, which, after defeating the powerful Leclerc/Rochambeau expedition that set out from France to re-establish slavery there in 1804, became the Haitian Republic. Though defeated, France was able, due to the young Republic's fear of a new war and a new French occupation, to impose reparations on the Haitian government as the price of its independence: an indemnity of 150 million gold francs to compensate the former colonists, and a guarantee of preferential trade terms for France. This debt contributed to the weakening and ultimate ruin of the first Black republic in history and remains a point of contention between the two countries to this day. The government of Charles X took cynicism still further by mobilizing French banks to finance the loan extended to the Haitian government to pay off its debt of independence! The relationship to debt was the converse of today's perception: not the debt owed by France for centuries of slavery in its colony, for crimes committed over generations against deported Africans, but the debt owed to France by its former slaves, to compensate for the economic loss incurred to the former colonists. In a way that seems intolerable to us today, the only "victims" who were compensated at the time were the former slave-owners. For the former slaves and their descendants, not a penny.

Whether war reparations or reparations for independence, one thing remains constant: demands for reparations are made between states, without involving legal proceedings. In other words, this dominant mode of historical reparation generally remains outside the law (criminal or civil), save perhaps the law of the strongest, at the scale of the geopolitical power relations of a Westphalian order. In their content, war reparations have the same properties as civil law reparations (guilt, tort, damages, compensation, etc.). But in their form, they are radically different: for one thing, because they take place between states (rather than between individuals), and for another, because they do not result from judicial procedures and decisions. Ultimately, war reparations borrow mechanisms from the law to pursue politics by other means. It is less a question of rendering justice than of extending domination (occupation of territories, weakening of a state, etc.) by means other than war. It is no coincidence that war reparations are experienced by the defeated as a second humiliation, following a military defeat, as was the "diktat" of the Treaty of Versailles.

While war reparations are governed by power politics and are generally part of a Westphalian order of relations between sovereign states, civil reparations for crimes against humanity belong to a post-Westphalian neo-liberal order through which victims' claims transcend state borders, and even seek to prosecute transgressor states. The former testify to the subjugation of the law to politics, the latter to the domestication of politics by (civil) law:

> Such upheavals were only made possible because these lawsuits succeeded in neutralizing the state-to-state treaties that had settled the matter of reparations. Legal actions on civil rather than public grounds succeeded in making the political non-binding. It is now conceivable to bring a claim for these rather special debts before any court in the world, for any time in history, without the political authorities being able to invoke any privilege of jurisdiction.[7]

International criminal law, from the Nuremberg trials through to the establishment of the international criminal courts (ICCs), also harbors an ambition to go beyond borders and beyond state sovereignty;[8] in short, to undermine what Garapon calls the Schmittian (or Westphalian) model of law, defined by the full, inalienable exercise of state power over a territory and a population (the national boundaries of law). In the Schmittian model, state criminals could remain largely immune from prosecution in the name of the principle of sovereignty. International criminal law, by establishing international courts of justice, already constitutes a major departure from the principle of national sovereignty, but in practice it comes up against the difficulty of arresting or extraditing (depending on the case) those charged with war crimes or crimes against humanity, as they are protected by complicit states. While some Nazi criminals were judged and sentenced as early as 1945, or at later trials such as Eichmann's, how many died without ever being importuned, thanks to the protection of a sympathetic government? In other words, international criminal law, for all its ambitions, still depends to a certain extent on the sovereignty of individual states.

The unprecedented innovation that has come into play since the 1990s is the international extension of civil law to obtain reparation for historical harms and compensate the victims. In addition to overcoming historical distance, civil law, from this period onward, transcends spatial distance and challenges, more radically even than international criminal law, the principle of state sovereignty and national borders: "In the context of globalization, civil law is called upon to organize the bonds that escape any jurisdiction and belong to no state. It is as if civil liability had the power to create legal bonds, however fragile, between people as foreign to each other as sweatshop workers and American consumers."[9]

It is worth dwelling on the historical genesis of this model of reparation, which Antoine Garapon skillfully retraces, this unprecedented *reparatio* that gave shape and meaning to the ambition of "repairing history." The project emerged from a particular context (the United States) and by means of a particular legal instrument (the class action[10]): lawsuits brought by American Jewish associations first against Swiss banks, then against other European companies and states for the losses suffered by Jewish victims during the Holocaust. The initial objective of the plaintiffs was to demand the restitution to the rightful owners of funds that had been improperly held by Swiss banks (so-called "unclaimed assets") since the Second World War. Initiatives in this direction, emanating from Jewish associations and from the US administration, date back to the end of the war, but at the time they were stonewalled by the Swiss banks. Starting in the mid-1990s, new lawsuits were filed jointly by the Jewish associations and the US Senate (under the impetus of Senator D'Amato), but this time with the threat of sanctions from the US administration: the non-renewal of the licenses of Swiss banks in the United States. After intense negotiations, an agreement was reached between the American associations and the Swiss banks for an amount of 1.25 billion dollars. In addition to this agreement, a Swiss Solidarity Fund was set up in 1997 to come to the aid of "Holocaust survivors in need." This was followed by subsequent agreements with Austria, Germany, the Netherlands and France,[11] based on a similar "class action" model.

The culmination of this process drew on a whole network of interacting players: Jewish associations, the World Jewish Congress, the Simon Wiesenthal Center, Senator D'Amato, lawyers (acting as private prosecutors), the US administration and judges. But the restitution of the unclaimed assets could not have happened without the influence of American politics, the power of the US market, and media coverage:

> Why did the Swiss banks fold? Because before they could even plead their case before a judge, they had lost in the court of public opinion. Not their own public opinion (as the referendum would later show) but the public opinion of their clients, who are global, and might have found themselves out of step. . . . In all of the identical cases in other European countries, no company wanted to see its name associated with Nazism, or to be suspected of having profited from the misfortune of the Jews. The main lever used by the American plaintiffs was that of naming and shaming.[12]

But is the Swiss bank affair really a case of reparation? Strictly speaking, no. It is about the restitution to the rightful owners of an asset unjustly held by an institution, rather than establishing an equivalent (in kind or in money) to compensate for the loss of something. The $1.25 billion set by the agreement is not strictly speaking a compensation award, but a demand for the return of funds. The same applies to Jewish property looted in France when it was returned to the victims and their descendants.[13] The distinction between restitution and reparation is, however, more complex in the cases in question. On the one hand, the demand for restitution may be accompanied by a claim for "damages for loss of enjoyment" for a given period of time. This additional amount is not restitution, but clearly reparation. On the other hand, the American Jewish associations decided to pay more than a third of the amount provided for in the agreement to Holocaust survivors, regardless of whether they had a claim to the assets held by the Swiss banks. Although this was not the rationale for the original settlement in the agreement, it changed the meaning of the compensation payment: "By moving from restitution to reparation, there was a surreptitious shift from liability for negligence or minor fault, or even no-fault liability, to criminal or quasi-criminal liability. At the outset, the case of the unclaimed assets was not one of reparations, but it became so, contrary to the formal agreement of one of the parties."[14] One may also wonder whether the creation of the Swiss Solidarity Fund for Holocaust survivors, which Garapon ascribes to a humanitarian logic, is not also part of a logic of reparation, at least implicitly (and at the same time an at least implicit recognition of Switzerland's responsibility). In France, the creation in 2000 of the Fondation pour la Mémoire de la Shoah, on the recommendation of the Mattéoli Commission, is also part of a process of reparation rather than restitution. Endowed with some of the unclaimed funds resulting from the spoliation of the Jews, the Foundation advocates for cultural and moral reparation (historical research into the Holocaust, duty of remembrance, etc.).[15]

Whether the demands are made for restitution or for reparation, successfully or otherwise, these actions testify to a transformation of international relations and of the way history is written. In the Westphalian or Schmittian model, states—especially the most powerful ones—enjoy immunity and relative impunity, and have the privilege of dictating the "direction" of history in line with their own interests. In the post-Westphalian model, thanks to an international extension of civil law, the victims, formerly reduced to silence, are taking their revenge on the power politics of states and large corporations. The state must now answer for the historical wrongs for which it is responsible. Economic globalization has deepened the indebtedness of states in financial terms; legal globalization has amplified their historical and moral debts. Two processes with one and the same consequence: a diminution of state sovereignty and power.

The legal transformation of power relations correlatively modifies the relations of meaning between history and memory. One of the chief manifestations of this is the contemporary invention of the "duty of remembrance" of victims, which has come to compete with the earlier "right of remembrance" of heroes who died for their country.[16] Up until the 1990s, national commemorations nourished the goal of glorifying the great figures and victorious events (revolutions, military victories, etc.) of a nation's history; but a new commemorative grammar was emerging, in which the "innocent victims," those who "died *because of* rather than [for] France" (Jews, descendants of slaves, former colonized peoples) became the new protagonists of a national counter-narrative. The law of 2000 (creating a day of homage to the victims of the racist and anti-Semitic crimes of the French state) or the law of 2017 (for a national day of homage to the victims of colonial slavery, every May 23), even more than the law of May 10, 2001 (which recognized the slave trade and slavery as a crime against humanity), clearly attest to this reconfiguration of official memory.

THE LONG TIME OF HISTORICAL INJUSTICE

The main obstacle that the project of historical reparation keeps running up against is that of the passage of time. Temporal distance is already a factor at the scale of common law crimes, where limitation periods apply. The possibility of obtaining legal reparation for a common law crime is constrained, in many legal systems, by time limits set by the legislator. This legal limitation on legal proceedings leaves a significant number of crimes in a state of irreparability, arouses a sense of injustice (particularly in the case of sexual or blood crimes), and recurrently revives debates over the extension of limitation periods. But the statute of limitations, which dates back to Roman law, nonetheless displays certain virtues, at least for its supporters. For one, when the alleged facts are significantly distant in time, the possibility of investigating, managing evidence, gathering testimony, and possibly prosecuting the criminals can prove perilous, directly threatening the fairness of the judicial decision. For another, the establishment of limitation periods is justified in the name of social harmony, without which lawsuits would multiply for all kinds of cases.

But these justifications no longer hold for certain categories of crime (war crimes and crimes against humanity, depending on the systems in force) for which the legislator considers, because of their extreme seriousness, that the passage of time cannot erase the criminal's debt to the victim and to the law. The legal imprescriptibility of the crime reinforces historical indebtedness and calls for still greater efforts of collective memory. It is in these terms that the French Parliament enacted Law no. 64–1326 of December 26, 1964, seeking to establish the imprescriptibility of crimes against humanity: "crimes against humanity as defined by the resolution of the United Nations of 13 February 1946, which takes note of the definition of crimes against humanity contained in the Charter of the International Military Tribunal dated 8 August 1945, are by their nature not subject to any period of limitation." However, the imprescriptible nature of crimes against humanity comes up against the reality of the temporal remoteness of certain deeds, for which the main perpetrators have disappeared, to say nothing of the victims, who have sometimes been dead for centuries, without ever having the opportunity to have their grievances heard. Legal reparation is therefore directly compromised, even when the descendants do their utmost to keep the case alive.

All reparation is based on several orders of temporality. The first order of temporality is entailed by the distance that separates a set of disruptive events from the lives of contemporaries. It is not yet directly a question of victims, let alone reparations. Any process of reparation nevertheless presupposes a significant change in the state of the world, even at the scale of an individual life. Reparation can only exist for a series of actions and events that have a before and an after, a bifurcation, a break in the normal course of things, a loss of physical integrity, a loss of freedom, a deprivation of material goods . . . . of course, not every disruption to the course of day-to-day life culminates in a sense of victimhood and a demand for reparations. But there can be no demand for reparations and for reparative mechanisms without some upheaval, on varying scales, in the state of the natural, social or political world. And the degree of temporal remoteness of such disruptions has direct implications for the way potential reparations are addressed.

To speak of upheaval in the state of the world is in no way reducible to a sudden and brief event: the upheaval can set in for the duration, with effects that reach far beyond its initial conditions of production. Moreover, upheavals in the state of the world, far from being raw data, are always hedged around by systems of perception and representation, and by individual and collective assessments. The African deported into slavery certainly experienced a major upheaval in his or her life-world; for the eighteenth-century slave trader, on the other hand, it was a normalized mode of economic production. This regime of temporality is not yet directly that of reparation. It is not yet the time of reparation, but an anterior form of temporality, an a priori condition of the former.

Nor is the second order of temporality directly that of the reparative process. It might be called the "temporality of victimhood," the time of the collective mobilization of the victims themselves, or of collectives that speak and act in their name. It is one thing to be able to determine a substantial transformation in the state of the world, quite another to be able to identify agents and patients, victims and perpetrators. Not every change in the state of the world will necessarily lead to the imputation of damage, harm and loss. To attribute such characteristics to a state of the living world supposes a whole series of symbolic, scientific and technical mediations, legal instruments, and social classifications. For example, before the invention of the category of post-traumatic stress, as Fassin and Rechtman have shown, veterans suffering from psychological distress could not be considered as victims of war.[17] But the degree of temporal distance affects the way in which the upheaval is problematized and presented as a harm, loss, offense, wound, or privation. The legal-medical category of post-traumatic stress may be very well suited to describing suffering that originates in the short time of an event (terror attack, natural disaster, etc.), but it is unsuited to the causal attribution of suffering or trauma that takes place over a longer period of time. In the case of the history and memory of slavery, as I have tried to show elsewhere,[18] the actors have relied mainly on the legal instrument of crimes against humanity, which, being free from statutory limitations, allows for causal imputation over a longer time frame.

The temporality of victimhood is not that of reparation as such. Victims' groups may press for the recognition of harms, offenses and suffering, without this leading to actual reparation. But there can be no reparation without this timeframe in which the victims are mobilized, except in specific cases where the public authorities directly take the initiative to set up a reparative mechanism, as for example when a "natural disaster" is officially declared.

Even in this case, reparation can only take place after the causal attribution of victims and harms, and an assessment of loss and damage.

The third order or regime of temporality is that of the actual reparation and reparations. It could not come about, however, without the two preceding levels: the originating temporality of a transformation in the state of the world, and the subsequent temporality of characterizing the upheaval in terms of harm, loss and privation. Here again, temporality is central: the time of reparation may be close to that of the harm, although there is generally a delay for evaluation, not to mention the slowness and bureaucratic red tape that always requires a suspension of time. The performative element of reparation ("the state undertakes to") imposes a waiting period that can last for years before the victims are partially compensated by the courts, by the state, or by the insurance companies.

In other cases, there may be a significant time gap between the events characterized as damaging and the actual reparations. This difficulty can be clearly seen in the case of demands for reparations relating to slavery, due to the temporal distance from the crimes committed, the duration (several centuries) over which the acts were perpetrated, and direct state involvement in that vile trade. In France, the controversies actually date back to the second abolition of slavery in 1848, but in reverse, so to speak: compensation was paid not to the slaves themselves or to their descendants, but to the wealthy planters for the economic losses incurred by abolition.[19] The possibility of reparations in favor of slaves was, by contrast, largely ignored in public debate and by the public authorities in France until very recently. Even in 1983, when the first law on the commemoration of the abolition of slavery was passed, the question of reparations for the descendants of slaves was barely touched upon in parliamentary debates. The decisive year, which marked a turning point, was undoubtedly 1998, the year of the official commemorations of the 150th anniversary of the abolition of slavery. It was in this commemorative context that new issues around slavery emerged in metropolitan and overseas France, championed by non-profit groups that uphold the memory of slavery, in which "reparations" were given special attention: Is it possible to repair what is sometimes represented as the irreparable, so great is the crime? Can we establish a (fair) equivalence between the harm suffered and the consequent reparations? What are the legitimate modalities of reparation? Who should make reparation (the former slave states, the companies that profited from the slave trade)? To whom should reparations be attributed (African states, descendants of slaves, former slave colonies)? These and other questions came to the fore in 1998, less—to begin with—in the media and in political circles than within the associative fabric of non-profit organizations.

The creation of the "Comité Devoir de Mémoire" (Duty of Remembrance Committee) or CDM in Martinique in 1997 can be analyzed, at least in retrospect, as just such a space of intermediation, for it is within this public space that the problematization of slavery in terms of reparation was most developed.[20] This committee served as a space of intermediation between the literary spaces where new grammars of the memory of slavery were being invented and the parliamentary bodies where draft legislation to recognize slavery as a crime against humanity was being discussed. In a series of conferences,[21] the CDM brought together writers and specialists on Antillean identity (Patrick Chamoiseau and Edouard Glissant joined the committee from the outset), along with legal professionals who helped translate this commemorative recognition into the legal terms of a crime against humanity and formulate the question of reparations and, finally, professional politicians (future French justice minister Christiane Taubira was present at the conferences organized by the committee).

Professor Emmanuel Jos, a specialist in international criminal law at the University of the French Antilles, was undoubtedly the figure who played the lead role in this mediation process, starting with the April 1998 conference held in Martinique. Jos unambiguously placed his legal expertise at the service of the cause of recognizing slavery and the slave trade as crimes against humanity. His methodological approach consisted in defining a space of legal possibilities for translating this recognition into legal terms, building on jurisprudence and on the recent extension of the concept of crimes against humanity to causes other than the Holocaust (the Rwandan genocide, ethnic cleansing in the former Yugoslavia,[22] recognition of the Armenian genocide). The aim was to seize upon this process of extending the scope of crimes against humanity and apply it, with amendments as required, to the particular case of slavery. Drawing on the existing law, Jos distinguishes between a narrow meaning, referring to inhuman acts committed on a large scale as part of a policy of ideological, racial or religious hegemony, and a broader meaning, referring to acts that deny the victim's humanity. While the first meaning has long predominated, because of the genocide committed against the Jews, national and international jurisprudence has evolved towards a broader understanding. Modern slavery, he points out, does not easily fit the narrow meaning, but it clearly falls within the broader meaning, while Afro-American slavery, stemming from the slave trade, fully satisfies both meanings, particularly in terms of the international jurisprudence of the Nuremberg Tribunal, which qualifies deportation into slavery as a crime against humanity. The law of December 1964 on the imprescriptibility of crimes against humanity "internalizes" into French law the legal meaning given by the London Agreement.[23] The qualification of African-American slavery as a crime against humanity should therefore not pose any legal difficulties, according to Professor Jos, even under the narrower definition: "The objective of the 'absolute' monarchies of the time was undoubtedly to enrich themselves economically, but also to consolidate the supremacy of a race—the white race—of European culture, and of a religion: the Roman Catholic Apostolic Church."[24]

The recognition of the Holocaust, under Article 6(c) of the Nuremberg Charter, can only provide a framework for the recognition of slavery by making a series of amendments. As Professor Jos explains, one cannot prosecute former slave-owners or slave-traders in the same way as former Nazi criminals, because of the temporal distance. In other words, African American slavery cannot give rise to legal prosecutions, at least in the criminal sense. The demand for reparation presupposes the legal qualification of the crime. The imprescriptibility enshrined in the 1964 law is of no use in prosecuting long-dead slavers. The legal possibility of recognizing slavery as a crime against humanity comes up against the legal impossibility of criminal prosecution and bringing the perpetrators to justice; an impossibility further reinforced by the principle of non-retroactivity of laws, even if this principle admits of certain exceptions (as was the case during the Nuremberg trials). We should note that Professor Jos is reasoning here as a criminal lawyer and not as a civil lawyer. His argument does not take account of international lawsuits that have mobilized civil law to overcome historical distance and the difficulty (or in some cases impossibility) of prosecuting the perpetrators. At the time of the conference organized by the CDM, the international class action movement was still in its infancy, despite media coverage of the Swiss bank case. The limitation of criminal law, as we saw, is that it remains dependent, in geopolitical space, on the sovereignty of states and, in historical time, on the availability of criminals for prosecution. The limitation of criminal law is that it deals with relationships between persons, whereas civil law deals above all with relationships between things, for which it seeks to establish equivalences.

It is therefore with regard to the limitations of international criminal law, despite its meteoric progress since 1945, that we should hear Jos' argument for opening up other opportunities for recognition and reparation, while the possibility of effective legal action is closed off. There is nothing to prevent this recognition from being posed in pedagogical, moral, political and cultural terms (i.e., in terms of moral reparation). This moral purpose of reparation, however, lies outside of civil law and of any retributive logic of compensation.

Professor Jos' legal opinion played a key role in the gestation of what would later become the Taubira Law (Jos and Taubira met at the CDM conferences). Although Jos did not participate directly in drafting the text of the law, the representative's report explicitly refers to his work, which precisely defined a space of legal and political openings to qualify slavery as a crime against humanity, by way of moral reparation, but without closing the door to material reparations. It emerges from the initial report presented by Taubira[25] that the issue of reparations was indeed on the parliamentary agenda. This was the whole purpose of Article 5 of the draft bill: "A committee of qualified persons is hereby established with the task of evaluating the damage and examining the conditions of reparations due for this crime. The competences and missions of this committee shall be determined by the Council of State."[26] However, the parliamentary committee modified the initial content of Article 5. It was Taubira herself who censored a key provision of her own draft law. The reason was that the government of Prime Minister Lionel Jospin, which was in favor of recognizing slavery as a crime against humanity, was not prepared to follow her on the matter of material reparations, so as not to open up the Pandora's box of compensation payments.

Struggles for material reparations to compensate for the harm caused by slavery are not over, however,[27] despite the reversal suffered at the time of the adoption of the Taubira Law. They regularly resurface in political debates and in the courts, as we have seen, though nowadays less on the model of criminal law than on that of civil law, directly inspired by the American legal system. The lawsuits pursued against the French state for several years now by MIR and CRAN go precisely in this direction, despite the setbacks experienced in court.[28]

The 1990s and 2000s saw a growing awareness of the question of slavery among elites of formerly colonized populations around the world, supported at the same time by studies concerned with producing a postcolonial narrative. Just as there was an internationalization and Americanization of the Holocaust in the 1970s and 1980s, so too the memory of slavery has been internationalized since the 1990s. This internationalization was initiated by the "Slave Route" project in 1994, implemented by UNESCO at Ouidah in Benin. The other important international event was the 2001 World Conference against Racism, held at Durban in South Africa. One of its strands directly concerned the request of African countries for slavery to be recognized as a crime against humanity, demanding that the former slave-owning powers make reparation for the harm (economic, social, cultural, etc.) suffered by the African continent, and canceling the debts of the countries that were formerly victims of slavery. Formerly colonized countries hoped that Durban would lead to a "generalized discharge of all the historical debts" relating to colonization: "The conference was supposed to allow some to formulate their debts, and others to assume them, on the postulate that the staging of this indebtedness would, at least symbolically, absolve international relations of their accumulated debts—whether financial debts or debts of blood."[29] Rather than a "symbolic refounding of the international community" on the basis of a generalized historical reparation, the Durban conference ended in relative failure, due to the opposition of the former colonial powers and to divisions between the former colonized countries, with the most radical pressing for financial reparations along the lines of the treatment of the victims of the Holocaust, while others (notably Senegal, Nigeria and Cape Verde) called for a development program for Africa and the restitution of looted artworks. The Western countries present at Durban agreed to a gesture of recognition (recognizing that slavery and the slave trade were "a crime against humanity, and should always have been so"), by way of moral reparation, but refused to be held solely responsible and, in particular, to make commitments on the financial component of reparation.

While France has hitherto favored a model of moral reparation (commemorative laws, memorials, the opening of archives, the Foundation for the Memory of the Shoah, the Committee for the Memory and History of Slavery, etc.) and has always been reticent about financial reparation, especially in the form of individual compensation, other countries, particularly in the English-speaking world, have mobilized civil law to bridge the historical gap and opted for material reparations through the mediation of the civil courts. The past (colonization, slavery, etc.), which the dominant thought was over, is being transformed into a debt that must be paid. Even before the Swiss bank affair, the "Black Hills" case set a precedent in American judicial history when the Supreme Court awarded the sum of 122 billion dollars in compensation for the damage suffered by the Sioux, whose territory, initially defined by the Treaty of Fort Laramie (1868), had been whittled down by the American government in 1874 following the discovery of gold mines (the administration pressured the Native Americans to sell their land). This case, like those that followed, is symptomatic of a difference in ethos from one country to another in its relationship to this debt:

> It is probably no coincidence that these cases originated in the United States: a Protestant country that has pushed the secularization of debt and the financialization of social relations further than any other. What worked for the economy must surely be applicable to such politically charged issues as slavery or crimes against humanity. May the market save us from the vicissitudes of history![30]

In practice, the distinction between material reparation and moral reparation is not always so clear-cut. Material reparation, for example in the form of financial compensation, may at the same time imply a gesture of moral recognition (apologies, requests for forgiveness, etc.) as was done by JP Morgan bank, after initially adopting a position of denial. Conversely, moral reparation may at the same time involve significant funding from public or private institutions, but without appealing to a "civil law" logic of retribution and compensation. The creation of the ACTe Memorial, for example, under the presidency of François Hollande, could be seen as a material commitment to moral reparation, independently of any civil procedure for judicial arbitration and financial reparation. The cost of building the memorial (over 80 million euros) corresponds neither to a logic of restitution, nor to a logic of corrective or retributive reparation by which some amount might have been set aside to compensate the descendants of the victims of slavery. The memorial was financed independently of any principle of legal equivalence.

The political application or use of moral reparation, with or without material implications, is clearly distinct from the kind of moral reparation in face-to-face interactions that we looked at with Goffman. Admittedly, we can find the same performative framework: apologies, requests for forgiveness, acts of atonement, and so on. On the one hand, however, the harm suffered in the case of moral-historical reparation is of a gravity that has no equivalent in the banal offenses of everyday life. The proportionality clause is put directly to the test when it comes to trying to make moral reparation (for example, by apologies alone) for crimes against humanity, which are out of all proportion to encroaching on someone's personal space or accidentally bumping into them in the street. On the other hand, the political use of moral reparation, while it may be expressed by a flesh-and-blood person, is always carried out in the name of a public institution. When President Jacques Chirac, in his speech of July 16, 1995, marking the commemoration of the Vel d'Hiv Roundup, acknowledged France's responsibility for the anti-Semitic crimes committed during the collaboration period, he was not acting in his own name, as a private person, but as the Head of State, as an institution. It is in this capacity that the political use of moral reparation is performed. Although he was officially making reparation, it was not Chirac who was responsible for the crimes committed during that period. The President was acting as a third-party repairer, as a substitute repairer, in the name of the continuity of the state, as a representative of France facing up to its past crimes, even if committed under a non-republican regime. In the same way, the "subject" to whom the act of reparation is addressed is not an individual person, but a partly virtual collective; the direct victims have largely disappeared, even if their descendants or relatives, to whom the act of reparation is actually addressed, may be present. This has little to do with the remedial exchanges that take place in the interactions of daily life, involving the face-to-face presence of offender and offended. There, the debt owed by one to the other can be settled in the very instant following the injury by a gesture of apology or remorse. Not so for crimes against humanity committed several generations ago: the debt is encumbered with the burden of history.

To speak of remedial exchanges in this case would be largely irrelevant, given that many of the victims are no longer there to receive the offer of reparation, and should they so wish, accept it. The ideal-typical cycle of remedial exchanges that punctuates ordinary life (offense/reparation/ acceptance/gratification) loses its meaning here. When, in 2008, the new Australian Prime Minister Kevin Rudd made an official apology to the Aborigines for all the injustices they had suffered over the centuries, he did not really expect an "acceptance" from the offended, most of whom are long gone, or even from their descendants, even though representatives of these collectives may acknowledge an important gesture of recognition, without necessarily speaking for all of their members. The acceptance of reparation, let alone gratification, will always be open to question. Historical distance, especially when it is remote, completely modifies the interplay of actors and remedial exchanges, as the victims and perpetrators are no longer present. The stage of historical moral reparation is peopled largely by third-party repairers and third-party repairees. Those who today call history and the once mighty to account are no longer the vanquished of yesteryear, but those who speak in their name, turning history into a debt passed down from generation to generation.

DEBT AND INCOMMENSURABILITY

Financial reparation mechanisms for historical wrongs aspire to a form of objectivity in their aim to establish a relationship between loss and compensation. This is the advantage of civil law over criminal law, in that it considers "objects" rather than "intentions," things rather than people, as Antoine Garapon reminds us: "The calculation of civil damages is supposed to be much more precise than criminal sentencing: we do not ask the same questions to evaluate the losses of the dispossessed owners of a mine (there are experts who do that all day long for courts around the world) as we do to decide whether Maurice Papon should be sentenced to ten years or to life in prison."[31]

When it comes to requests for restitution in the strict sense, civil law has adequate means to respond. The obstacles that might emerge are both procedural and technical: they depend, on the one hand, on the possibility of going beyond national borders in order to bring a case to trial, and on the other, on the possibility of evaluating assets that have been improperly appropriated. With the exception of possible claims for damages for loss of enjoyment of property (which initiates a reparation process), the restitution of assets kept "as is" does not involve the determination of monetary equivalents. In other words, the problem of the commensurability of reparation does not really arise: what was looted, plundered or stolen must be returned in its original state to its rightful owners or their beneficiaries. This is precisely the aim of the action taken by the American Jewish associations against the Swiss banks, or the demand by African countries for the restitution of artworks looted by the former colonial powers.

The question of reparation does arise, however, when looted property, such as artworks, has been partially damaged, or when land has been unjustifiably appropriated, as was the case during Western colonization (as we saw with the Black Hills affair). In such cases, restitution cannot be made, either because the damaged property cannot be materially repaired, or because returning the land would raise new legal issues (e.g., expropriating "new" owners of land that may have been acquired generations ago). The restitution mechanism must then be replaced by a reparation mechanism, determining principles of equivalence for compensation. The procedural and technical issues here are much more sensitive than in the case of straightforward restitution: how, for example, can the loss of ancestral lands be evaluated for indigenous populations? How is the principle of equivalence to be established? Despite these difficulties, civil law has its own specific resources, insofar as it is a matter of evaluating, comparing and measuring things against other things in order to establish equivalences. These specific resources consist in being able to convert any material prejudice into a supposedly universal equivalent: money. The ambition of civil law is to be able to compensate for any harm by means of a monetary value.

Monetary symbolism, however, does not have the same cultural valency across different countries and cultural areas, even within Western countries. It is not hard to imagine that things get still more difficult outside the Western cultural area. Artworks or lands are not necessarily material "things" for the populations who were deprived of them, or for those who claim them back today. They may also have a cosmic, religious or identity-related meaning. The secularized Western meaning of an artwork (such as an African mask), in its aesthetic dimension, is not the same as the meanings encountered in traditional non-Western societies. Repatriating an "artwork" looted from the native land is not only "giving back" a thing, but also bringing back the "soul" of an ancestor and reestablishing a sacred order. Likewise for the loss of ancestral lands, which are not only "property" but also signs of belonging to an imaginary community. We see here the limits of simply converting historical injustices into monetary equivalents. Anthropologically, in Descola's terms,[32] we are faced with the problem of the frontier between the human and the non-human, whether for things that refer to persons (a funerary mask, a sarcophagus, etc.) or for things (or beings) that are from the outset equivalent to persons or divinities (the garden plants seen by Achuar women as children to be cared for). The ontological and moral boundary between persons and things, between the spiritual and the material, between the soul and the body, is the first anthropological challenge to civil law's supposed ability to translate any harm, universally and uniformly, into monetary compensation.

This incommensurable aspect of the element of soul that inhabits the lost "thing" already represents an initial form of historical irreparability. Financial compensation, however generous, will never bring back the sacred land of the ancestors of the Sioux or the Maoris. We are confronted with the irreparable at its two constitutive levels: time and debt. Time, in that granting compensation is in no way equivalent to returning the victims of expropriation to their previous situation; here, the irreparable is expressed as irreversible. Debt, in that no monetary value will be able to compensate for the harm suffered, especially if the loss of the thing is felt as a loss of its inherent soul; here, the irreparable is expressed as irredeemable. Civil law, for all its claims, can never pay off a debt that cannot entirely be converted into monetary value.

When the harm concerns things, even things imbued with soul, the irreparable is only relative; in the case of a purely objective relationship to things (if that is possible), it does not arise at all. In such cases, admittedly, the irreparable of time will always remain, but without necessarily implying an irreparable of debt, at least if the civil parties feel that the monetary compensation meets their expectations (which inevitably depends on social and cultural frameworks of evaluation). The memory of the harm persists, even if the debt can be forgiven.

The question of the irreparable arises with far greater gravity when the harm concerns a crime against humanity, especially one committed on a large scale, over long periods of time, and with state complicity. Of course, civil law can still aspire to repair that part of the crime that can be quantified in economic terms. If, for example, we consider slavery from the quantifiable angle of unpaid work, civil law could perhaps evaluate—albeit by means of an expert assessment that defies mortal understanding—the monetary compensation that should be awarded to compensate for the economic and social damage inflicted, including on much of the African continent, impoverished because of slavery. But even if such an assessment were possible, the problem would immediately arise of the status of repairers and repaired. Who should make reparation? When companies that are still in existence have profited from slavery and the slave trade, legal proceedings are possible, as we have seen with American banks such as JP Morgan. However, because of historical distance, most of the businesses that thrived on that crime no longer exist and so cannot be prosecuted.

So should we "nationalize" the debts of history? It would then be up to states—in part because they directly benefited from slavery and the slave trade—to take on the burden of historical debt. But at the cost of new difficulties: should African states (such as present-day Benin) that participated in the slave trade (at the time of the kingdom of Dahomey) also be included)? The nationalization of historical debt, because it would ultimately be funded by the taxpayer, would impose upon current generations a duty to make reparation for a crime they did not commit. In the name of an ideal of justice, the nationalization of historical debt would at the same time risk generating a new injustice, affecting today's generations. Moreover, if the repayment of historical debt is funded through taxation, we would, by a cynical irony of history, have to ask the descendants of the victims of slavery to help pay off the debt themselves; in short, forcing them to pay today for the harm suffered yesterday by their ancestors.

The problem of the status of the repairers is compounded by that of the repaired. To whom should compensation be attributed when the direct victims are no longer with us, when the crime was committed several centuries ago? A process of individual compensation would be a very tricky proposition due to the distance of time, without taking account of intermixing (largely forced intermixing between masters and slaves during the time of slavery) which means that some descendants of slaves are, genealogically, also descendants of slave-owners.

There are, however, as we noted, other forms of material reparation beside individual financial compensation, such as renegotiating the (economic) debt of African countries that were victims of slavery or colonialism, granting scholarships for African American or West Indian students, and creating a reparations bank for the economic and social development of impoverished countries or regions (such as the Antilles). These reparations mechanisms, despite the irreducible persistence of the irreparable of time and debt, attest to the possibility of repairing that part of a crime against humanity that is amenable to quantification in economic and monetary terms. This is where civil law can have its say.

The same cannot be said for the part of the crime that is incommensurable with economic and monetary values, where the very idea of humanity is directly affected in its foundation. How could civil law hope to find a "just" monetary equivalent? We can only acknowledge a conflict between monetary value and moral value (relating to the dignity of the human person), which are deemed to be morally incommensurable. The problem is not only technical: how do we determine an "objective" monetary value that represents a fair equivalent to the suffering of the victims of human trafficking, or the inmates of the death camps, or the Tutsis who died under the machetes of their torturers? Must we establish hierarchies of crime and suffering? It is also a moral problem. Even if a metric could be established to determine a monetary equivalent, the payment of a sum of money could have the effect of "trivializing evil," as Garapon calls it, after Arendt, or of sullying the memory of the victims, making crimes against humanity "measurable" in monetary terms, and ultimately seeking to rid ourselves of a historical debt.

THE POLITICAL USE OF MORAL REPARATION

The paradox of the historical reparation of crimes against humanity by monetary equivalent is that it undermines its very gravity. If the reparation for the crime is "quantifiable," commensurable, can the crime really be so terrible? To measure it, to compare it, to evaluate it in monetary terms is to deny its radicality. In other words, there is a kind of contradiction in wanting, on the one hand, to recognize the moral disproportionality of the crime against humanity, while on the other wanting to assign it a monetary value. The ambition of using money as a medium of universal equivalence is discredited from the outset.

It is for these reasons that commemorative activists consider any form of reparation by monetary equivalent for crimes against humanity to be indecent. Among them Aimé Césaire, the key figure of the Négritude movement and anti-colonialism, when he said, in an interview with Françoise Vergès, that slavery falls into the category of the irreparable: "It would be too easy: 'So you were a slave for so many years, a long time ago, so we multiply that by so much: here's your reparation.' And that would be the end of it? It's irreparable. It's done, it's history, there's nothing I can do about it."[33] Césaire was speaking out against reparations that could be expressed in an accounting logic, which would amount to determining an equivalent to compensate for the immensity of the crime. As a consequence, the former slave-owning nations would be considered absolved of their crimes after paying a certain amount, and the historical debt would be deemed to be settled. To affirm the irreparable character of slavery and the slave trade and, more generally, to treat historical wrongs as crimes against humanity, is to assert that the debt can never be paid off because of the gravity of the crime. Paradoxically, this acknowledgement of debt can have a positive function, which lies precisely in the recognition of the exceptional nature of the crime. The only way to attest to the radical nature of crimes against humanity is to refuse to make or accept any reparation based on accounting principles.

Should we argue then, by analogy with the more eccentric forms of living matter, for a kind of a-reparability? For refusing to repair a-nomal living forms in the name of the creativity and diversity of life and refusing to repair historical injustices so as not to reduce them to an accounting schedule? In either case, it is about justifying non-reparation in order to resist either a statistical norm (in biology), or a norm of monetary equivalence (in civil law). The paradox of the historically a-reparable, at least in a logic of monetary equivalence, is that it opposes reparation in the name of respect for the victims of crimes against humanity. Not only non-reparation by default (due to technical impossibility) but also non-reparation by design (as a moral protest).

But surely the historically a-reparable leads to the persistence of debt, potentially generating festering resentment among representatives of the victims, and festering guilt among representatives of the perpetrators? On the one hand, as Garapon points out, following the work of Jacques Godbout,[34] moral (and not only economic) indebtedness is part of the moral structure of social relations. Who can claim to have no moral debt toward their family, friends or colleagues? The social fact of reparation does not mean that we could ever "pay off" all our debts. It is another social fact that we live in a world of mutual indebtedness:

> To dream of a world that is totally "quits," that could start again "with a clean sheet" once its liabilities have been cleared and its accounts settled, is as illusory as to imagine a world without guilt, a world restored to its original innocence. Better to accept that these historical debts cannot be paid, that no country can claim to be definitively free of debt, and that we will never be even with each other.[35]

On the other hand, acknowledging a historical debt does not necessarily presuppose that the burden should be placed on present and future generations who are in no way responsible for the crimes committed by their forebears. Contemporaries and successors are not accountable for the debts left by their predecessors.

The (positive) recognition of an a-reparable—of an unpaid debt, according to a retributive accounting logic—with the aim of attesting to its radical nature and paradoxically paying homage to the victims, is not, however, incompatible with other forms of material reparation (such as development aid, educational grants, or the cancellation of debts, to cite our earlier examples). As Césaire pleads in the same interview: "The West must do something, help countries to develop, to be reborn. It owes us this aid, but I don't think we need to present a bill for reparations. It is aid, not a contract."[36] While not all debt can—nor should—be paid, in the name of the a-reparable, this in no way diminishes the duty of the former criminal states to engage in economic and social development assistance programs to countries that have endured historical injustice.

The obligation may be more moral than legal, but this form of material reparation, free from any logic of equivalence, presupposes an act of recognition of the historical facts and of the harm suffered, a sharing of responsibilities by all parties (not only the former colonial powers) toward the victims of the past. Any policy of reparation is always, at the same time, a policy of recognition. Though one may sometimes doubt the sincerity of third-party-repairers, because of the ever-present possibly of abuses and instrumentalization of the memory of the victims, the political use of moral reparation—through apologies, regrets or requests for forgiveness—can nonetheless provide a lever for calming a troubled past and rebuilding a new future.

That was the motivation behind the gesture of Willy Brandt, one of the first heads of state to presage the political use of moral reparation for historical injustices, when, on December 7, 1970, he knelt before the memorial to the dead of the former Warsaw Ghetto. The Federal Republic of Germany was a pioneer in Europe in recognizing the historical responsibility of Nazism for crimes perpetrated during the Second World War. The chancellor went beyond the customary placing of a wreath on a monument (already an act of recognition): his gesture of genuflection, which historically refers to religious ritual, accentuated the intention of moral reparation in the sense both of respect and homage to the victims and, on the part of a German political leader, of regret for past crimes. It was as a third-party repairer, like Jacques Chirac at the Vel d'Hiv a quarter-century later, that Willy Brandt performed his gesture, having never himself adhered to Nazi ideology. He had no need to apologize as an individual for the crimes committed by the Nazis, but as a representative of the German nation, which bears its collective share of responsibility for the genocide perpetrated against the Jews.

This could be called an act of "institutional repentance"—as distinct from "individual repentance,"[37] where the government official also carries some personal responsibility for the criminal past. This political use of moral reparation by no means aims to settle the entire historical debt; it does not lay to rest the irreparable and a-reparable parts of the historical wrong; nor does it imply forgetting, unlike practices such as amnesties, nor does it in any way exclude other political objectives and motivations (restoring Germany's image among the nations, rapprochement with the State of Israel, recognition of the Oder-Neisse border which had separated (East) Germany from Poland since 1945, etc.). While it assumed a part of the historical debt, Brandt's gesture did not correspond to any logic of accounting equivalence. Given the proliferation in Canada, Australia, New Zealand and France, especially from the 1990s onward, of political speeches with moral connotations at the initiative of government officials, caution must be exercised as to their true scope and motivation: do they represent a political instrumentalization of the memory of victims, or an attempt to wipe clean a historical debt simply through the rhetorical use of institutional apologies or requests for forgiveness?

The ritual of institutional apology does not have the same performative force as that of institutional forgiveness. Apology, to be effective, relies entirely on the initiative of the offender, or of the third party speaking on their behalf. While an apology invites, at least implicitly, an acceptance on the part of the offended, or of those who speak in their name, it can be made without any *de facto* acceptance. Forgiveness is expressed first as a request, as a wish from the offender (or their representative) addressed to the victim, who may legitimately reject it. Unlike an apology, there is no forgiveness, as a performative act, without the final response of the victim. The offender can apologize (and may ask for forgiveness), but only the offended can forgive— or not. But as Vladimir Jankélévitch points out,[38] institutional forgiveness does not give the victims the opportunity—especially, of course, when they are no more—to accept or reject the request; in short, to respond. The political use of forgiveness is inherently biased: it cannot really fulfill its performative function, and ultimately leads to a second form of violence (reducing the victims to silence). For this reason, as Sandrine Lefranc has observed, associations of relatives of the "disappeared" in Argentina, Uruguay and Chile, notably the "Mothers of the Plaza de Mayo," have turned down these skewed requests for forgiveness when they come from representatives of the state.[39]

The difficulty is compounded when the interpretation of the historical wrong is controversial. Who should bear the burden of the debt? Even in the case of the Second World War, where the designation of the main culprits should be beyond doubt, what are we to say about the responsibility of the Allies in the bombing of civilians (not only in Germany but also on France's Atlantic coast), sometimes with no strategic targets, not to mention the atomic destruction of Hiroshima and Nagasaki? We know that, in the case of the Algerian War, for example—officially recognized as such by the French Parliament in 1999—there is no consensus about the interpretation of the historical debt, whether on either side of the Mediterranean or among those who keep the memory alive in France. Who should recognize and assume their share of responsibility? France, for its bloody reprisals (such as Sétif), the official use of torture, and the abandonment of its local allies, the Harkis? Or Algeria, whose ruling party is a direct product of the War of Independence, for its attacks committed against the Pieds Noirs and its massacres of Harkis? Rivalries over memory are, at the same time, evidence of a mutual debt that is far from being settled, despite President Macron's recent recognition of French colonization in Algeria as a crime against humanity and of the use of torture (notably against the communist activist Pierre Audin).

The political use of moral reparation is by no means the only possible expression of a desire to repair history. Art provides another channel. Among contemporary artists who openly present their art as a way of repairing history, the work of Kader Attia deserves particular attention. Born in 1970 in the suburbs of Paris, Attia, a French-Algerian national, soon became interested in the way objects are repaired in non-Western societies. According to the artist, the Western mode of repair is singular in the way it erases the signs of fracture and covers over the cracks in an object to recreate its initial pre-damaged state, as if nothing had happened. By contrast, non-Western modes of repair, such as those found in Japan (the practice of *kintsugi*, which consists of repairing broken pottery with lacquer mixed with powdered gold) or in certain African societies, take a very different approach. After a visit to the Congo, Attia brought back a wraparound with holes that had been carefully patched by sewing in fabric from France. This mode of repair, he suggests, points above all to a "hybrid culture," creatively reappropriating foreign materials at a time when Western art is often uncomfortable about its non-Western sources of inspiration (such as African art for Picasso, or the North African architecture of the medina for Le Corbusier). It is a mode of repair that does not seek to hide the passage of time, to erase the damage, to smooth over the traces of cracking, tearing and breaking, but seeks instead to display them, continuing the process of creation by a further aesthetic gesture.[40] Rather than returning the object to its initial state, it makes it into another, yet more beautiful, object, typical of creative repair. While Western repair assumes a continuity of time in which the present reenacts the past by seeking to bring the thing back as it was, non-Western repair assumes a heterogeneity of temporalities, exalting the difference between the before and the after of the thing, while signaling a creative relationship between them.

At an exhibition entitled "Repairing the Invisible" at S.M.A.K., the Museum of Contemporary Art in Ghent in 2017, at which he presented old textiles gleaned from Africa, Attia explained the rationale behind his approach:

> Traditional repair has always signed the passage of time, accepting it, through relief, with colour sometimes, the subtlety of pronounced detail which covers the injury to reveal it . . . as if it were necessary to live with it, accept it, not to be in denial; which is probably what our contemporary society ought to learn from these everyday objects: a metaphysics of everyday life.[41]

We might reasonably question whether there is really only one Western mode of repair, given the persistence in our societies of practices of repair and making do that also testify to inventiveness, to the creative transformation of the object.

Attia's ethnographic reflection on esthetic repair is at the same time part of a political orientation that directly takes on the question of repairing history. This is not a political use of moral reparation, as found in commemorations and the speeches of government officials, but an artistic use of moral reparation for political ends. The artist does not speak on behalf of a nation, apologizing for past crimes committed by a state, but instead seeks to spotlight the suffering of the victims and showcase historical traumas in order to make his contemporaries think, as with his *J'accuse* (2016). Through his art, Attia practices bottom-up politics.

That much is clear from the installation presented by the artist in 2012 at the 13th Documenta in Kassel, entitled, "The Repair, from Occident to Extra-Western cultures." This multi-faceted exhibit comprised traditional African sculptures, damaged objects with visible repairs, the faces of Africans with deliberate esthetic alterations and the mutilated faces of soldiers (European and African) from the First World War. The meaning that Attia sought to give to his presentation was itself reparative, in a non-Western sense, by not seeking to erase the past, with its crimes, traumas and painful separations, and acting as if all had been repaired and nothing had happened. The paradox of artistic repair lies in revealing the irreparable, in exhibiting the scars of the past, in the image of the *gueules cassées* (broken faces), the facially disfigured European and African soldiers of the First World War. An analogy emerges between the way Westerners seek, on the one hand, to mask or erase the traces of broken objects, or to hide them away and, on the other, the way Europeans continue to gloss over their colonial history and render it invisible. By a reverse process, with a militant anticolonial stance, the artist makes the breakages visible, but without trying, unlike some traditional modes of repair, to embellish them:

> What the artist is advocating is a non-Western type of repair, which neither denies nor renders invisible the harm caused to dominated peoples but preserves the trace of it and recognizes the debt contracted by the West. "Repairing history" would mean, for example, recognizing that today's undocumented migrants—depicted in the slide show mobilizing as a group, or being expelled—are the descendants of Africans enlisted in the European contingents of the First World War.[42]

The debt still weighs upon the present through its impact on the victims' descendants (e.g., the effects of the slave system on race relations in post-slavery societies).

While some of the objects exhibited by Attia have indeed been repaired—creatively—how should we understand the artist's own claims to historical reparation? Is it not rather a kind of historical irreparable (or a-reparable) that he seeks to reveal through the historical fractures that have, precisely, not been repaired? If this proposed reading is accurate, we can at the same time justify two others that are not incompatible with the first. The first is to say that by displaying the scars of the unrepaired past, the artist clearly seeks to alert his contemporaries and draw their attention to their duty to repair both the past in itself and its effects on the present (for example in the form of policies towards the descendants of colonized peoples). The second is to say that by putting the past on display, the artist is performing a sort of symbolic reparation, calling for an effort and a duty of remembrance towards the beings and the faces that others have sought to efface, erase, expunge from history. In a way radically different from any government official, Attia, as an artist, acts as a third-party-repairer paying homage to the unrepaired, without himself being directly responsible for the harm they suffered.

RECONCILIATION AND TRANSITIONAL JUSTICE

Crimes of state committed on a massive scale do not only affect the destiny of individual lives: they also threaten social cohesion and coexistence in the process of democratic transition. How are we to overcome national divisions, the risks of civil conflict, and a pervasive sense of resentment? How are we to judge crimes that involve an entire state bureaucracy, or even a part of civil society? How are we to guarantee independent justice when the new regime is still in its infancy, or when the state apparatus becomes judge and jury? Such are the problems that commonly arise in situations of "transitional justice."[43]

Restorative justice, which, as we saw in the previous chapter, has been experimented with for dealing with common law crimes, in a strictly judicial framework and with the aim of restoring interpersonal relationships, has been transposed to certain forms of "transitional justice" when dealing with mass crimes. They are driven by the same end purpose of justice: social peace or national reconciliation. Reparation is no longer limited to broken interpersonal relationships but extends to the whole social body. In this respect, we can speak of a political use of reparative justice, and by derivation, of reparations policies.

Among the most significant contemporary experiments in reparations policy, the Truth and Reconciliation Commission (TRC) set up in South Africa to bring an end to the Apartheid regime, deserves special attention. The principles of restorative justice in many ways resonate with the principles of transitional justice:

Restorative justice aims to achieve fairness in the application of a sentence or solution that will serve not to punish perpetrators, but to hold them accountable (which may involve imposing a sanction); not to provide pecuniary reparations for victims, but to ensure their overall reparation; not to protect society, but to involve it in resolving the conflict.[44]

One of the procedures that distinguishes them, however, is the status granted to amnesty in the TRC framework, which is conditional on a confession by the perpetrators, whose "sincerity is hard to gauge."

The key difference between the two processes of justice, however, goes much deeper. In as much as there has never really been a "we" in South Africa, but rather racially separate "nations," one of which used to exercise unchallengeable dominance over the other, the goal of the Commission was to invent a new "Rainbow Nation" rather than to restore or reinvent one (the model typically found in the Truth Commissions of Latin America). What would "restore" mean in the case of transitional justice in South Africa? Even before the TRC came into being, the Interim Constitution (which would give it legal form) clearly set out its terms of reference:

> The pursuit of national unity, the well-being of all South African citizens and peace require reconciliation between the people of South Africa and the reconstruction of society. The adoption of this Constitution lays the secure foundation for the people of South Africa to transcend the divisions and strife of the past, which generated gross violations of human rights, the transgression of humanitarian principles in violent conflicts and a legacy of hatred, fear, guilt and revenge. These can now be addressed on the basis that there is a need for understanding but not for vengeance, a need for reparation but not for retaliation, a need for ubuntu but not for victimization.[45]

The "national" dimension of reconciliation was all the more necessary in that the victims heard by the Commission were not only those of the Apartheid regime (the government, the army, the police, etc.) but also the victims of violence perpetrated by the African National Congress (ANC) and the (largely Zulu) Inkatha Freedom Party (IFP). The Interim Constitution therefore adopted a very broad conception of victimhood.

Unlike other, sometimes older, transitional justice mechanisms (such as in Chile), the South African experiment was original in its refusal to prosecute the alleged perpetrators of crimes, albeit with certain conditions. It is not unusual, of course, to grant amnesties in order to end national discord, but the Interim Constitution made it conditional on the former criminals acknowledging the facts. That was, indeed, the key mechanism of the TRC. There was nothing automatic or unilateral about the amnesty it offered. The objective of reconciliation was conditioned by a requirement of historical truth, quite the opposite of the oblivion instituted by amnesty:

so that the break with the culture of violence, which involves refraining from using even the legal violence of criminal repression—granting amnesty, in other words—does not lead to forgetting and to the concealment of forgotten deeds— i.e. to amnesia. On the contrary, it is about facing up to it, just as the Epilogue says, in order to become fully aware of its past reality.[46]

For the purposes of our analysis, the major interest of South Africa's TRC, which sat from 1996 to 1998, lies in the way it mobilized several models of repair, some of which intermeshed and reinforced each other, sometimes even merging together. Despite its very limited means, and although it fell outside the civil law model and any logic of equivalence, legal repair (as retribution) was present in the TRC in the form of the Committee on Reparation and Rehabilitation, one of the three committees that made up the Commission.[47] The main innovation of the TRC was that it transposed different models of repair—psychological (therapy), moral (apology) and religious (atonement, forgiveness)— into a *dispositif* of reparative justice. These three models were inspired partly by traditional South-African conflict resolution practices used to redress social equilibria and restore broken relationships,[48] and partly by religious, mainly Christian, peacemaking practices (notably "the Old Testament tradition of 'returning' wrongdoers to justice and the common good").[49] The model of moral repair is here associated with a religious model of repair: by acknowledging their faults, by expiating them, by asking for forgiveness, the guilty put themselves on the path to salvation and can aspire to find the way of virtue once again, and at the same time contribute to national reconciliation.

The personality of Anglican archbishop and 1984 Nobel Peace Prize winner Desmond Tutu played a decisive role, as chairman of the TRC, in transposing the Christian ritual of forgiveness into the kind of collective catharsis that the committee hearings eventually became. While "memorial candles" were lit during the sessions, the archbishop often began each keynote address with prayers:

> For Tutu, this was nothing less than a way of counting the tears, to enable a form of catharsis, which occasionally earned the Commission the nickname "The Kleenex Commission." Victims were systematically thanked by the representatives of the TRC, who insisted on acknowledging their suffering and the contribution of their dead to the betterment of the country, and often made use of religious ritual.[50]

Although forgiveness was not necessary to protect the perpetrators from potential prosecution (recognition of the facts was, however, required), it was often requested, and sometimes that request was granted: "While the law did not require the expression of any remorse, many candidates slid from testimony into repentant confession, thus echoing one of the aims of the members of the

TRC, who were keen to move on from explanations of the facts to an attempt to understand the underlying motivations."[51]

The ethical-religious model of repair (confession, apology, forgiveness, atonement, etc.) was intended from the outset to generate psychological (therapeutic) repercussions, mainly on the victims but also on the perpetrators. Psychological repair to some extent obeys its own independent logic when victims are encouraged to relate their experiences, to express their pain; the mechanism then has the function of relieving the suffering of the wronged (repairing oneself; being repaired by another). But in as much as the therapeutic mechanism is embedded in religious ritual and mobilizes ethical-religious *reparatio* (forgiveness, atonement, confession), the modes of repair tend to become conflated. A confusion reinforced, reciprocally, by the psychological impact of the ethical-religious *reparatio*: the acknowledgement of the facts and of the status of victim, and the partial self-absolution of the perpetrators when their plea for forgiveness is heard, can have reparative effects on the psychological well-being of the witnesses. The expression "collective catharsis," sometimes used to describe how the TRC worked, says a great deal about how these reparative horizons (moral, religious, and psychological) merged together.

The ultimate goal of the Commission, however, remained national reconciliation (even at the cost of the truth); that is, a mode of political repair. While moral, religious, and psychological repair came into their own at the individual scale of the victims and perpetrators, in a dyadic relationship, as a means of self-reconstruction, they were at the same time instruments at the service of a truly political conception of repair (repairing the sick, perverted, divided body of the nation). It was as if the thousands of witnesses, acting as a single party, were expected to play out and imbue with meaning, by metonymy, the whole imagination of the nation, especially given the intense media coverage of the TRC's work. The television set became the medium of national catharsis. The "little us," in search of moral, religious and psychological repair, was to symbolically represent the "big us" of the nation, in search of political repair. And a paradoxical kind of political repair at that, as we noted earlier, since—unlike in Latin America with its Truth Commissions—the "Rainbow Nation" did not exist before the Constitution was adopted.[52] The idea of returning to some earlier status quo, taken as a point of reference, would have made no sense here. Strictly speaking, even the expression "national reconciliation" is spurious. The process of political repair was built on the embryonic ideal of a "Rainbow Nation."[53] In short, whatever political repair there was, it was in no way restorative, but rather constructive.

This is not the place for an exhaustive assessment of the work of the TRC or a discussion about the future of South Africa. We must acknowledge, however, that certain real phenomena, beyond even the "historical truth," observed among the "little us"—in terms of providing moral, religious, and psychological repair for the victims of Apartheid—have not produced the hoped-for effects at the national scale of the "big us." The process of political repair has been a relative failure, despite the end of the official Apartheid regime and the avoidance of civil war. South African society, far from becoming a "rainbow," remains one of the most violent and racist societies in the world. The virtue of restorative justice also has its downside: many criminals, suspected of serious crimes, have been able to escape any criminal sanction, generating a sense of impunity and resentment that is still perceptible. Though the work of the Commission, as Lefranc tells us, has enabled a degree of rapprochement between black and white elites, and even between some of the victims and agents of repression, reconciliation is still a distant prospect:

> The dispute over the crimes committed by the Apartheid regime is compounded by the *a priori* irreducible character of "ethno-racial" misunderstandings, and consolidated by glaring social inequalities that follow the same fault lines: South Africans continue to define themselves—and to justify their mutual misunderstandings—in terms of the racial categories forged by Apartheid. The most senior members of the repressive system, who often did not apply for amnesty, have either retrained . . . or continue to work for the security services of the new regime.[54]

The desire to repair history must preserve its highly paradoxical, not to say absurd, nature. Strictly speaking, history—especially for the historian—is done, and cannot be undone, or even repaired. From the perspective of time, it is an absolute irreparable. From the perspective of debt, however, the ambition to repair history has taken shape in response to a category of crimes, generally mass crimes, whose extreme seriousness defies the typical modes of moral and legal reparation of harm. The phenomenon is a relatively recent one (emerging mainly since the 1990s). The great trials set up after the Second World War, with their penal logic, were not directly intended to repair history, or at least its victims. The objective was first and foremost to punish the criminals.

The innovative phenomenon is the transposition of the logic of equivalence from civil law in order to hold history, or at least those responsible for historical crimes, accountable for the suffering of the victims and their descendants. Trials for historical reparation are inseparable from a process of internationalization of American lawsuit culture, as part of a post-Westphalian order. When it is enmeshed in a logic of restitution, reparation does not raise major legal or philosophical problems, apart from procedural and technical questions around the possibility of restituting what was stolen. But when reparation concerns not simply things, but the suffering of injured, damaged, broken lives, the logic of equivalence proper to corrective justice and civil law comes up against formidable obstacles. The first is the long distance of time for certain categories of mass crime, whose immediate victims have long since disappeared; the difficulty being to trace the causal chain of responsibility back in time and to identify the victims. The second and even greater obstacle is the sheer incommensurability of the harm suffered—due to its radical nature—with any accounting logic and any translation into monetary value.

The aporia inherent in historical reparation, conceived of in terms of corrective justice, can nonetheless be overcome if we make room for reparation conceived of in more moral or cultural terms (official acknowledgement of crimes, erection of memorials, opening of archives, etc.), while remaining wary of attempts to instrumentalize the political uses of moral reparation by way of "institutional repentance." Historical moral reparation is not in itself incompatible with material reparations (development aid, educational grants, etc.) if we look beyond the limitations of civil law. It remains only to plead for a kind of a-reparable, as an act of resistance against any bid to compensate for or resolve historical crimes and tragedies whose enormity defies any possibility of full reparation. Accepting the a-reparable is not about forgetting; it is about recognizing the abyss of history.

NOTES

1. Born in 1942, Garcin Malsa is one of the founders, along with Alfred Marie-Jeanne, of the "Mouvement indépendantiste martiniquais." He was elected mayor of the municipality of Saint-Anne for twenty-five years.
2. The anti-colonialist commemorative regime of slavery emerged in the French Antilles during the 1950s and 1960s within the pro-independence and nationalist movement (notably the Martinique Progressive Party founded by Aimé Césaire). With the aim of building a new nation, the memorial narrative no longer emphasizes the Republic that freed the slaves from their chains by "decree," but the anti-slavery struggles, the maroons, the insurrections, etc. (see J. Michel, *Devenir descendant d'esclave. Enquête sur les régimes mémoriels*. Rennes: PUR, 2015).
3. F. Hartog, *Régimes d'historicité. Présentisme et expériences du temps*. Paris: Seuil, 2003.
4. Antoine Garapon, *Peut-on réparer l'histoire? op. cit.*
5. *Ibid.*, p. 58.
6. Quoted in *Le Monde*, September 3, 2019.
7. Antoine Garapon, *Peut-on réparer l'histoire? op. cit.*, p. 109.

8. For a legal and philosophical discussion of the procedures for obtaining reparation for victims of crimes against humanity within the ICC framework, see Jean-Baptiste Jeangène Vilmer, *Réparer l'irréparable. Les réparations aux victimes devant la CPI*. Paris: PUF, 2015.

9. A. Garapon, *Peut-on réparer l'histoire? op. cit.*, p. 114.

10. A class action is a lawsuit or procedure that allows a large number of people to sue a company or public institution for financial compensation. The advantage of this procedure is that it allows a large number of individual claims to be brought together into a single lawsuit, thus increasing the chances of success at the end of the trial.

11. The French case is distinct, however, in that—in accordance with the wishes of President Jacques Chirac and under pressure from part of France's Jewish "community"—a process of restituting looted Jewish property was undertaken at the initiative of the government of Prime Minister Alain Juppé, with the establishment of the Mattéoli Commission (1997), tasked with evaluating the unclaimed assets. The commission's report estimated the amount of confiscated Jewish property at 5.2 billion francs, not counting the looting of apartments and works of art by the Germans. Subsequently, a "Commission for the Compensation of Victims of Spoliation Resulting from the Anti-Semitic Legislation in Force during the Occupation," chaired by Pierre Drai, was set up in September 1999 to respond to the individual claims of victims and their heirs (*Guide des recherches dans les archives des spoliations et des restitutions* / Mission d'étude *sur la spoliation des Juifs de France* (ed. Caroline Piketty with the collaboration of Christophe Dubois and Fabrice Launay). Paris: La Documentation française, coll. "Mission étude spoliation Juifs," 2000).

12. A. Garapon, *Peut-on réparer l'histoire?, op. cit.*, p. 42.

13. In another context, the same procedure has been initiated with Western museums by formerly colonized African countries. It is not about *reparation*, but about the *restitution* of looted works. In November 2018, for example, the governor of Easter Island requested the return of a Moai basalt monolith that had been kept at the British Museum for 150 years.

14. A. Garapon, *Peut-on réparer l'histoire, op. cit.*, p. 49.

15. The creation of the Foundation (followed a few years later, in 2005, by the inauguration of the Holocaust Memorial in Paris) took place in the same year (2000) as the adoption of a "National Day in Memory of the Victims of Racist and Anti-Semitic Crimes committed by the French State and in Homage to the 'Righteous' of France," which, following a landmark speech by President Chirac, recognized France's responsibility in the Holocaust.

16. J. Michel, *Le devoir de mémoire. Paris*: Que sais-je? 2018.

17. D. Fassin, R. Rechtman, *The Empire of Trauma, op. cit.*

18. J. Michel, *Devenir descendant d'esclave, op. cit.*

19. F. Ade Ajayi, "La politique de Réparation dans le contexte de la mondialisation," *Cahiers d'études africaines*, no. 173–74, 2004, pp. 41–63.

20. The CDM was founded by Serge Chalons, a medical doctor, member of Médecins du Monde and of the Mouvement des Autonomistes et Progressistes (close to the Parti Progressiste Martiniquais founded by Césaire) and by the geographer Christian

Jean-Etienne, a faculty member of the IUFM teacher-training college in the French Antilles.

21. The conference papers, a valuable archive document, were published in a volume that is now out of print: *De l'esclavage aux réparations* (ed. S. Chalons, Ch. Jean-Etienne, S. Landan, A. Yébakima) Paris: Karthala, 2000.

22. For a multidisciplinary approach to the Yugoslav case, see the work coordinated by Isabelle Delpla and Magali Bessone (eds.) *Peines de guerre: la justice pénale internationale et l'ex-Yougoslavie*. Paris: Éditions de l'EHESS, 2010.

23. Pierre Truche, who acted as public prosecutor at the trial of Klaus Barbie, later confirmed this qualification: "The enslavement of African peoples to work in the American colonies, regulated by the French state in its 'Code Noir,' was a crime against humanity" (P. Truche, "Les facteurs d'évolution de la notion de crime contre l'humanité," *Le Crime contre l'humanité*, texts collected by Bruno Gravier and Jean-Marc Elchardus, under the direction of Marcel Colin. Ramonville: Erès, 1996, p. 34.).

24. E. Jos, "Esclavage et crime contre l'humanité," *De l'esclavage aux réparations* (eds. S. Chalons, Ch. Jean-Etienne, S. Landan, A. Yébakima) Paris: Karthala, 2000, pp. 144–45.

25. Report no. 1378 filed on February 10, 1999, with the National Assembly, Archives of the 11th Legislature.

26. Draft bill no. 1297 submitted to the National Assembly by Christiane Taubira on December 22, 1998.

27. Demands for material reparations resurfaced in the national debate at the very beginning of President François Hollande's five-year term. Taking advantage of the appointment as Prime Minister of Jean-Marc Ayrault (hailed for his action in favor of the memory of slavery in Nantes), Louis-George Tin's CRAN (accompanied by representatives from MIR) hoped to find a sympathetic ear in the new administration for the opening of discussions about material reparations for slavery. President Hollande was quick to close this window of opportunity, at least in terms of financial compensation, especially in a context of government spending cuts. The Head of State was nevertheless favorable, as a form of moral and cultural reparation, to the creation of the ACTe Memorial or "Caribbean Center of Expression and Memory of Human Trafficking and Slavery" which he inaugurated in Pointe-à-Pitre, Guadeloupe, on May 10, 2015.

28. On this point, see the contribution of Magalie Bessone, who seeks to design a model of reparation that goes beyond corrective justice alone by taking as a basis the decision rendered on April 29, 2014, by the court of Fort-de-France, Martinique, regarding the lawsuit filed by certain associations (The International Movement for Reparations and The World Council of the Pan-African Diaspora) against the French state for its "responsibility" in slavery and the slave trade. While acknowledging France's responsibility in slavery and the slave trade, the judges dismissed all the claims of the parties. One of the arguments put forward by the judges was that the law of May 10, 2001 (recognizing slavery as a crime against humanity) is not a reparative law (in the sense of civil law) but a declarative law, with no normative implications (M. Bessone, "Les réparations au titre de l'esclavage colonial: l'impossible paradigme judiciaire," *Droit et société*, 2019/2 (no. 102), pp. 357–77).

29. A. Garapon, *Peut-on réparer l'histoire?, op. cit.*, p. 239.
30. *Ibid.*, p. 93.
31. *Ibid.*, p. 83.
32. P. Descola, *Beyond Nature and Culture*, trans. J. Lloyd, Chicago: University of Chicago Press, 2013.
33. A. Césaire, *Nègre je suis, nègre je resterai* (conversation with F. Vergès). Paris: Albin Michel, 2005. Extracts of the conversation are reproduced on the *Creoleways* website: https://creoleways.com/2015/03/31/aime-cesaire-esclavage-et-reparations-sortir-de-la-victimisation-est-fondamental/.
34. Jacques Godbout, *Le don, la dette et l'identité: homo donator versus homo oeconomicus*. Paris: Éd. La Découverte, 2000.
35. A. Garapon, *Peut-on réparer l'histoire?, op. cit.*, p. 247.
36. A. Césaire, *Nègre je suis, nègre je resterai, op. cit.*
37. S. Lefranc, *Politiques du pardon*. Paris: PUF, 2002, p. 16.
38. V. Jankélévitch, *Le pardon*. Paris: Champs Essais, 2019.
39. S. Lefranc, *op. cit.*, p. 252.
40. See the excellent study by Brigitte Derlon and Monique Jeudy-Ballini, "Appropriations et réparations dans l'oeuvre de Kader Attia" in B. Derlon and M. Jeudy-Ballini (eds), *L'Art en transfert*. Paris: L'Herne, Cahiers d'anthropologie sociale, pp. 77–94, 2015.
41. K. Attia, Presentation of the exhibition at SMAK, March 27, 2017 (https://smak.be/fr/exposition/10994).
42. B. Derlon and M. Jeudy-Ballini, "Appropriations et réparations dans l'oeuvre de Kader Attia," *op. cit.*, p. 83. Derlon and Jeudy-Ballini partly turn Attia's own argument against him by showing that the artist uses and exhibits works from countries that are not his own, without always indicating their provenance or their original creators, thus opening himself up to the criticism of adopting a "colonialist" attitude in a professedly anticolonialist artistic initiative.
43. "Transitional Justice refers to a set of judicial and non-judicial measures and mechanisms aimed at overcoming a legacy of violence, abuse of power, and state crimes in societies emerging from armed conflict or authoritarian rule. The guidelines of the International Center for Transitional Justice (ICTJ) outline four main areas of intervention: prosecutions, truth-seeking mechanisms, reparations programs, and institutional reforms. Reconciliation and commemoration transcend these four themes, while at the same time representing the goals of Transitional Justice." (Emilie Matignon, "Dispositifs restauratifs et victimisation de masse," *La justice restaurative. Une utopie qui marche? op. cit.*, p. 71).
44. *Ibid.*, p. 84.
45. From the Epilogue to the Interim Constitution of South Africa (1993).
46. B. Cassin, O. Cayla, Ph. Salazar, "Dire la vérité, faire la réconciliation, manquer la réparation," *Le genre humain*, no. 2, 2004, p. 14.
47. The two others being the Committee on Human Rights Violations and the Committee on Amnesty.

48. The Epilogue to the Interim Constitution refers explicitly to the concept of *ubuntu*, which, in Bantu societies, defines the quality of a person in terms of their bonds to others.

49. B. Cassin, O. Cayla, Ph. Salazar, op. cit., p. 17.

50. S. Lefranc, *Politiques du pardon, op. cit.*, p. 62.

51. *Ibid.*, p. 63.

52. As Cassin, Cayla and Salazar point out, before the completion of the TRC's work, the terms of an agreement between the conflicting parties had to be reached, if only to draft an interim constitution and the Commission's frame of reference. Without speaking of a pre-existing nation, the objective of national reconciliation was based on a draft conciliation agreement, if not at national level, then at least between the institutional protagonists, after lengthy negotiations and bargaining (B. Cassin, O. Cayla, Ph. Salazar, "Dire la vérité, faire la réconciliation, manquer la réparation," *op. cit.*, p. 20).

53. All else being equal, this is the same process that we encountered in the context of the repair of certain living beings (for example, people born with disabilities) when the therapeutic project is constructed according to an ideal (or statistical) norm rather than according to a previous situation, held up as a dominant standard, from which something is supposed to be restored.

54. S. Lefranc, *Politiques du pardon, op. cit.*, p. 346.

Conclusion

Repair is a global phenomenon of the human condition, though with no single, unified character. Only a philosophical approach, with its reflective and all-encompassing vocation, can grasp the concept in all its anthropological depth. Philosophical tradition is rich in insights that help us outline its basic contours, but it is not sufficient for an appreciation of its particular expressions. To analyze the specific processes and mechanisms involved in repair, in its diverse manifestations, we need to integrate the "positive knowledges" of the natural sciences, psychology, sociology, and law.

The fact that repair affects all human activities, indeed all living beings, does not necessarily imply that it we are constantly repairing and being repaired. There are other regulatory mechanisms that monitor natural and social organisms in order to prevent the need for repair, such as prophylaxis in the medical field, or social rituals of avoidance. It is when these preventive measures fail, when a set of events negatively affects the organism's functionality and equilibrium, that repair comes into play. Generally, repair is a *response* to the experience of *loss*: loss of the use of something, of the functioning of an organ, of the love of a another, of one's self-esteem, of the purity of an order. It can also, in other cases, be a response that does not look back to a prior state that needs to be reestablished, but rather to a social norm that needs to be complied with. Repairing birth defects does not make sense in terms of restoring an earlier situation and is not a response to an original loss; it is understood as bringing the individual into conformity with a prevailing norm.

Only an analogical method allows us to envisage repair both as a general phenomenon and in its particular forms, with their similarities and differences. Viewed solely from the perspective of the Other, acts of repair appear simply to be about language games or about fragmented and heterogeneous forms of life that have nothing fundamental to say about being human. But if repair is omnipresent, it is because it bears witness, in each of its domains of application, to human vulnerability, fallibility and fragility, and to our efforts to remedy them. Viewed solely from the perspective of the Same, acts of repair are reduced to a single level of analysis, overlooking its specific expressions. The analogical method, on the other hand, enables us to identify ideal-typical models of repair that have both common characteristics and distinctive features: the biological model (scarring), the psychological model (the work of mourning), the religious model (atonement), the moral and social model (apology), and the legal model (compensation for harm).

The use of analogy also helps to guard against the risk of naturalizing or essentializing repair, for example by making one model the basis of all the others. Each model has a degree of autonomy that prevents us from elevating any one of them to an overarching position. But along the common thread that runs from simple self-repair of living things to historical reparations for crimes against humanity, the scale of gravity changes, and with it the complexity of the reparative mechanisms. This change of scale makes any attempt at reduction meaningless, when we consider the importance of the *reparatio* as a set of technical objects and action sequences, from the most rudimentary to the most complex, which are rigorously distinguished from one model to another.

Investigating the uses of repair in the living world enables us at the same time to focus on how certain ideal-typical models of repair borrow from one another, and sometimes intermesh. The way, for example, in which the psychological and therapeutic model of repair (relief of suffering) has been imported into law (reparations for harm). Or the way religious models (forgiveness and atonement) and moral models (apologies) of repair have been transferred into certain mechanisms of historical reparation. Even scarring is sometimes used, at least as a metaphor, to describe the healing of a wound of the soul in the psychological domain. It is precisely because there is a *sameness-in-difference* across the various reparative models that such boundary transgressions are possible. The advantage of talking about ideal-typical models of repair is that it does not cement each model into a fixed set of practices, and allows us to be attentive to the discrepancies and boundary crossings that are often observed in their actual use.

Favoring an anthropological approach enables us to affirm that repair affects humans in every dimension of their humanity (economic, biological, psychological, social, religious, legal, and political). Phenomena of repair, in each field of application, are nevertheless undergoing historical transformations that only positive knowledge can help us explain. In the field of medicine and the manipulation of living organisms, unprecedented scientific and technological innovations are making the boundary between repair and augmentation ever more permeable. In the field of psychology, there is a growing demand, even an injunction, for self-repair, against the backdrop of the increasing individualization of Western societies. In the field of law, the aims of justice are being transformed to converge with the therapeutic age of repair. In the field of historical reparation, exceptional measures are being deployed to respond to the enormity of crimes against humanity.

Does this mean that we repair more today than in the past? In some fields, due to technological innovations and legal transformations, that is indeed the predominant trend, at least for Western societies. But even more than the actual practice of repair, it is the incessant *demand* for repair that seems to be the hallmark of our time. This is not true in every domain, however. One cannot evade the fact that in most Western societies, as a result of secularization, religious reparation is in relative decline. Equally, it is obvious that, due to transformations in our modes of production, items are less repairable and more prone to obsolescence. The analogical method therefore prevents us from concluding that repair is growing exponentially at every level of expression.

Not everything can be repaired. Such an affirmation does not only mean, trivially, that there are things, beings and situations that have not been repaired and which, in many cases, probably never will be, whether deliberately, or through negligence, or due to technical incapacity. Our world is constantly being populated, and will continue to be, with damaged things left in a state of abandonment, with living things heading for extinction, with people in a state of psychological distress, with wrongs that remain unforgiven and with crimes left unpunished. To say that not everything can be repaired means, moreover, that when repair does take place, it always leaves, to varying degrees, a residue, a trace, an absence; in short, its share of the irreparable. Repair, in other words, however successful, is never in every respect a pure and simple return to the initial situation. The restoration of a work of art, even by the best specialists, will never return the work to its pristine state, although the repair may be creative and may reconfigure the initial object in an original way. The lesion of an organ, once healed, will always leave a mark. Even when forgiven, an offense will still leave a trace.

A distinction must be drawn between the irreparable of time and the irreparable of debt. A debt may be partially forgiven (though liable to resurface) in the case, for example, of an offense, but without the initial misdeed disappearing from the face of time. To repair does not mean to return to a previous state as if nothing had happened, but rather to reestablish the use of a thing (after it was damaged), to revive the functionality of an organism (after a lesion), to renew the capacity to live and to love (after a psychological shock), to reinstate oneself in a sacred order (after defilement), to restore self-esteem (after an offense), or to remedy the loss of property (after it was stolen).

Repair undoubtedly takes its most dramatic and aporetic turn when confronted with irreversible destruction (of human or natural origin), and when there is no real mechanism to compensate for the loss suffered. From the inability of an organism to recover its functionality, or of an ecosystem to regain its equilibrium, to the paroxysm of crimes against humanity, no principle of equivalence, not even among those that can be translated into monetary values, can ever measure and counterbalance the harm. The irreparable is a direct expression of the incommensurable. Seeking at all costs to find an equivalent for something that defies all measurement could, paradoxically, detract from the extreme seriousness of the crime (and denigrate the memory of the victims) by reducing it to a convertible quantity (such as money). To break free from this aporia we must bring in a third term, one that has permeated our entire investigation: that of the a-reparable, as an alternative to the reparable and the irreparable. The a-reparable is irreparable not by default (because one cannot), but by design (because one must not); it points not to a deficit of reparability, but to the danger of excess. The a-reparable does not imply forgetting, still less denial; it implies the full recognition of the incommensurability of loss, and resistance to any possibility of measurement. It is doubtless the most difficult position to hold—worthy of the spiritual exercises practiced by the Ancients—given that humanity, no less than Nature, abhors a vacuum.

Bibliography

Aberdam Daniel, "Réparer ou régénérer, il faut choisir," *Médecines/sciences*, 23, pp. 783–807, 2007.
Ade Ajayi Jacob Festus, "La politique de Réparation dans le contexte de la mondialisation," *Cahiers d'études africaines*, no. 173–74, 2004, pp. 41–63.
Ameisen Jean-Claude, *La sculpture du vivant. Le suicide cellulaire ou la mort créatrice*. Paris: Seuil, 1999.
Andler Daniel, *La silhouette de l'humain. Quelle place pour le naturalisme aujourd'hui ?* Paris: Gallimard, 2016.
Aristotle, *History of Animals*. London: Bell, 1887.
———. *The Nicomachean Ethics*, trans. D. Ross, Oxford: Oxford University Press, 2009.
———. *On Rhetoric*, trans. G.A. Kennedy. New York: Oxford University Press, 2007.
Augustine (Saint), *Confessions and Enchiridion*, ed., trans. A.C. Outler, Louisville: Westminster John Knox Press, 2006.
Badot Pierre-Marie & Richard Hervé, "Est-il possible et loisible de 'réparer' la Nature?," *De la réparation* (Jean-Marie Schaeffer ed.). Paris: L'Harmattan, 2010.
Barbot Janine & Dodier Nicolas, "The Force of *Dispositifs*," trans. M.C. Behrent, *Annales. Histoire, Sciences Sociales*, vol. 71e année, no. 2, 2016, pp. 421–50.
———. "Dealing with compassion at work. Strategic reflexivity among court lawyers," trans. C. Hinton, *Sociologie du travail*, 57, 56, 2014, pp. 365–85.
Bardhoshi Nebi, On the Anthropology of Blood-Feuds During a Time of 'Total Crisis'" *Ethnologie française*, 2017/2 (no. 166), pp. 331–40.
Bastien Joseph, *Healers of the Andes: Kallawaya Herbalists and Their Medicinal Plants*. Salt Lake City: University of Utah Press, 1988.
Benvenuto Andrea, "De quoi parlons-nous quand nous parlons de 'sourds'?" *Télémaque*, 25, pp. 73–86, 2004/1.
Bernard Claude, *Principes de médecine expérimentale*. Paris: PUF, 2008.
Besnier Jean-Michel, *Demain, les posthumains*. Paris: Fayard, 2012.

Bessone Magalie & Delpha Isabelle (eds.) *Peines de guerre: la justice pénale internationale et l'ex-Yougoslavie*. Paris: Éditions de l'EHESS, 2010.

Bessone Magalie, "Les réparations au titre de l'esclavage colonial: l'impossible paradigme judiciaire," *Droit et société*, 2019/2 (no. 102), pp. 357–77.

Beuchot Mauricio & González Jorge Enrique, *Diversité et dialogue interculturel*. Paris: Editions des archives contemporaines, 2018.

Bloch Marc, *The Royal Touch*, trans. J.E. Anderson. London: Routledge, 2015.

Boltanski Luc & Chiapello Eve, *The New Spirit of Capitalism*, trans. G. Elliott. London: Verso, 2007.

Bouffartigue Jean, "L'automédication des animaux chez les auteurs antiques," Isabelle Boehm & Pascal Luccioni (eds.), *Le médecin initié par l'animal*. Lyon: Maison de l'Orient et de la Méditerranée, 2008, pp. 79–96.

Bougerol Charles, "La sorcellerie aux Antilles : Interactions et malheurs," *Socio-anthropologie* [online], 5 | 1999, posted January 15, 2003, accessed April 25, 2018.

Bowlby John, *Attachment and Loss*. New York: Basic Books, 1980.

Camproux-Duffrène Marie-Pierre, "La réparation du dommage environnemental," *De la Réparation*, (Christophe Schaeffer ed.). Paris: L'Harmattan, 2010.

Canguilhem George, *Knowledge of Life*, ed. P. Marrati, T. Meyers, trans S. Geroulanos, D. Ginsburg. New York: Fordham University Press, 2008.

———. *The Normal and the Pathological*, trans. C.R. Fawcett. New York: Zone Books, 1991

Cario Robert (ed.), *La justice restaurative. Une utopie qui marche*? Paris: L'Harmattan, 2010.

Caroli J., Hecht Y., André J., "Foie," *Encyclopædia Universalis* [online, in French], accessed on April 5, 2018. URL: http://www.universalis.fr/encyclopedie/foie//.

Cassin Barbara, Cayla Olivier, Salazar Philippe, "Dire la vérité, faire la réconciliation, manquer la réparation," *Le genre humain*, no. 2, 2004.

Centemeri Laura, "Reframing problems of incommensurability in environmental conflicts through pragmatic sociology. From value pluralism to the plurality of modes of engagement with the environment," *Environmental Values*, 24, (3), 299–320, 2015.

Césaire Aimé, *Nègre je suis, nègre je resterai* (conversation with F. Vergès). Paris: Albin Michel, 2005.

Chalons Serge., Jean-Etienne Christian., Landan S., Yébakima A., *De l'esclavage aux réparations*. Paris: Karthala, 2000.

Changeux Jean-Pierre & Ricœur Paul, *What Makes Us Think?* Trans. M.B. Debevoise. Princeton, NJ: Princeton University Press, 2010.

Chappoz Y & Pupion P-Ch., "Le New Public Management," *Gestion et management public*, vol. 1/2, no. 2, 2012, pp. 1–3.

Churchland Patricia, *Neurophilosophy: Toward a Unified Science of the Mind-Brain*, Cambridge, MA, MIT Press, 1986.

Cingolani Patrick, *L'exil du précaire*. Paris: Klincksiek, 1986.

Clerget Joël, "L'irréparable outrage," *De la réparation* (Christophe Schaeffer ed.). Paris: L'Harmattan, 2010.

Costa-Neto E.M., "Zoopharmacognosy, the self-medication behavior of animals," *Interfaces Científicas-Saúde e Ambiente*, vol. 1, no. 1, 2012, pp. 61–72.

Cotsarelis George, "Epithelial stem cells: a folliculocentric view," *J Invest Dermatol*, 126, pp. 1459–68, 2006.

Cyrulnik Boris, *Resilience: How Your Inner Strength Can Set You Free from the Past*, trans. D. Macey. New York: Tarcher, 2011.

———. *Les âmes blessées*. Paris: Odile Jacob, 2014.

Damasio Antonio, *Self Comes to Mind*. New York: Pantheon Books, 2010.

David Victor, "La lente consécration de la nature, sujet de droit: le monde est-il stone?," *Revue juridique de l'Environnement*, 3, 2012, pp. 469–85.

Dawkins Richard, *The extended phenotype: The gene as the unit of selection*, Oxford: W.H. Freeman and Company, 1982.

Deleuze Gilles & Guattari Felix, *A Thousand Plateaus*, trans. B. Massumi. Minneapolis: University of Minnesota Press, 1987.

———. *Kafka: Toward a Minor Literature*, Minneapolis: University of Minnesota Press, 1986.

Derlon Brigitte & Jeudy-Ballini Monique, "Appropriations et réparations dans l'oeuvre de Kader Attia," in B. Derlon & M. Jeudy-Ballini (eds.), *L'Art en transfert*. Paris: L'Herne, Cahiers d'anthropologie sociale, pp. 77–94, 2015.

Descola Philippe, *Beyond Nature and Culture*, trans. J. Lloyd, Chicago: University of Chicago Press, 2013.

Descombes Vincent, *Les institutions du sens*. Paris: Editions de Minuit, 1996.

Diaz Paola, "Les chemins de la publicisation de la torture au Chili," *Sociologie* [online], Dossiers, L'expérience latino-américaine de la sociologie pragmatique francophone, posted May 23, 2017, accessed March 28, 2019. http:// journals.openedition.org/sociologies/6281.

Douglas Mary, *Purity and Danger: An analysis of the concepts of pollution and taboo*. London: Routledge, 2001.

Dutreuil Sébastien, "Lovelock, Gaïa et la pollution: un scientifique entrepreneur à l'origine d'une nouvelle science et d'une philosophie politique de la nature," *Zilsel science, technique, société*, Editions du Croquant, 2017, pp. 19–61.

———. "L'hypothèse Gaïa : pourquoi s'y intéresser même si l'on pense que la Terre n'est pas un organisme?," *Bulletin de la Société d'Histoire et d'Épistémologie des Sciences de la Vie* (SHESVIE), 19 (2): 229–41.

Ehrenberg Alain, *The Weariness of the Self: Diagnosing the History of Depression in the Contemporary Age*, trans. D. Homel *et al.* Montreal: McGill-Queen's University Press, 2010.

———. *Le culte de la performance*. Paris: Fayard, 2011.

Elferink Jan, "The Inca healer: empirical medical knowledge and magic in pre-Columbian Peru," *Revista de Indias*, 2015, vol. LXXV, no. 264, pp. 323–50.

Epicurus, *La Lettre à Ménécée*. Paris: Hatier, 1999.

Fassin Didier & Rechtman Richard, *The Empire of Trauma: An Inquiry into the Condition of Victimhood*, trans. R. Gomme. Princeton: Princeton University Press, 2007.

Favret-Saada Jeanne, *Deadly Words*, trans. Catherine Cullen, Cambridge: Cambridge University Press, 2010.

Ferry Luc, *La révolution transhumaniste*. Paris: Plon, 2016.

Fischbach Franck, *Manifeste pour une philosophie sociale*. Paris: La Découverte, 2009.

Foessel Michael, *Le temps de la consolation*. Paris: Seuil, 2015.

Fornari Giuseppe, "Labyrinthine Strategies of Sacrifice: The *Cretans* by Euripides." *Contagion: Journal of Violence, Mimesis, and Culture*, vol. 4, 1997, pp. 163–88.

Foucault Michel, *Madness and Civilization: A History of Insanity in the Age of Reason*, trans. R. Howard. New York: Vintage, 1988.

———. *Discipline and Punish*, trans. A. Sheridan. New York: Vintage Books, 1991.

———. *The History of Sexuality, Vol. 1*, trans. R. Hurley. New York: Pantheon, 1978.

———. *L'herméneutique du sujet*. Paris: Gallimard, 2001.

———. *Naissance de la biopolitique*. Paris: Gallimard, 2004.

———. *Mal faire, dire vrai*, edition compiled by Fabienne Brion and Bernard E. Harcourt. Louvain: Presses universitaires de Louvain, 2012.

———. *About the Beginning of the Hermeneutics of the Self*, trans. G. Burchell. Chicago: University of Chicago Press, 2016.

Francour Patrice, "Les mesures compensatoires permettent-elles une réelle réparation des milieux naturels?," *De la réparation* (Jean-Marie Schaeffer ed.). Paris: L'Harmattan, 2010.

Fraser N and Gordon L, "A Genealogy of Dependency: Tracing a keyword of the US Welfare State," *Signs* 19(21), pp. 309–36, 1994.

Frazer James, *The Golden Bough*. New York: Oxford University Press, 1998.

Freud Sigmund, *Papers on Metapsychology and Other Works*, London: Hogarth, 1957.

Gage F.H., "Stem cells of the central nervous system," *Current Opinion in Neurobiology* 8, pp. 671–76, 1998.

Gaillard-Seux Patricia, "L'automédication animale: le serpent et le fenouil, l'hirondelle et la chélidoine. Du mythe à l'indication médicale," *Histoire, médecine et santé* [online], 8 | Winter 2015, posted July 3, 2017, accessed April 20, 2018. http://journals.openedition.org/hms/862; DOI : 10.4000/hms.862.

Garapon Antoine, *Peut-on réparer l'histoire?* Paris: Odile Jacob, 2008.

Garapon Antoine, Puech Thierry, Gros Frédéric, *Et ce sera Justice. Punir en démocratie*. Paris: Odile Jacob, 2001.

Garrau Marie & Le Goff Alice, *Care, Justice et dépendance*. Paris: PUF, 2010.

Gefen Alexandre, *Réparer le monde*. Paris: Editions Corti, 2017.

Gernet Louis, *Droit et institutions en Grèce antique*. Paris: Flammarion, 1982.

Gilbert Scott, *Developmental Biology*. Sunderland: Sinauer Associates Inc., 2000.

Gilligan Carol, *In a Different Voice: Psychological Theory and Women's Development*. Cambridge, MA: Harvard University Press, 2016.

Girard René, *Violence and the Sacred*, trans. P. Gregory. London: Bloomsbury Academic, 2013.

———. *Evolution and Conversion: Dialogues on the Origins of Culture*. London: Bloomsbury Academic, 2007.

Godbout Jacques, *Le don, la dette et l'identité : homo donator versus homo oeconomicus*. Paris: La Découverte, 2000.

Goffman Ervin, *Asylums*. New York: Anchor, 1961.

———. *Relations in Public: Microstudies of the Public Order*. New York: Basic Books, 1971.

———. *Interaction Ritual*. New York: Pantheon, 1961.

Golse Bernard, "Le concept de réparation dans le champ de la Pédopsychiatrie et de la Psychopathologie Infanto-juvénile," in *De la réparation* (Christophe Schaeffer ed.). Paris: L'Harmattan, 2010.

Gondard Eric, "Visages de la médecine," *Sociétés*, 2013/3 (no. 121), pp. 127–35.

Goody Jack, *The Domestication of the Savage Mind*, Cambridge University Press, 1977.

Gros Frédéric, *A Philosophy of Walking*, trans. John Howe. London: Verso, 2014.

Habermas Jürgen, *The Future of Human Nature*, Cambridge: Polity, 2003.

Hadot Pierre, *What is Ancient Philosophy?* Trans. M. Chase. Cambridge, MA: Belknap Press, 2004.

Hartog François, *Régimes d'historicité. Présentisme et expériences du temps*. Paris: Seuil, 2003.

Hegel Georg W.F., *Elements of the Philosophy of Right*, trans. H.B. Nisbet. Cambridge: Cambridge University Press, 2003.

Hénaff Marcel, *The Philosophers' Gift*, trans. J-L. Morhange, New York: Fordham University Press, 2020.

Hermitte Marie-Angèle, "La nature, sujet de droit?," *Annales. Histoire, Sciences Sociales*, vol. 66e année, no. 1, 2011, pp. 173–212.

Heuzé Vincent, "Une reconsidération du principe de la réparation intégrale," https://www.courdecassation.fr/colloques_activites_formation_4/2005_2033/repartion_integrale_8065.html#_ftn1.

Honneth Axel, *Ce que social veut dire. II Les pathologies de la raison*. Paris: Gallimard, 2015.

Hottois Gilbert, *Philosophie et idéologies trans/posthumanistes*, foreword by Jean-Yves Goffi. Paris: Vrin, coll. "Pour demain," 2017.

Hutchins, E.D., Markov, G.J., Eckalbar, W.L., George, R.M., King, J.M, et al., "Transcriptomic Analysis of Tail Regeneration in the Lizard *Anolis carolinensis* Reveals Activation of Conserved Vertebrate Developmental and Repair Mechanisms," *PLOS ONE* 9(8), e105004, 2014.

Jankélévitch Vladimir, *Le pardon*. Paris: Champs Essais, 2019.

Joas Hans, *The Sacredness of the Person*. Washington, DC: Georgetown University Press, 2013.

Jonas Hans, *The Imperative of Responsibility: In search of an ethics for the technological age*. Chicago: Chicago University Press, 1984.

Jos Emmanuel, "Esclavage et crime contre l'humanité," *De l'esclavage aux réparations* (ed. S. Chalons, Ch. Jean-Etienne, S. Landan, A. Yébakima). Paris: Karthala, 2000.

Karsenti Bruno, *L'homme total—Sociologie, anthropologie et philosophie chez Marcel Mauss*. Paris: PUF, 2011.

Klein Melanie (with Joan Rivière), *Love, Hate and Reparation*, London: Hogarth Press, 1953.

Korff-Sausse Simone, *Le miroir brisé*. Paris: Calmann-Lévy. Paris: 1996.

———. "La femme du pervers narcissique," Revue française de psychanalyse, 2003/3 (Vol. 67), pp. 925–42.

Kurzweil Ray, *The Singularity is Near: When Humans Transcend Biology*. New York: Penguin, 2005.

Latour Bruno, *Nous n'avons jamais été modernes*. Paris: La découverte, 1991.

———. *Facing Gaia: Eight Lectures on the New Climatic Regime*, trans. C. Porter. Cambridge: Polity, 2017.

Le Blanc Guillaume, *Vies ordinaires, vies précaires*. Paris: Seuil, 2007.

———. *L'invisibilité sociale*. Paris: PUF, 2009.

Le Breton David, "La marche est souvent guérison," *La philosophie de la marche* (ed. N. Truong), Editions Aube/Le Monde, 2018.

Lefranc Sandrine, *Politiques du pardon*. Paris: PUF, 2002.

Legendre Stéphane, "La résilience des écosystèmes," *De la Réparation* (Christophe Schaeffer ed.). Paris: L'Harmattan, 2010.

Lévi-Strauss Claude, *Mythologiques. Le cru et le cuit*, tome 1. Paris: Plon, 1978.

———. *La pensée sauvage*. Paris: Plon, 1962.

Lovelock, James, *Gaia: A New Look at Life on Earth*. Oxford: Oxford University Press, 2000.

———. *Gaia, the Practical Science of Planetary Medicine*. Oxford: Oxford University Press, 2000.

———. *The Revenge of Gaia: Why the Earth is Fighting Back—and How We Can Still Save Humanity*. New York: Allen Lane, 2006.

Lovelock James & Epton Sidney, "The Quest for Gaia," *New Scientist*, February 6, 1975, p. 305.

Lovelock James & Margulis Louis, "Atmospheric homeostasis by and for the biosphere: the Gaia hypothesis," *Tellus*, 1974, 26(1–2), 2–10.

Lucas David, "La philosophie antique comme soin de l'âme," *Le Portique* [online], 4–2007 | Soin et éducation (II), posted June 14, 2007, accessed October 9, 2018. http://journals.openedition.org/leportique/948.

Magnin Thierry, *Penser l'humain au temps de l'Homme augmenté*. Paris: Albin Michel, 2017.

Matignon Emilie, "Dispositifs restauratifs et victimisation de masse," *La justice restaurative. Une utopie qui marche ?* Paris: L'Harmattan, 2010.

Mauss Marcel, *Sociologie et anthropologie*. Paris: Presses universitaires de France, 1950.

Mbanzoulou Paul, "La médiation pénale en France à l'aune de la loi du 9 juillet 2010," *La justice restaurative. Une utopie qui marche?* Paris: L'Harmattan, 2010, pp. 16–32.

Michel Johann, *Devenir descendant d'esclave. Enquête sur les régimes mémoriels*, Rennes, PUR, 2015.

———. *Le devoir de mémoire*. Paris: Que sais-je? 2018.

Mottez Bernard, *Les sourds existent-ils?* (texts collected by Andréa Benvenuto). Paris: L'Harmattan, 2006.
Mouralis Guillaume, "Retrouver les victimes. Naufragés et rescapés au procès de Nuremberg," *Droit et société*, 2019/2 (no. 102), pp. 243–60.
Nabert Jean, *Eléments pour une* éthique. Paris: Aubier, 1971.
Nietzsche Friedrich, *Twilight of the Idols*, trans. D. Large, Oxford: Oxford University Press, 2008.
Olmer Fabienne, "La médecine dans l'Antiquité : professionnels et pratiques," *Sociétés & Représentations*, vol. 28, no. 2, 2009.
Palier Bruno, *Les réformes de l'Etat providence*. Paris: PUF, 2009.
Parfit Derek, *Reasons and Persons*. Oxford: Oxford University Press, 1986.
Pascal Blaise, *Pensées and Other Writings*, trans. H. Levi. Oxford: Oxford University Press, 1999.
Paugam Serge, *La disqualification sociale. Essai sur la nouvelle pauvreté*. Paris: PUF, 2004.
Peirce Charles Sanders, *Reasoning and the Logic of Things*. Cambridge, MA: Harvard University Press, 1992.
Piketty Caroline (ed.), with the collaboration of Christophe Dubois and Fabrice Launay. *Guide des recherches dans les archives des spoliations et des restitutions / Mission d'étude sur la spoliation des Juifs de France*. Paris: La Documentation française, coll. "Mission étude spoliation Juifs," 2000.
Pingaud Bernard, *Ecrire jour et nuit*. Paris: Gallimard, 2000.
Plato, *The Last Days of Socrates*, trans. H. Tredennick, H. Tarrant. London: Penguin, 1993.
———. *Alcibiades*, N. Denyer (ed.). Cambridge: Cambridge University Press, 2001.
———. *Timaeus and Critias*, trans. R. Waterfield. Oxford: Oxford University Press, 2008.
———. *Meno and Other Dialogues*, ed./trans. R. Waterfield. Oxford: Oxford University Press, 2009.
Plutarch, *On the Intelligence of Animals*. Cambridge, MA: Loeb Classical Library, 1957.
Porée Jérôme, "Justice et réparation," in *Corpo, saúde e espaço público*, volume 1. Coimbra: Ariadne, 2006.
———. *Phénoménologie de l'aveu*. Paris: Hermann, 2018.
Ricœur Paul, *Freedom and Nature: The Voluntary and the Involuntary*, trans. E.V. Kohák. Evanston: Northwestern University Press, 1966.
———. *Oneself as Another*, trans. K. Blamey. Chicago: University of Chicago Press, 1994.
———. "Le juste, la justice et son échec," *Cahiers de l'Herne* (spécial Ricœur). Paris: 2004.
———. *Le juste*. Paris: Ed. Esprit, 1995.
———. *The Symbolism of Evil*, trans. E. Buchanan, New York: Harper & Row, 1967.
Ritchie B.G. & Fragaszy D.M., "Capuchin monkey (*Cebus apella*) grooms her infant's wound with tools," *American Journal of Primatology*, vol. 16, no. 4, 1988, pp. 345–48.

Robion Jacques, *Les réparations thérapeutiques*. Paris: L'Harmattan, 2017.

Rodriguez E & Wrangham R, "Zoopharmacognosy: The use of medicinal plants by animals," *Phytochemical Potential of Tropical Plants*, vol. 27, 1993, pp. 89–10.

Ryle Gilbert, *The Concept of Mind*. Chicago: University of Chicago Press, 2000 [1949].

Straus Erwin, *The Primary World of Senses*. New York: Free Press of Glencoe, 1935.

Strawson Peter, *Individuals: An Essay in Descriptive Metaphysics*. London: Methuen, 1959.

Taylor Charles, *The Sources of the Self*, Cambridge, MA: Harvard University Press, 1992.

Tesson Sylvain, *Sur les chemins noirs*. Paris: Gallimard, 2016 [*On the Wandering Paths*, trans. Drew Tesson. Minnesota University Press, 2022, forthcoming].

———. "La marche est une critique en mouvement," *La philosophie de la marche* (ed. N. Truong), Editions Aube/Le Monde, 2018.

Thiebaut de Schotten M., Urbanski M., Duffau H., Volle E., Levy R., Dubois B. & Bartolomeo P., "Direct evidence for a parietal-frontal pathway subserving spatial awareness in humans," *Science*, 309 (5744), pp. 2226–28, 2005.

Tisseron Serge, "La réparation, des chemins inattendus," *De la réparation* (Christophe Schaeffer ed.). Paris: L'Harmattan, 2010.

Tracy David, *The Analogical Imagination*. New York: Crossroad, 1991.

Tronto Joan, *Moral Boundaries: A Political Argument for an Ethic of Care*, London: Routledge, 1993.

Truche Pierre, "Les facteurs d'évolution de la notion de crime contre l'humanité," *Le Crime contre l'humanité*, texts collected by Bruno Gravier and Jean-Marc Elchardus, under the direction of Marcel Colin. Ramonville: Érès, 1996.

Truong Jean-Michel, *Totalement inhumaine*. Paris: Les empêcheurs de tourner en rond, 2003.

Tyrrell Toby, *On Gaia: A Critical Investigation of the Relationship Between Life and Earth*. Princeton: Princeton University Press, 2013.

Verdier Raymond, *Vengeance. Le face-à-face victime/agresseur*. Paris: Ed. Autrement, 2004.

Vilmer Jean-Baptiste Jeangène, *Réparer l'irréparable. Les réparations aux victimes devant la CPI*. Paris: PUF, 2015.

Wenzel Eric, "Quelle place pour la victime dans l'ancien droit pénal ?" In: *Les victimes, des oubliées de l'histoire ?* [online]. Rennes: Presses universitaires de Rennes, 2000.

Werner E. & Smith R., *Overcoming the Odds: High-Risk Children from Birth to Adulthood*. New York, Cornell University Press, 1992.

Wieviorka Annette, *The Era of the Witness*, trans. J. Stark. Ithaca: Cornell University Press, 2006

Winnicott Donald, *Human Nature*. Philadelphia: Brunner/Mazel, 1988.

Wittgenstein Ludwig, *Remarks on Frazer's Golden Bough*. Brynmill: Humanities, 1983.

———. *Philosophical Investigations*. Englewood Cliffs, NJ: Prentice Hall, 1973.

Zehr Howard, *The Little Book of Restorative justice*. New York: Good Books, 2014.

Ziller C., Paraf A., Cruickshank A., "Régénération et cicatrisation," *Encyclopædia Universalis* [online, in French], accessed on April 5, 2018. http://www.universalis.fr/encyclopedie/regeneration-et-cicatrisation

Zwierlein-Diehl Erika, "Les intailles magiques," *Pallas*, 2007, vol. 75, pp. 249–62.

Index

Analogical hermeneutics, XV
Anomal, 19, 20, 22, 24
Apologies, XIV, 59, 93, 112–15, 121, 123, 129, 195, 196, 203, 204, 218
Anthropocene, 26, 27, 30–32, 38, 40
A-reparable, 24, 26, 40, 139, 202, 203, 207, 212, 220
Aristotle, XV, 6, 7, 41n13, 82, 132, 141–46, 163, 164, 167, 171, 173n14, 176n63
Augustine (Saint), 105, 126n22, 221
Avoidance rituals, 118, 119, 122, 125, 128

Barbot, Janine., XVIn4, 151, 158, 174n34, 174n36, 176n53, 221
Bernard, Claude., 13, 19, 42, 221
Besnier, Jean-Michel., 43n42, 43n50
Bessone, Magalie., 214n22, 214n28, 222
Beuchot, Mauricio., XVII n6, 222
Bloch, Marc., 9, 41n23, 41n25, 222

Canguilhem, George., XIV, 1, 19–24, 37, 40n1, 43n55, 43n56, 43n58, 77, 138, 222
Cario, Robert., 166, 177n72, 222
Césaire, Aimé., 180, 201, 202, 212n2, 213n20, 215n33, 215n36, 222
Civil Code, 145, 157, 222

Confession, 68, 93, 102–10, 126n20, 126n22, 126 n28, 126n34, 155, 208–10, 221, 222
Corrective justice, 132, 141–45, 165, 167, 168, 173n17, 212, 214, 222
Creative reparation, 106–8, 222
Cyrulnik, Boris, 73, 74, 89n63, 89n64, 89n66, 90n77, 223

Damasio, Antonio., XII, XVIn2, 50, 83, 86n12, 86n14, 86n15, 86n19, 223
Deleuze, Gilles., 63, 77, 78, 88n48, 90n78, 91n86, 223
Dependence, 131–37, 158, 172n7,
Depressive position, 57–59, 68, 87n27
Descola, Philippe., 41n27, 198, 215n32, 223
Descombes, Vincent., 112, 126n37, 223
Destructive repair, 76, 90n71, 90n73, 107
Dodier, Nicolas., XVIn4, 151, 158, 174n34, 174n36, 176n53, 221
Douglas, Mary., 95, 96, 99, 125n7, 125n11, 223
Dutreuil Sébastien, 32, 44n67, 45n78, 223

Ehrenberg, Alain., 80, 91n80, 91n82, 223

Enhancement, XVI, 2, 14, 17, 23, 46n91, 74
Epicurus, 67, 68, 223
Exagoreusis, 108, 109, 223
Expiation, 98, 101, 102, 104
Exomologesis, 107, 108, 223

Favret-Saada, Jeanne., 11, 42n33, 224
Ferry, Luc., 15, 43n45, 165, 224
Fischbach, Franck., 135, 172n4, 172n6, 224
Flagellation, 98–99
Foucault, Michel., 22, 62, 65, 76, 81, 88n50, 90n74, 104, 107, 109, 124, 126n21, 126n27, 126n28, 126n31, 126n32, 153, 156, 159, 172n2, 174n39, 175n45, 175n46, 224
Frazer, James., 9, 10, 41n21, 41n22, 224
Freud, Sigmund., 54–61, 66, 69, 70, 74, 75, 83, 86n19, 86n20, 87n21, 88n32, 103, 150, 224

Garapon, Antoine., XVIIn9, 165, 166, 177n65, 183, 185–87, 197, 201, 202, 212n4, 212n7, 213n9, 213n12, 213n14, 215n29, 215n35, 224
Gefen, Alexandre., 81–83, 91n85, 91n91, 91n98, 91n99, 91n100, 91n100, 91n101, 224
Girard, René., 98, 100, 125n12, 126n13, 126n16, 224.
Godbout, Jacques., 202, 215n34, 225
Goffman, Ervin., 77, 90, 111, 116–21, 126n35, 127n45, 128n47, 128n47, 128n48, 128n49, 128n50, 128n51, 128n52, 128n53, 128n55, 129n56, 131, 132, 196, 225
Goody, Jack., 11, 42n30, 42n32, 225
Guilty, XIV, 35, 58, 68, 87, 100–2, 104–10, 120, 124, 134, 143, 145, 148, 150, 154, 157–61, 164, 165, 171, 209,

Habermas, Jürgen., 43n44, 225
Hadot, Pierre., 62, 65, 88n45, 88n51, 225
Handicap, 16, 17, 25, 42n39

Harm, XIII, 34, 36, 45, 83, 123, 124, 131–53, 156–72, 176n50, 176n51, 176n52, 177n78, 179, 182, 183, 186, 190, 191, 194, 196, 198, 199–203, 207, 211, 218, 220
Hegel, Georg W.F., 103, 112, 148–50, 157, 162, 163, 164, 174n28, 176n62, 177n64, 181, 225
Hénaff, Marcel., 113, 127n40, 127n43, 225
Heuzé, Vincent., 146, 148, 173n20, 225
Honneth, Axel., 133, 136, 172n1, 225
Hottois, Gilbert., 14, 42n40, 225

Incommensurability, 46n94, 144, 149, 150, 152, 197, 212, 220, 222
Irreparable, VIII, XIV, XVI, 2, 6, 13, 21, 23, 24, 27, 35, 38–40, 49, 53, 64, 66, 71, 83, 87n25, 90n71, 93, 102, 103, 111, 119, 122–25, 132, 138, 140, 144, 147, 149, 153, 171, 181, 182, 191, 199–203, 206, 207, 211, 219–20, 222, 228

Jankélévitch, Vladimir., 204, 215n38, 225
Joas, Hans., 175n45, 225
Jonas, Hans., 33, 45n79, 49, 225

Kanun, 160
Klein, Melanie., 57–58, 68, 70, 72, 76, 87n26, 87n27, 87n29, 226
Korff-Sausse, Simone., 25, 42n39, 44n63, 60, 87n31, 226
Kurzweil, Ray., 17, 43n48, 226

Latour, Bruno., 28, 29, 32, 42n32, 44n69, 44n73, 226
Le Blanc, Guillaume., 135, 136, 139, 172n5, 173n9, 226
Lefranc, Sandrine., 204, 211, 215n37, 215n39, 216n50, 216n54, 226
Lévi-Strauss, Claude., XV, XVIIn7, 11, 226
Lovelock, James., 27–32, 40, 44n66, 44n67, 44n68, 44n72, 45n77, 45n78, 223, 226

Magical-religious repair, 101, 103, 104, 107, 109, 124,
Magnin, Thierry., 43n41, 43n52, 226
Matignon, Emilie., 215n43, 226
Mauss, Marcel., XI, XVIn1, 62, 112, 113n36, 225, 226
Mottez, Bernard., 44n61, 227.

Nietzsche, Friedrich., 88n47, 88n48, 103–5, 107, 227

Other-repair, XIV, XVIn1, 2, 6, 14, 39, 51, 60, 69, 70, 71

Parfit, Derek., 84n3, 227
Pascal, Blaise., 94–95, 125n2, 125n4, 227
Penance, 98, 108
Plato, XV, 65–68, 88n42, 88n43, 88n44, 88n46, 88n49, 94, 227
Plutarch,. 7, 41n14, 227
Pollution, 95, 125n6, 223,
Porée, Jérôme., 104, 106, 109–10, 126n19, 126n20, 126n25, 126n33, 147, 150, 152–53, 174n32, 174n38, 227
Posthuman, 43n42, 221
Prophylaxis, 8, 64, 217
Purification, 21, 66, 93–104, 124, 181

Redemption, XIV, 93, 97–98, 101, 106–8, 124, 155, 181
Redress, XI, XVIn4, 140–41, 153–54, 209
Regeneration., XVI, 2–6, 40n3, 40n4, 41n8, 41n9, 48–49, 105, 150, 152, 155, 225, 229
Rehabilitation, 19, 46n91, 63, 106, 153–55, 165–66, 177n69, 177n70, 209
Repairing oneself, 60, 62, 67–70, 210
Reparative rituals, 115, 125, 129n55,
Resilience, XVI, 30, 38, 44n74, 72–76, 89n63, 89n64, 223
Restitution, XVI, 34, 35, 58, 128, 143, 147, 166, 181, 183, 186–88, 195–98, 211, 213, 227
Restorative justice, 165–72, 177n71, 177n73, 177n78, 207–11,
Retribution of the victim, 157, 164, 171

Ricœur, Paul., 55, 82, 84n3, 85n4, 87n23, 94, 97, 102–7, 125n1, 125n5, 125n9, 126n17, 126n24, 159, 161, 165–66, 176n55, 176n57, 177n66, 177n69, 222, 227
Robion, Jacques., 70, 89n55, 228

Sacrifice, XV, 3, 21, 59–60, 98–102, 108–9, 121, 124, 126n15, 152, 154, 162, 175, 181, 224
Scar, XIII, 5–6, 55
self-care, 61–66, 80, 106
Self-repair, XIV, 1–6, 14, 17, 27–32, 37–40, 48, 49–52, 55, 60–83, 171, 218, 219
Sin, 97–104
Social repair, 93, 123, 131–39

Taylor, Charles., 80, 91n84, 228
Tesson, Sylvain., 63–64, 88n38, 88n39, 228
Territories of the self, 117
Therapeutic age of reparation, 147, 150–52, 171, 181
Third-party repairer, 113, 134, 196, 197, 203, 207
Tisseron, Serge, 75–76, 90n72, 228
Tracy, David., XVI, 228
Transitional justice, 173n13, 207–8, 215n43,
Tronto, Joan., 136, 172n8, 228
Truche, Pierre., 214n23, 228
Truong, Jean-Michel., 16, 43, 228.

Vengeance, 31, 154, 159–65, 176n58, 208, 228

Winnicott, Donald., 25, 57–58, 70, 72, 87n30, 228
Wittgenstein, Ludwig., XV, XVIIn8, 41n22, 228
Work of mourning, XIV, XV, 53–61, 66, 73, 74, 80–83, 93, 99, 181, 218

Zehr, Howard., 167–70, 177n73, 228
Zoopharmacognosy, 7, 41n16, 223

About the Author

Johann Michel is professor at the University of Poitiers, a researcher at EHESS (Paris) and a member of the Institut Universitaire de France. He specializes in hermeneutics and social theory, and he is the author of many books in French, translated into several languages (including *Ricoeur and the Post-Structuralists*, Rowman & Littlefield, 2014 and *Homo Interpretans*, Rowman & Littlefield, 2019).

Lightning Source UK Ltd.
Milton Keynes UK
UKHW041510030123
414759UK00003B/60